How India Loves

Praise for *The Water Phoenix*

'Deliberately and lovingly written . . . Devastating . . . Chatterjee can write beautifully and vividly' *Mumbai Mirror*

'Chatterjee is courage personified' *The Times of India*

'Illuminated with wonder and curiosity and humour; and a child's utter honesty about people, places and relationships . . . strongly reminds one of Charles Dickens' Scroll.in

'Rituparna Chatterjee's brave memoir *The Water Phoenix* has helped to bring the issue of child sexual abuse into the open in India. And that can only benefit the many Indian children who are still suffering in unknowing silence' Nikkei Asia

'Rituparna Chatterjee's vivid and brave memoir *The Water Phoenix* soars without fear past the angry eyes of society' *India Today*

'Chatterjee has managed to love herself radically enough to be comfortable in her own skin and to speak her truth through her works' *The Telegraph*

'Chatterjee belongs to that growing pantheon of Indian writers in the English language whose style is a new movement in literature that has quietly developed, almost unseen. This is a very intimate book that deeply delves into many subjects. For instance, the body's storage of trauma, processing that one has been abused, the business of forgiveness, and so on. Her life is indeed a coexistence of peace and friction, of hope and giving up, of affection and domination. But in a more concise sense, her life is an unadulterated, concentrated version of the various demons and angels that life can conjure in front of us. The book is brilliantly penned and it carries a warrior within itself' *Outlook*

'The most crucial lesson you learn is that which the author gives you after having gone through it all: Healing is important. More importantly, that healing is possible. You don't always have to burn yourself to your regeneration. It is possible to be a water phoenix too. *The Water Phoenix* is not just a book for victims of sexual or physical abuse. It is a book for everyone . . . because it is a book about healing from your hurts' The Daily O

'Brilliantly written! *The Water Phoenix* offers solutions, offers hope, offers voice, and offers the ray of sun to hundreds of thousands of victims of abuse who lack voice and power, and cannot talk about their trauma in India' *The Sunday Guardian*

'Steeped in a dancing range of stunning visual imagery, emanating from the active imagination of an isolated but hugely resilient six-year-old child, Chatterjee's *The Water Phoenix* is a disarmingly honest memoir, empathetic and nuanced in its telling, providing a space for the reader to reflect and grieve along with the writer' Firstpost

'*The Water Phoenix* may help many child sex abuse victims open up about their own horrors. Chatterjee's take on forgiveness ("You cannot just wake up one day and decide to forgive. You can only forgive when you are ready.") will resonate with many. More than relevant!' *India Today*

'An extraordinary exposition of the journey of a child who was sexually abused several times during her childhood. The book portrays the young girl's trauma, her growing up in an echo chamber of self-doubt and her catharsis as she rejects the accepted norms to rise through the morass and emerge a healed person' National Laadli Media and Advertising Awards for Gender Sensitivity

How India Loves

Love Stories from the World's Largest Democracy

RITUPARNA CHATTERJEE

BLOOMSBURY

NEW DELHI • LONDON • OXFORD • NEW YORK • SYDNEY

BLOOMSBURY INDIA
Bloomsbury Publishing India Pvt. Ltd
Second Floor, LSC Building No. 4, DDA Complex, Pocket C – 6 & 7,
Vasant Kunj, New Delhi, 110070

BLOOMSBURY, BLOOMSBURY INDIA and the Diana logo
are trademarks of Bloomsbury Publishing Plc

First published in India 2025
This edition published 2025

Some names and details of individuals have been changed to preserve their anonymity

ISBN: PB: 978-93-56408-03-6; eBook: 978-93-56407-17-6
2 4 6 8 10 9 7 5 3 1

Typeset in Adobe Garamond by Manipal Technologies Limited
Printed and bound in India by Gopsons Papers Pvt. Ltd., Noida

FSC www.fsc.org
MIX
Paper | Supporting responsible forestry
FSC® C191020

For the romantic nincompoops who wasted four years of my life

Contents

b) Love

Author's Note

HOW IS A BOOK born? Where does it begin? Where does it end? These are questions that every writer of books is asked – by the readers, by the press as well as by themselves. And the truth is, not a single one of us knows. Nor will we ever know. The ancient Greeks and Romans, as well as Renaissance men, may have attributed the genesis of literary works to various muses and whimsical gods. And we Indians our epics to sages who had divine scribes, such as Ved Vyasa, who had Ganesha for his scribe, who we believe co-wrote the Mahabharata. We also worship and seek the blessings of the compassionate, gentle goddess Saraswati for wisdom and inspiration in all matters of learning, whether it is for school or public service examinations (no less than the epic battles of yore). Students of Jungian psychology and fans of quantum physics, like yours truly, may say that like all of reality and life books too – whether gigantic epics, works of fantasy or even short, realistic stories based on research – hail from the subconscious. Our beliefs and observations – which as many string theories, thought experiments such as Schrodinger's Cat, the Holographic Principle and Stephen Hawking's final theory of the Big Bang and even Hindu philosophies of Advaita Vedanta or the Bhagavad Gita's teaching that the world is maya or illusion suggest – create a quantum hologram, a hallucination in which we live. In other words, physical reality is not real. A bunch of atoms become matter. But this matter is just a construct of our inner worlds. And unless we inspect ourselves like scientists, we won't know why we do what we do like what we do, dislike what we do. Really basic. Much like dream interpretations. How then, without endless digging, can we know where stories and ideas come from? The truth is, nobody knows the answer to the question of where writing arises from.

When the writer Neil Gaiman was asked at an event where his ideas came from, he said, 'You have asked the one question no one must ask of writers,' admitting, after a long, delightful chat about werewolves and other horror elements, that the truth was that nobody knew.

As a writer, you must first become a non-judgemental space and allow things to come to you, to unfold of their own accord. People then automatically begin telling you their stories. This was something I was already used to, even before I started work on this book. In the spring of 2021, I was dealing with a mountain of paperwork (immigration, taxes, finances and property mostly) to ensure a life between California and India. Now that my son was older, busier and needed me for just fifteen minutes a day, if at all, and that too when I wasn't losing my endless battle for his attention with video games, friends, soccer, judo and other activities, Oculus and virtual realities. In other words, he didn't need me as much as he did some years ago, when he was still mama's little boy, and I was free to and could live what every expat only talked about, that is, a life in their homeland, or at least a life lived equally between their birth and adopted home countries. So I decided not to wait until he got a driver's license, went to university, got a job, got married, and so on. I did what I needed to. Right away. I'd spend six months spread out in India. This would include all school vacations and the months when my in-laws lived in California, insisting on spoiling both boys rotten, theirs and mine, ruining my hard work, returning both boys back to being Indian raja beta and laadla – what I worked so hard to undo and return them to being independent men fit for the upcoming twenty-second century, when such roles would be fiction. This way, with this schedule, no one was in anyone's way. Everyone won. And our sanity remained intact. All of this paperwork was happening in IST (Indian Standard Time, synonymous with Indian stretchable time), giving me the time to simultaneously do the launch tours in India for my second book, *The Water Phoenix*, at a leisurely pace. I spent months in various Indian cities, interacting with people on the streets, getting to know the real India, deeply aware that thanks to my endless duties and responsibilities that are every adult's life, I'd never have this kind of luxury of time and headspace perhaps ever again. Due to the deeply intimate nature of *The Water Phoenix* (the story of a gentle and highly imaginative child who has suffered abuse and her lifelong search to find out what love is and what it is not), readers began to tell me their own stories. To say that they were moving, overwhelming or unnerving would be an understatement. People were telling me things they had not told their spouses, their children, their dearest and nearest. I felt like I had become the journal pages of an entire country. Weeping, strong-looking grown men with bulging biceps were the most disconcerting for me. Because I had addressed those men too in *The Water Phoenix*, in my talks and in my column, insisting again and again that contrary to the popular myth that only girls are abused, the truth is that abuse knows no gender or stereotype. They felt seen, heard and validated in a way they had never been before. This is why I always echo Jung – that we are all archetypes, and hence the personal story is everyone's story. Readers began to take me out after book signings. And I had the time for them. They began to bring along their children, their mothers – often senior citizens – who too began opening up about their own stories of what they now knew was marital rape, domestic violence or intimate partner violence (IPV). Or their stories were of subtler forms of abuse, of feeling isolated in the shams that passed off as perfect marriages, which had seen their silver, even golden jubilees. It came to a point where I could not even enter the powder room of a hotel after book events without being accosted by people who had such stories to tell. This began to happen randomly at bookstores, hotel buffets or restaurants, where they'd recognise me, introducing themselves as readers who had followed my journalistic work, columns, books, social media posts, and so on. And they'd go on to share how they had found themselves in my work. Writing is a deeply solitary process and writers live for this kind of connection with their readers. I was touched, overwhelmed and, most of all, very grateful. I wondered what would have happened if I were to frequent a local salon, or 'beauty parlour', as they used to be called in the 1990s in the India I grew up in, which were treasure troves of secrets that might render the drama and shenanigans of reality television and soap operas, even with their quintessential dramatic sound effects, tame and blah.

These stories knew no class, caste, gender or other social or economic boundaries that dictate our lives lived in little bubbles. Maids, drivers, labourers, policemen and women, wealthy housewives, sugar babies, trust fund kids, hawkers, rickshaw-pullers . . . anyone and everyone told me their stories. The stories seemed to come from nowhere and everywhere, from no one and everyone. Many of them made it to my column in *The Times of India*, 'California Dreaming', on my life as a global Indian writing about the vagaries of living between India and America. But even up to 1,500 words per week (which was unnatural generosity on the part of the newspaper editors) were not enough to tell their stories. Before Shraddha Walkar's gruesome murder by her boyfriend shook the country, my column had featured hundreds of love stories gone wrong. My editors suddenly realised the gravity of the trends my stories reflected, which were going completely undocumented. They suggested that I focus more on love, sex and relationships, and I was happy to, given the tsunami of love stories that had completely taken over my life, bringing the research for the novel I was writing to a complete halt. Stories have to go somewhere. They can't be bottled up. After all, every work of art is a possession. It is a complete haunting. The work chooses the artist, the writer, until the two aren't separate, at least not for the duration of the work. Incidentally, my first book, *An Ordinary Life*, was a study of this, but only of the art of acting. As for books, we may still not know where the ideas come from. And how. That's the irony. But ultimately, this possession that comes from god alone knows where is how all books are written, this is how all art is created.

After having written two deeply intense and intimate books – incidentally, both memoirs – and a newspaper column on my life, I knew by now that one must respect the work, even if one did not quite know the work. Or what the work itself was. That's the irony. It was, is and will always remain an endless act of discovery. That was the fun of writing. The sheer joy of creating. It also meant abandoning one's own notions of what the work should be. Trusting the work enough, especially when you had no idea whatsoever of even what the next sentence, leave alone the total work, would be. It was like being a child, playing with mud, building sandcastles . . . somehow, it all does come together. All of this made sense to me while painting my watercolours. Or the intuitive piano I played sometimes. Or how I cooked or baked, not knowing what I would. Learning to live and see the world with the trust, openness of a child who knew nothing. And had the courage to be lost. To not want to make sense and use logic, all signs of adult cowardice and the brainwashing of the business of growing up.

The Spanish painter and sculptor Pablo Picasso himself referred to this process several times. 'Every child is an artist.

The problem is how to remain an artist once we grow up.' And later, 'It took me four years to paint like Raphael but a lifetime to paint like a child.'

But something as logical as non-fiction is something else. Or the systems had subliminally brainwashed us without meaning to perhaps. The systems of publishing, media, sales and marketing, and so on that decided this is fiction, this is non-fiction, this is this genre and this is how you go about it. Forgetting all along that the ancients did not have these boxes. Perhaps that's why their art is truer and timeless. I suppose this is also why the ancient ones called it worshipping the muse. It wasn't just the one body of work. You had to live a certain way. In the flow state. And what was meant to come, to be, would. And that meant all projects, all works. I had to abandon my novel. It was pointless. I put all of those sheets of paper containing the notes for the book into a navy vegan-leather folder and slid it into the drawer of my white writing desk overlooking the almond tree in the backyard of my Santa Clara home. Much of the research I had done, the hundreds of interviews, are the many love stories you will find in this book. 'California Dreaming' had become from a column on my life to a safe space for Indians to share their love lives. Thanks to it, more and more people wanted to share their stories with me, and my social media DMs too became flooded, as my life had, with them. Ultimately, after thousands (at some point I lost count) of such stories in all forms, some published, many just happily told to me and having been left at that, some as DMs and some as feedback to the columns (more stories!) over four whole years, *How India Loves* was born.

In books, we try to fit our material into chapters. But how does one categorise the ways in which a nation loves? For instance, where do I fit the stories of extramarital affairs of self-aware people? Do I place them in the chapter on extramarital affairs or in the one on therapy affecting relationships? Or in the chapter on IPV or marriage? This was the dilemma I faced with each and every love story featured here.

Most notably, I do not have a separate chapter on the LGBTQA community, for all they want is to be considered normal, to fit in, which is where they are headed in India, just like in the rest of the world. Several of my son's classmates are children of gay families with two dads or two moms, and because it is as normal and mundane in California as the sun rising every morning, nobody even notices this. India too is headed this way, and I wanted to tell the stories about the community – beyond the gay parades – that we don't see in the media. Many LGBTQA people, for instance, are members of India's growing BDSM community. Just as much as heterosexual couples in both short-term situationships, bonds with no names and formal long-term relationships and marriages are. And like those, the LGBTQA folk too have had situationships that you will see in chapters like the ones on when great sex was not enough or the reign of porn or the army of single women. So I have included them there instead of having a separate chapter on LGBTQA. This was extremely difficult to segregate, but I felt that it was our fragility, our humanity, which was most important in all of these love stories and ultimately what this book is about. Our fragile humanity transcends the necessary labels of gender and sexuality.

For this reason, I have not done a separate chapter on the grand Indian marriage either, for like the love stories of the LGBTQA community, stories of the grand Indian marriage too are everywhere in the book, across chapters.

Life is fluid, love even more so. Especially in the world's largest democracy, which is evolving far more rapidly than the other country, the world's most powerful democracy, which I call my second home.

This book is a testament to the trust and bond between the reader and the writer, both of whom are looking for a connection to something specific. And this something specific is ourselves. Ultimately, it is always ourselves we are looking for. It is ourselves we are yearning to connect with. These stories of love, sex and relationships in the world's largest and, arguably, most important democracy are anthropological tales of the heart and soul of India. Take away the surface tags, status, houses, labels and jobs. Who are Indians at their core? Like all peoples of the world, we are who we love, what we love, how we love, why we love. In journalism school, we are taught the four Ws (who, what, where, when) as the core of any story. I had always added 'why' and, even though it did not begin with a W, 'how', which explains why I skipped news entirely and entered directly into feature stories in my first job, ripping apart the whys and hows. But with the stories featured in this book, I kept asking myself again and again about the four Ws (and the whys and the hows): Are these questions? Or are these entire lives? Perhaps both. But these are who we are at our most intimate core. Always unsaid, unseen, unless someone takes the time to come out of their own stories to notice, which too, as we will see later in this book, communities and strangers do most often. As did this writer. Thank you to the thousands of Indians who trusted me as a safe space, as the holder of their deepest love stories and secrets.

This book, *How India Loves*, was born out of you, dear reader. And for that I will forever remain grateful.

Part I

Places

1

America

DEAREST READER,

Twenty years.

That is how long it took me to make peace with the Pacific. It happened on a starless night in Maui, at one of the infinite, nameless beaches across Hawaii, this one right next to the cottage we had rented that June for the beginning of Fussy's summer break. Every single time I had dipped a few fingers or toes into the serene but unforgiving blue waters in San Francisco, in Santa Cruz, in Half Moon Bay, in Monterey – really all over northern California, especially on the nameless beaches dotting Highway 1 – I had shuddered and pulled back, frozen. My bones would turn into ice instantly, even in the summer when my husband would go windsurfing in the tamed versions of the same waters locally, at Shoreline, and return cold – very cold but not frozen. I'd watch him and stay on the beach writing. This was my relationship with the Pacific – deeply intimate, beautiful, abusive.

So when my body instinctively responded the way it last had decades ago, I wasn't surprised. Bodies are the ultimate databases, built for storage, literally. Bodies store memories we have chosen to forget and forget so masterfully as to suggest they had never existed. I knew this well. Since Fussy's birth in the year of the Dragon, all of my writing was about this. My toes, ankles and eventually my legs almost fully dipped themselves in the sea of their own free will.

I only watched and was soon watching in shock. Instead of the waters turning my bones to ice, as always, sometimes without us even touching – just the Pacific breeze was enough for that – the unthinkable happened. The same ocean thawed my feet – which, like my fingers, are usually cold. The same Pacific waters were like the soothing salt baths I was so addicted to and that my son Fussy loved drawing up for me – rarely out of the goodness of his heart but whenever he wanted something or had done something he wasn't supposed to have, or had not done something he was supposed to have. Schools of little unnamed fish nibbled at my feet. Under sunlight they had colours, they had names. In the moonlight they were lost in the brilliance of the shimmering waters – so lost that they might have not existed at all. Like figments of the imagination. Like ghosts, like spirits, like the ones Hawaiian myths and folklore were so abundant in. Still, their nibbling felt like affection, even if from the invisible. My fingers had to touch the water to know what was happening, and like the wise blind ones, I did touch the water with them. I was in shock. Or, like Fussy said, as his friend Third Grade Matteo had taught him, 'I was shooketh.' Not so much by the fish, which ignored my fingers, which were somehow still soft in spite of decades of housework and dishwashing, choosing to bite my harder toes instead. The water was warm. I closed my eyes. And I let my fingers become the water, like they had wanted to for so long. I knew it then. It was not this ocean, the mightiest ocean on Earth, but another sea, one few might have known the name of in Hawaii or California. The sea that had raised me which I had forgotten but clearly my body had not. It was that sea that my hands and feet had felt. Not the Pacific Ocean but the Arabian Sea – opposite which I had grown up in small towns on India's west coast, eventually moving to the big city of Mumbai. The Arabian Sea was warm and loving, watching me in my home, filling it with a soothing breeze and playing peekaboo as it wrapped itself around the island city everywhere I went. I rarely touched it. You weren't supposed to. It was filthy, full of faeces, plastic, trash and once even floating corpses of buffaloes. But it went everywhere I went, day after day, from home to college and back. Through my dates and first job and back. Protecting me, keeping me safe. Keeping all of us safe from losing ourselves in the chaos of the big city. But I had never spent hours, years, decades, gazing into it or even trying to befriend it.

In Maui, it wasn't the Pacific I had befriended but my warm old friend who had come calling. That's what dreams do. That's what ghosts do. You really don't have a choice but to listen to them the easy way. You don't want to put them in situations where they have to be assertive, taking over your life, covering it with grief enough to fill an ocean, with rage enough to create a tsunami. In that instant, a decision was made. Many if not all of life's greatest decisions happen in subtle moments like these, with no ceremony. I knew I had to move back, not be halfway California, halfway India, like Hawaii was. Its mangoes tasted like Alphonso, its vibe was like Goa's, the welcoming hearts of its people full of love, like those of Bengalis from rural Bengal. But of course it wasn't India. No, I could not live a half-life any more. Suddenly, the emptiness that had been gnawing at me, which I had mistaken for peace and calm, came like the tsunami, engulfing me, reminding me that it was always there, and so not only was I to expect it, I also had no choice but to obey it. To live a full life, I must divide my life, which is another word for time. The husband and I had chatted many times about it. But so did every first-generation immigrant couple from every country. My California was that – full of highly educated, privileged immigrants who were not escaping wars but here, just because . . . They could have been anywhere, but somehow they had stayed on here.

It was the pull of the Pacific. Our mortgage and our son's life had so taken over our lives that we had forgotten our own wishes, like all parents. I could not wait till he was seventeen, like I had initially planned to. Anyway he was a nineteen-year-old in a ten-year-old's body – independent, so much so that I got barely fifteen minutes of his time daily, at the end of each day, when I was not ferrying him around like a taxi, again something that could be outsourced. And so it began, propelled by my simple wish which would not let me rest. Things began to take care of themselves. Fussy's school, my husband's work, my consultancies, immigration, finances, property, United States Citizen and Immigration Services (USCIS) formalities, all of it. In the process of surrendering my immigration, I requested the USCIS AI-powered voice software, which was becoming the ubiquitous customer service provider everywhere, to kindly allow me talk to a human so I may explain my unusual situation, which it could not find in its database. I tried again and again until the AI service finally said, 'I will have to hang up and report you.' I got yelled at by a robot! I, who as a journalist had covered robotics for over a decade, had seen them grow, had hung out with them, had loved and welcomed them, had done photo shoots with them; I, whose husband worked in AI and with whom AI and humans were daily dinner table talk, could not believe it. I looked around. I saw that my whole house was AI-powered. Rotis for my Punjabi husband were now made by a robot and my personal frenemy, whom I had named Rosie Roti Aunty. Rotis came out of it like paper printouts out of a regular printer. Our security systems alerted us no matter where we were in the world, no matter who walked past our house at what hour and would alert the security in the locality and the police if necessary. Our smoke alarms – certainly not made for Indian cooking which, as a college friend described, was about meals full of roti and charcoal (*subzi* which had to transform into charcoal to turn into irresistible deliciousness) – screeched and alerted the local fire station and emergency services if necessary. Google Assistant and its comrades entertained my son and me with detailed conversation. It was to an Android AI-powered tablet in my son's room that I had outsourced much of my nagging, like the million repetitions of 'Wake up! We are getting late for school!', 'Clean your room', 'Flush the toilet', 'Wash your hands', 'In the sink'. And some others he might kill me for mentioning. Even our water sprinklers, slow cooking and laundry were now courtesy of AI, able to be controlled from anywhere in the world. Really, AI had become that banal already. Soon it would be all of our cooking. In all of this glam and convenience, where was the human touch? Where was that most precious thing worth living for – human connection? What was the point of anything then? I longed for this connection. Everyone does. But few move their lives around for it. This is why we watch movies, read books, consume art and stories, even the ones on social media. Human connection is the most basic human need, occupying a higher place than even food and water. Because when our hearts break and we are alienated, we care for neither food nor water. With every passing day, I became surer and surer that I had to move to India. Not for calamity, like I was seeing people around me returning to their home countries for, not just India but also Turkey, Belgium, and so on. America's endless gun violence, terrifying shooter drills that I myself had sat through with my son and his classmates through every year of his elementary school, political climate, and so on were making immigrants return. Many Indians were returning to India, tired of the endless immigration processes I had written about in great depth during my years as a foreign correspondent for *The Economic Times*. It took an entire generation to truly settle down properly, and then there were ageing parents, friends, family back in India. Ripe climate to build and fund startups freely. Instead of being stuck with expensive mortgages, visa-tied up jobs that held you down. Spouse visas that didn't let you work. Degrees and experiences that went unrecognised, stories no immigrant wanted to tell even to themselves, leave alone to the media or anyone else. And of course, America's spectrum of endless natural disasters. On our part of the coast, it was just wildfires and earthquakes. Elsewhere, it was tornadoes. Unlike those fleeing calamities, I wanted to return, not for calamity. I wanted to return for joy. I suppose like those stereotypical Bollywood movies calling the NRI back home. The general isolation of America – living there was like being in an internal lockdown for fifteen years – had gotten to me. I craved spontaneity, the joy of not planning everything, of fewer boundaries. Of not having to make appointments in advance to have deep conversations.

Of making mistakes. Of being audacious.

2

New Delhi

I BOARDED THE FLIGHT from San Francisco International Airport to New Delhi like a calm puppy, full of awe and wonder. As one might when they know they are about to be reborn. I had boarded countless flights to and from these two airports, taking routes spanning most of the important cities in Western Europe and Asia. But it had felt like this just once before, when I had landed for the first time in America. All the world's shortest journeys are the longest ones – like a baby's passing through her mother's birth canal, the shortest distance of inches taking the longest.

I pondered over these things as my friend Snigdha's driver picked me up and drove me through central Delhi – its leafy lanes the only sights that had more or less remained the same from my childhood visits to the Indian capital in the 1980s. They were a source of comfort in an ever-changing world, where little made sense. I began to notice more changes the moment the driver opened the door to the government bungalow that would be my base for the next couple of months as I shopped for a second home in the country of my birth. Like most civil servants' homes, this one too had old-world elegance, antiques, vintage furniture, books and a few splashes of south Delhi opulence – a random crystal chandelier here, gaudy cushions and dining chairs there, shiny curtains, bizarre fuchsia polyester upholstery, with prints of the Eiffel Tower, completely out of place on antique dark-stained teak wood chaise longues (and yet very much in place in South Delhi). My suitcases were deposited in the guest room. Opposite were two bedrooms. One, distinctly His. One, distinctly Hers. Like hotel bathrooms. This was my first shock. I thought my middle-aged friend was happily married. I had known Snigdha for two decades, though I had not seen her for a decade and a half. She spoke normally about her husband, their social media photos showed happy couple photos of their travels, and news about them was always regular. I was not to pry, for it was none of my business, but every time I passed the hallway, I couldn't escape the two doors. Thick, tall, made of dark wood, the doors were ominous, like the monuments all over Delhi, the ones history has forgotten but you know are special, holding secrets in plain sight. My friends lived like housemates: Happily bantering about at their daily meals, allocating chores to servants, discussing work, goals, fitness, news, restaurants, food, movies and web series, trips and common friends. And then there were the other flavours of marriage – responsibilities, caregiving, medicines and hospital visits for themselves, parents, children and relatives.

Because you are an outsider in the home, you notice these subtleties that pass off as daily life to insiders. Moreover, the novel I was writing at the time featured seventeen houses. So I was in default research mode, observing every slight thing about homes. Barring the time when we were hunting for our own home to buy during the COVID-19 pandemic, I had never paid more attention to houses.

It was the same as at Snigdha's in a cousin's house. At the homes I was invited to for meals and functions. At the homes to which I was taken along by those who were invited. These were the homes of couples in the age range of late thirties to seventies. But age did not seem to matter too much in this respect, and my tours of house after house that I visited revealed the same situation. This, right here, was the modern Indian marriage – hidden like a secret in a safe space, which is what houses are – and yet, right there, revealing itself like a secret hidden in a pyramid. People went on frequent holidays with platonic friends from the same gender (girls' trips, boys' trips, as they were called) or with large groups of common friends, school or college friends, or attended family functions, like weddings. But the quiet intimacy of the 'romantic getaways' with spouses (that they worked so hard, battling all kinds of schedules of respective work, caregiving, kids, and so on, to make happen) or the scheduled sacred date nights that kept marriages alive in California were missing. These required deep connection, which required vulnerability, something that was increasingly becoming very, very scary and very, very rare. They had everything we did not. Most of all, they had delivery services and an army of staff – drivers, cooks, nannies, maids, gardeners – to replace our entire existence. Our lives were chores, and we served as taxi drivers carting our children and pets from one activity and appointment to another. But the couples here did not seem to be unhappy either. They were just distracted, constantly searching, barely present with each other. Perhaps they were searching for themselves. For our marriages, the most important of all of our relationships, are extensions of our relationship with ourselves. There was a togetherness in their separate lives under the same roof. Like two separate saris in a sari shop that just exist together peacefully, having neither love, nor malice, nothing at all, for each other. They lived like objects, in the sense that while they coexisted, inhabiting the same space, they appeared detached from each other. It is attachment to the country, a place or a person that makes us give or take lives. Without attachment, what is the point?

That night, after speaking with my husband and son, I called my friend Kristen. We had become friends in a small mothers' group in Mountain View when our sons were less than two years old. Over the years, our friendship became more about us than our children. At the time she was married to a man. Sometime during her postpartum depression, alienation and loss of identity, which affects, to some extent, every mother in the isolated West, the tensions between them grew and, propelled as a rocket is with liquid oxygen, Kristen grew closer and closer to her neighbour, with whom she had a 'nanny share' – both sharing a common nanny who watched their children at the same time. Her husband had installed a GPS on her phone, which he could access, because he did not believe she was with us at the hot yoga studio during the brief hours of the day when she was not with her son. Their relationship got bitter, and over months of fights and his stalking of her and painful chaos, Kristen finally left him for the woman, eventually finding her too very possessive and leaving her after some years. Now she was about to marry a woman this year, also a writer, like her, who understood her perfectly and allowed her to breathe. That was the California I knew. Everyone lived for love: even if it meant possessive, romantic intensity, like my friend's husband's and her first girlfriend's; even when children were involved or when there were mortgages or financial, social and emotional dependence, people still moved their entire lives, turning the most impossible situations around for love. I suppose that's what living in a wildfire and earthquake zone does to you. You know life is short, too short to live like machines or corpses, at least in your personal life if not at work. I myself had eloped from Bombay to Delhi and married a Punjabi when I was merely twenty-one, as both sets of parents were against our getting together. So I couldn't understand this new wave of Indian marriages, and I could not understand my friends, cousins – people I had known for years, or at least thought I knew. Kristen said, 'They don't care. That's the worst. You stop caring. So there's nothing to fight for. You just go on. That's why I too had to leave (my marriage) then.'

She nailed it. Somewhere in the infinite showing up for relatives, the *havans*, the weddings, the roles as the perfect bahu, wife and child, Indian women had forgotten who they truly were.

Not just the women, Indian men too never knew who they were, because this life of obligations and fake showing up was all that Indians had known – this life of being the classic good boys and good girls. Many chose to forget their authentic selves and had fallen into this cycle of drudgery.

But there was no animosity, no stonewalling, nothing whatsoever between the couples in India. But how was it possible to keep on living the way they were? Like props on stage? That is what blew my mind. And they were not our parents' generation; they had social media, they could see what lives others were living, they had freedom and support and, comparatively speaking, a society that was in many ways less judgemental than it had ever been.

We are sifting through crockery at Khan Market and then at GK1 M Block market. Snigdha wants to get a tea set for one of the infinite number of relatives we Indians seem to have. And I ask her then, 'What is it?'

'What is what?' she asks.

'Your marriage. You guys are okay?'

'Define okay.'

'I don't know. Something's off. And yet it seems okay.'

'You're all such romantics. Of course, we are okay. We are more than okay.'

'Well, what's the secret then? Because we certainly are not okay there.'

'Oh my god! What happened?'

'Well, we bicker and fight. It's always chores. Or the infinite demands of being a bahu and whose family wronged whose boundaries during their six-month-long stays. We are never as calm or "okay" as you guys.'

'Ah!' Gently putting away the white and gold porcelain cup and saucer set she is examining, she looks at me and smiles, 'There's a secret.'

'What's the secret? Are you on a certain drug? I may not have tried any, but being in California I think I know about most of the medicinal ones by now.'

'Yes!' She smiles mischievously. I look confused. Time changes everyone.

'A human drug.'

'Oh-kay! Tell me more.'

'His name is Ashish, and he is twenty-eight.'

'What?'

'Yes, I know I am sixty-one.'

'No. Wait. What?'

'What what?'

'You mean your driver?' Utterly defeated by chores that is all I can think of. Superman to us was a great driver with jugaad. 'You are talking about your driver?'

'A journalist!'

'Oh! Is it that bad here?' I think of our cycle of layoffs that turn Silicon Valley's millionaires into burger flippers and suddenly, in the next cycle, see them back in the Valley. Looking at the condition of media offices, I wonder if that has happened and the journalist has turned into a driver now. Really, I cannot think of anything beyond a driver. No greater luxury exists for my worn-out brain and body, having been a human taxi to my twelve-year-old and his friends for years. So that's where my imagination ends.

'No! My god!' Snigdha looks at me. 'What are you on? Did you smuggle in those gummies you guys have for your mental health? You know that shit's illegal here, and you'll get into trouble.'

'Driver! Driver! Driver! Uff! Ashish is my lover.'

'Oh! I just did not . . .'

'. . . did not what?' she quips, cutting me short. 'That I could take a lover? What a prude you are! For all of your talks of nude yoga and whatnot.'

'No! I am sorry. I just . . .'

'Well, if he can have her, why can't I have him?'

'He?'

'Raman has had a string of them. Young girls fawning over His Highness. You know how men are. Stroke them right and they are your little boys.'

'You mean stroke their egos?'

'Yes, that too!'

'Gosh! Okay, all this is too much! I am used to therapists prescribing open marriages. Friends having polyamorous relationships. But this is India. You guys are as traditional as it gets. Yours was an arranged marriage. What is all of this? Sorry, no judgement, but explain please, because I am really lost here. As are all of my ideas about India and Indian marriages.'

'Well, he fawns over me. I teach Ashish things. I love him like both a son and a pupil. I feel desired. But not just my body. My mind. I come alive. I remember who I was.'

'So Ashish doesn't matter. You just love how he makes you feel?'

'Same as the men, no? Raman or all of those editors, big men we know. They have these twenty-somethings, star-struck and looking at them like they are gods. They want to learn something. They want to feel safe. In a way, they don't feel safe with their own age group.'

'Right!' I say. It makes total sense of course. Just that I cannot picture her at all like this.

'So then, why can't I do it as a woman? If I do it, I am a slut? A whore who cuckolds her husband?' Snigdha is beginning to lose her patience and get angry. 'Come on, Ritu!'

'No, of course not! I am sorry, I didn't mean to make you feel that way.'

'Ashish makes me *feel*. It's not about how he makes me come. I am able to come like this because I am myself. Who am I? I am so lost otherwise. And look at our marriage. We are perfect. Every ask is met. I am the perfect bahu. Have you ever heard a complaint?'

'So how many years have you had Ashish?'

'My love, you are so naive. Ashishes come and go.'

So Ashish then is like an iPhone. Perpetually getting upgraded to the latest one, but it is always an iPhone, which makes you feel, well, like getting the latest iPhone does, I guess. Just when they come out.

'Thank you! You have given me an education.'

'You should try it too, darling. You are wasting your beauty away.'

'What does that even mean! Jesus!'

'You don't know until you have tried. Wait, let me make a call.'

'Nooooo!' I say sternly, holding her hand, which has gone into her purse to pull out her phone. Which, of course, is an iPhone. I look at the screen of my phone. Battered, of course, in spite of multiple gorilla glass covers, which shatter every few months and need to be replaced. My life is all kids, especially rambunctious boys – my son and his friends. And my phone is an Android. Traditional, boring. An ancient OnePlus. I hate upgrading. I only upgrade when my son's gymnastics or shenanigans (like accidentally tipping his glass and spilling his entire drink on my phone or Kindle or computer or iPad) has rendered the device dead. I remember how even Siri had once yelled at me. That's who I am. Old Android grandma. No iPhone for me. No Ashish for me.

That night, at 4 a.m. IST, during our video-call, my son tells me that the world's largest spider web is built by a spider called Darwin's bark spider. Our WhatsApp texts are full of cute animal gifs, and now, suddenly we have pictures of these giant 80-foot supernatural webs made in the wild too. And now I can explain to him that the amount of paperwork I was battling was just as big. From having no Aadhaar to RBI blocking my Indian bank accounts for their having been dormant for so long and all the work I had done at USCIS in America not showing up, to running to the US Embassy frequently for family immigration, both American and Indian . . . My ten-year-old may not understood the details thoroughly, but he understands the volume of the paperwork I have to do because of the gigantic webs of the Darwin's bark spider. Just like I understand the concept of Ashish only through iPhones.

Somewhere between my abnormal schedule – this enormous web of paperwork, book signings, events and interviews for my last book, *The Water Phoenix* – and her own rather normal schedule of work and household commitments, Snigdha and I manage to meet outside the two separate His and Hers bedroom doors, drive away to sneak in a few minutes together on morning walks in Siri Fort before our various lives beckon us. Ashishes and iPhones are more than metaphors. They enable each other. There is constant texting throughout the day and even at odd hours at night, conversations that range from fun and forwarded memes to serious advice and help in matters of work, financial planning to plumbing and, of course, romance, organising getaways and the occasional, 'Want to go?' Meaning, on a holiday, mostly a weekend getaway to someplace close by, that might not raise eyebrows or the faintest whiff of curiosity at all, getting lost in the sea of already abundant existing getaways with girlfriends and, of course, endless work trips so nobody suspects anything. Or 'Come?/Let's go' on drives when the harsh, judgemental sun has set and one can be lost, anonymous and free, in the shelter and safety the darkness of the hazy night offers, parking on the sides of isolated roads by India Gate or some neighbourhood or highway in the National Capital Region (NCR).

Or the rather frequent, 'Want to do a hotel?'

'When?'

'Tonight?'

'Lunch hour?'

'Two to five? I have work after.'

It had been seven years since I had made my annual pilgrimage to India – a brief, hectic khichdi of bahu duties, work meetings, meetings with the numberless relatives from my in-laws' side and the caretaking of our son, who being a baby at the time was always falling sick, all sprinkled with heavy doses of overwhelm and jetlag that the huge 13.5-hour time difference was bound to induce. It had been twenty years since I had lived here. But even in these seven years away, with no brief visits in between, India had grown beyond recognition. Something called OYO rooms had sprouted in India behind my back. Literally meaning On Your Own, OYO[1] provided safe, clean, small single rooms for budget-friendly travellers, often solo, but also welcomed couples of all kinds who could check in hassle-free, safely and leave, sometimes within hours. Though its valuation had fallen to $2.5 billion by mid-2024, the company was once valued at $10 billion.[2] I wondered if these taboo affairs had something to do with these projections. Off the record, the mention of OYO seemed to set off a mischievous glint in people's eyes. Safe spaces were nice. Safe spaces were necessary. But who would go on the record and admit just how much affairs contributed to this business?

The affairs were everywhere! I met my old friend ABC – a nickname that had stuck years after we had both quit working together. ABC was one of the most senior editors in the Indian national media. We were meeting at the bar at the beautiful ancient Imperial Hotel on Janpath. He was bound to know what was up on the streets of Delhi. I asked him what on earth was going on. Because I stuck with the name Ashish, he said he had had several Ashimas. And pretty much for the exact same reason my friend had had a string of Ashishes. And her husband his own curated museum of lovers. I was even more shocked to hear this from my editor. Here was someone I had worked with, respected and looked up to, whose wife I knew and had met many times, whose daughter had confided in me many times about her own boyfriends. As journalists, writers and artists, our conversations do tend to be less shallow and fake than one may find elsewhere. It was their role I donned all the time when I played *bari* bahu duties or met with venture capitalists and entrepreneurs in Silicon Valley or my son's teachers, my neighbours, the parents of my son's friends, and so on. But still, this was too much.

'How would you feel if Seema took on an Ashish?' I confronted him.

'I'd actually be very happy. I want my wife to be happy. I love her.'

What was love?

Friends told me that senior editors like ABC had Ashimas everywhere – doe-eyed, waif-like young girls looking up to their professional role models and heroes in awe and wonder and worship. Some were sugar daddies to younger Ashimas. The hero factor and the knight in shining armour are deeply entrenched in women's subconscious. But there were the so-called raging feminists too! Independent women who took no shit from anyone. Warriors who fought against these ancient subliminals tattooed into female minds so they could be free, truly free. As free as a man.

Those are the ones my hyper-masculine friend Shantanu said he preferred for his escapades. His own woman, his latest wife, whom he constantly referred to as 'My Love', was the opposite. She was a slightly upgraded version of the *sunder, sushil, ghareloo* archetype, a TV journalist who had quit her life to be a stay-at-home mom to their children. Clearly, we were all iPhones. Shantanu was married once before, to one of the feminist types, and of course, with both of them being alpha, their marriage had not worked out. So he had strategically decided to have the stability of a domestic married life with 'a tamer woman' who was easier to love and to take care of, which really helped calm him down so he could work and rise in his career more peacefully.

'So then, your marriage is successful?'

'Absolutely!' He beamed, showing me his not-so-gleaming *battisi* (thirty-two teeth).

'What, then, is the secret of a successful marriage?' I asked him.

'Lots of sex and zero lies,' he said, now distracted, looking into his phone. For work texts and emails? Or lovers' texts? Or both? I don't know.

'But . . .' I tried to waft together words as politely as I could about his marriage.

'Sorry, I have to take this!' He cut me short, taking a call on his phone. 'It is My Love.' He smiled, turning his phone to me for a second to show me that it was indeed she – fair-skinned, smiling, happily married – at least in the picture, where the phone indeed read My Love.

'Hi jaan,' he said into the phone. 'Tell me baby . . .' This was most amusing, and I was trying very, very hard not to laugh out aloud. Luckily, he walked off for privacy, leaving me to smile and giggle to myself, much to the waiters' amusement, but of course they were too polite to show it. When done, I calmed down and took it all in again.

Shantanu's description of his marriage still rang in my ears and in my head. 'Lots of sex and zero lies.'

His marriage was the exact opposite. In fact, his no-strings-attached dalliances were what matched this very description. His life and his marriage were a facade. They were completely based on the opposite. But his extramarital affairs were indeed 'lots of sex and zero lies'.

Google searches and Quora forums revealed page after page of material on extramarital affairs in India. The reasons for them were, primarily, sexual dissatisfaction to the wish for a no-strings-attached kind of association that I was seeing with my friend. Almost 50 per cent of those having extramarital affairs were, like my friend Snigdha, moms. The French extramarital dating app Gleeden was thriving in India. So much so that it claimed that 20 per cent of its 10 million users were Indian![3] The number of Indians on the app increased by 11 per cent from September 2022. And as early as in 2018, India had ranked tenth among fifty-three countries in membership of another popular extramarital dating app, Ashley Madison; this one based out of Canada. Gleeden – which, like the dating site Bumble is designed for women – says their Indian-mom users are aged between thirty and sixty. Almost 80 per cent of them are well-educated, in great jobs that allow them economic independence. These women consider themselves attractive, yet they are sexually dissatisfied, so seek excitement and thrill. Guilt, insecurities or the tradition of the sacrosanct Indian marriage does not plague them. But it did plague us in California, where there was no social taboos and where nudity and polyamory abounded. So if something faded out, we simply exited, worked on ourselves and our inner psychological patterns, healed ourselves and simply went into a new relationship, perhaps a marriage, perhaps not.

It was deeply ironic that the openness of society helped us keep our marriages more sacred than people could in a country like India, famous for its arranged marriages, where you married not just a person but his or her entire family. This just blew my mind.

In postpartum depression, with her husband choosing his work and evening beer with friends over helping her out as much as he should have with their highly colicky baby, my friend Sarah had struck up an intense emotional affair with an old friend who had just got divorced. She felt seen, cared for and validated, and though they never physically met, she felt 'held'. But she soon decided to end it. Her marriage was more important. She could have had the affair on the side, very, very easily, but she chose not to. 'How very Indian you are!' I had told her then. *Sundar, sushil, ghareloo* (beautiful, docile, domesticated). She had laughed when I translated the phrase for her. These are the three things an Indian woman must be, if she were to be a bahu. It was rare to see Sarah laugh during those days. But over time she began to again. She and her husband are still 'very happily married', hitting their second decade together; it is a marriage full of flaws and fights, but they are together out of *choice*.

That was the single word that decided the fates of marriages and those in it – choice.

My world was made of people of privilege. Their secrets were revealed in privileged places, in posh South Delhi markets, posh homes, posh five-star hotels. Was this an elitist phenomenon? The age-old classic case of the bored, idle rich – rich being highly variable, not determined as much by bank balances as by availability of free time, lifestyle and luxuries like drivers. (Really, I couldn't and still cannot and probably never will get over this ultimate luxury. Anyone from the first world, no matter how much they love to drive, who has experienced this, would know.)

For my umpteenth trip to the US Embassy, I decided to ask Josh, another media friend, for a favour. I asked for his driver, as that would spare me the bother of having to stand in queues for checking in my phone and whatnot. And from the little I had seen, private Indian chauffeurs were not only highly reliable but were also often smarter than their employers. Everyone seemed to be married to their drivers more than to their spouses. And of course the drivers were extremely resourceful and trustworthy. So I thought that instead of hailing an Uber, I would reach out to my friend for this favour so I could clear my mind and focus on the paperwork for my son's passport. I texted him. He was out of town and said his driver was not available.

'He is on *chhutti*.'

'Oh, why?'

'He is getting a divorce.'

'What? Why?' Nothing like curiosity about people you have never known and will never know or meet. 'Is this a joke for not helping me out because you love your driver?'

'Yeah!'

'Mope.'

'Mope, meaning?'

'Nope.'

'Can I interview him?'

'Hahaha, no. He is sad.'

'But I am very empathetic. And I am tired of only featuring women. We need more male voices.'

'Why is he getting a divorce?'

'His wife fucks his cousin.'

'What! I am sorry, but this is too funny. Why?'

'How do I know?'

'How do you not know? He is your driver.'

'I don't pry into people's lives.'

'But he is not people. He is your driver. More important than your spouse.'

'I don't have a spouse.'

'That's right. Sorry, I forgot. Some people have several. Now, both your driver and you are divorced men. Please let me do a story,' I said. 'Poor thing, though. Why do people have extramarital thingies?'

'I don't know . . . boredom, maybe.'

Back to Ubers. I wore saris 24x7 in India for no reason other than the sheer joy of it and the weather. I was crazy about India, like a stereotypical NRI, and seemed to have become a subject of great fascination wherever I went. That baffled me, but that was how it was. This meant Indians from India, being Indians from India, put me into their boxes openly. I became the picture of Hinduism, of *sanskari* in a *non-sanskari* younger world. Uber drivers began greeting me with smiles and were even more elated to learn, upon constant interrogation, that I was indeed married with a kid, which my looks did not suggest. I felt like a packet of Parle-G. I wonder what or who fit this bill of being married with a kid. Did all of us come out of a factory, and if so, were we products meant to match the ideas of products in people's heads? Nevertheless, my *sanskari* looks coaxed them into opening up about the numerous married men or women who got into their taxis with their lovers and made phone calls to their spouses, in-laws, relatives, children's teachers, saying they were busy with made-up chores. He would hear excuses such as:

'My mother is sick. I am out to get medicines and won't be home before nine.'

'I am at the school.'

'Work meeting. Later.'

'Doctor's appointment.'

'Friend is depressed and suicidal. I am with her.'

'They are not like you,' they would say, pleased, as if signing a character certificate nobody had asked for. Apparently, my wearing a sari meant that I was neither an Ashima nor had an Ashish.

Snigdha was out. Perhaps with Ashish and her iPhone? Her existence on earth had now suddenly become a reminder of how I had neither. Sushila, her maid, made me a classic Indian chai tea with ginger, lemongrass and tons of milk and sugar. You could laugh all you wanted at this combined use of two words for tea by the Americans, as if they were toddlers. Naan bread, chai tea, and so on. But they do say pita bread, lavash bread . . . for so many types of flatbreads; and matcha tea, sencha tea, oolong tea, earl grey tea, Ceylon tea, Darjeeling tea and its subsets (first flush, second flush, orange pekoe) . . . and of course, chai tea – the most special of them all, made with so much time, skill and care that it became a love language.

Just like the many types of tea, there are many types of extramarital affairs. To my aid came the newspaper I wrote for, for it had compiled lists of the types of extramarital affairs:[4]

1. Casual (Based on lust, could be one-night stands)
2. Romantic
3. Emotional (Like my friend Sarah's, this could be platonic too)
4. Cyber (No physical cheating happens)
5. Sanctioned (What we might call an open marriage. Polyamory, ethical non-monogamy, swinging, dating, where the couples allow each other to be involved with others romantically or sexually, or both)

Then, just like the ever-growing subsets of chai, from the classic ginger chai tea, cardamom chai tea to tandoori chai, chocolate chai, chili chai, etc., there are special subsets of extramarital affairs too, though I'm not quite sure where they fit:

1. One-night stand: apparently its own category under 'casual', because 'it just happened' and 'in the heat of the moment' because I was 'drunk'/'vulnerable'/'just not in my senses, yaar'
2. Love-addict affair: The participants believe they are married to the 'wrong person' and are addicted to the idea of 'the one'
3. Repeated-sex-addict affair: Jumping from person to person just for sex, with no emotional attachment, remaining perpetually unfulfilled (I made a mental note to text this to my friend discussing strange Bengali politicians, putting them in the same subcategory, even if he said he had not acted yet on his urges.)
4. Revenge affair: Perhaps the most dangerous, because it's to show that one is desirable and to make the spouse feel insecure
5. Exit-strategy affair: Like any business wanting to shut down may have an exit strategy, a person has an affair of any type from the list above, with the intention of getting caught so that their spouse or partner leaves them

'*Didi, aap kya dekh rahe ho?*'

Sushila, the maid, asked me what I was browsing on my phone as she set down the tall porcelain cup of wonderfully fragrant, steamy tea. She could read English. The list was in a large font and had accompanying pictures, making it easier for her to get the gist of what I was reading at a glance. '*Aap bhi?*' She blushed, smiling at me with a mischievous glint in her eye.

'*Aap bhi matlab?*' I asked her. What do you mean by you too?

'Main bhi.' She smiled. Me too.

'What do you mean?'

'*Side mein matlab hain koi* (I have someone on the side),' she said.

'Aap itne sundaar ho. Aap bhi kar lo, jab yahan ho kuch time ke liye (You are so pretty. While you're here for a while, you too should get a side piece),' she continued. She had seen my WhatsApp video calls to my son. My family had said hi to her. Sushila too made video calls to the son she had left behind in her village with her in-laws in Bihar to be able to work in the country's capital. And she too had an iPhone – she used WhatsApp and not Facetime, for whatever cultural and economic reasons, and her iPhone was a pre-loved one, as we call it in America, having had three or four users before her. It was ancient, bought from the phone-walla. Nevertheless, it was an iPhone. Both madam and maid had iPhones and Ashishes.

Affairs were everywhere. But why. My friend Tinku had just texted me a meme about the strange, self-proclaimed sexual appetite a Bengali politician was boasting about on a local TV channel. Tinku's wife had had many men while they were married. Her mother-in-law, that is, Tinku's mother, had been approving of these relationships. The couple themselves had never had a conversation on the subject. Naturally, like all difficult things, it is most human to avoid difficult conversations. Often, the longevity and success of marriages were simply due to avoiding. So of course they never spoke about it. But she knew he knew. He knew she knew he knew. So I couldn't think of a better person to answer me. I texted him:

'Why do people have extramarital affairs?'

'Because it's boring with the other person.'

'Other? You mean same? As in same person, your partner?'

'Same', 'other'. Same difference. (Other becomes same. The novelty gets lost eventually even with a new person. You get used to the person and then get bored. So there is no point of a new person or a partner of many years.) Basically, it becomes muscle memory. Just like amputees get used to loss of limb. Same way.'

'Huh?' I was lost. 'You feel like an amputee in your marriage? Should I talk to your wife?'

'No! She doesn't know I know.'

'She knows. And she knows you know she knows. Anyway, what's with this hyper-dark amputee metaphor?'

'Muscle memory of having sex with the same person. Familiar motions.'

'Whatever. People are just bodies at the end of the day. What's the difference? Loyalty is sexy to me. Monogamy is hot. It takes courage. It's a heroic act now perhaps more than ever before.'

'I know!' he says. 'But sex is a conversation, and the same conversation is boring to me. To everyone actually. I couldn't disagree with you more. Monogamy is a social construct. It's like socialism.'

'Socialism?' I ask. 'How Bengali of you. Might as well say Marxism, bring in CPI-M history.'

'We have been trained to glorify a most unnatural thing,' he says.

'Glorify socialism? Or monogamy?'

'Both!' he says, slightly impatient at my naivety. 'Boredom isn't courage. It is surrendering to social hypocrisy.'

'To each their own, I guess. Look at the Americans. They sleep with a lot of people, have their adventures, then marry their love, move to the suburbs to have a perfectly content, boring, monogamous life in peace and joy.'

'Yes, many people go vegetarian and then go on to hospital food.'

The sarcasm failed to pierce my thick hide.

'I love sex. The more illicit, the better.'

'Once the taboo is removed, it loses its charm and you realise the more mature, peaceful joys of monogamy,' I said.

'Nope. That's why one does it with many. With one it's boring. Anyway, we were discussing Bengal politics.'

On the side, I discovered a host of statistics and surveys on extramarital affairs in India, Gleeden once again leading these absurd, fascinating surveys. Trust the French on these matters. After all, theirs is the language with the highest number of euphemisms for orgasm, the term *la petite mort* literally translating into 'little death'. A Business Insider India article cited Gleeden surveys which had found that most extramarital affairs occurred during the honeymoon phase itself.[5] There were many other interesting findings. Infidelity knew no gender; the percentage of survey respondents from both genders who were unfaithful to their partners was almost the same – 59 per cent of men and 53 per cent of women. And the rate of extramarital affairs was almost the same in the big metros, like the national capital (that was revealing itself to me), as in the smaller towns – 58 per cent in the biggest metropolitan cities versus 56 per cent in the small towns. The biggest contributor to extramarital affairs had been the pandemic. During the lockdown, not knowing what to do with themselves, many had resorted to fantasising about being with someone other than their spouses and about the charms of complete infidelity. Gleeden discovered that almost a quarter of Indians were no longer against the idea of cheating in their marriage. Over 50 per cent of survey respondents said the lockdown had changed their minds about extramarital affairs. Four out of ten respondents fancied being with someone who wasn't their partner. Gleeden's findings were also in line with my own discovery – that people tend to cheat mostly with people they know, with those in their circle of friends and workers or with those they meet at parties and private events. Online affairs were also happening. I had already seen Shantanu, who had become Mr Jaan in my head now, constantly texting his lover. Many meetings were engineered through social media and of course there were online apps like Gleeden itself.

My son and husband came visiting briefly. We looked for a house that would suit our needs. In California, you could get a basic apartment in an hour's time. Or even less. It's not Silicon Valley for nothing. We had forgotten just how long everything took in India and how everything came with infinite doses of drama, entertainment and connection. And that it would take us a few tiny trips until we found the perfect place. Until then I found myself with my eleven-year-old in the backseat of scores of Uber Premiers, all an assortment of white sedans and numberless new brands that I couldn't recognise. Unlike NRI kids, he spoke no Hindi and had no love for Bollywood, Indian festivals, sweets, cricket and other Indian passions. But his essence was more Indian than all of them, having been raised on a diet of Advaita Vedanta philosophy and meditation, as well as yoga and Ayurvedic practices since birth, giving him a Zen sage-like aura, according to many who met him. Having to translate the country for him, even in the PG-rated bubble I had made for his world, made me even more aware of everything around me. On the streets, I found myself unable to escape romance even a single day! We drove past several random auto-rickshaws, which my son called by the pan-Asian name of tuk-tuks, which he had learned from his Asian-American friends on trips to their parents' home countries in Southeast Asia. And past random Indian trucks, decorated like only Indian trucks can be. He asked me to translate the signs on them. All of India, north India especially, was always hilarious to me; the signs there giving away more about the anthropology or current vibe of the country than any of the news channels, and every single one of them unbearable in its own way. Like the one we had just passed by, a giant billboard advertising 'Status: India's tallest mall'. Perfect for a country based heavily on *Jaanta hain main kaun hu? Mera baap kaun hain?* (Do you have any idea who I am? Who my father is?) A country based on name-calling, who knew who or whose cousin or uncle, obsessed with status. But no signage was as hilarious as the famous truck signs of India. There were of course the ubiquitous 'Horn OK please', 'Dipper at Night' (sometimes 'Use Diaper at Nite'), 'Blow Horn', 'Keep Distance', we had grown up with. All amusements in themselves that have been much recorded and sold as merchandise making for cute gifts. But there are unique expressions too, each one a work of art that brought a smile to my face and utter bafflement to my son's. Signs such as:

1. *Pyaar karo to jaano:* Fall in love first, and then you will truly know (the magic)
2. *Dekho magar pyaar se:* Please do look but with tenderness and love
3. *Chaila Miya:* Mr Romeo in love
4. *Mera sona babu:* My golden beloved
5. LOVE Jatt: Each of the letters of LOVE consisting of puzzle pieces of painted weapons, like pistols, knives and an AK-47. Jatt is a north Indian community known for their warrior spirit and pride, made famous by the actor Sunny Deol's dialogues, such as 'No if. No but. *Sirf* (only) *Jatt*, while referring to the FBI as not the US Federal Bureau of Investigation but a 'Fully Bewkoof Insaan', a complete fool.[6]
6. *Pyaar karo, bache nahee:* A potent, unsolicited ad for contraception, which condom and other protection companies should have spent millions on, which translates into 'make love, not kids'
7. *Pehle thhe ladki ke diwane, ab lage kamani, akal aa gayi thikane:* First, we were crazy about women, then we began to earn money and returned right back to our senses

8. *Pehle thi Pooja, ab kaam hi pooja:* First, there was Pooja (a girl). Now work is the only pooja (worship)
9. *Din mein bhaiya raat mein sayiaan:* Brother by day, lover by night

I did not know then that a year later, when we did find a house, I'd have to translate Indian love once again to my son when our maid would elope with her boyfriend to Uttar Pradesh of all places, the land of honour killings, sending us the message through another maid, whom I'd discover was the boyfriend's ex. Or that the gentle-mannered teenage delivery boy at the local super-mart in our gated community, who lugged our cart for us to our apartment (the joys of a service economy, which only those who have lived in the so-called first world, where you had to do every single thing yourself, appreciate every minute!), would narrate to us tales of his own heartbreak, and how he had now shifted his love from girls to his buffaloes, whose milk and the ghee he made from it he would try to sell to me, and which I had to gently refuse because of my lactose intolerance. And he'd say, '*Bhains best hain.*' The buffalo is the best!

Not a day would go by when we could escape the subject of love. But I did not know that then. Back then, US President Donald Trump's indictment, courtesy of adult entertainment film star Stormy Daniels, was all over the news. Apparently, this was shocking. It was consensual, paid for, and yet it was considered a scandal. And here were so many of the commoners in a conservative country doing just that. What was scandal and what wasn't? It was all surreal. I found it difficult to wrap my mind around all of it. I was shocked at the strange ways in which these marriages of others began to affect me. Challenging my beliefs. Sneaking into my mind to make me question my own 'perfect' marriage of decades. And like ancient histories, be it pyramids, doors of houses or personal relationships of many years, there were cobwebs that needed to be cleaned out. Sometimes skeletons. With difficult conversations about the hurts and betrayals of bygone times that daily life rendered redundant, but the hurt remained. But like cobwebs, dust, and in some cases skeletons, we ignored them, pretending they did not exist. It was far easier. I thought of Tinku's marriage. I may not have had skeletons like that but I did not have the courage for more cobwebs. That too, giant cobwebs. Not now. So like all good Indian women, I swept the questions away and pretended they did not exist. At least for now. It was much easier to focus on people around me than on myself. A new-found curiosity grew in me, engulfing me completely. I wanted . . . no, wanted is an understatement . . . because I had just moved my own picture-perfect NRI life around to live here out of choice, I was not merely curious, I did not merely want to know more, I was dying to understand this new India. To me, it was an anthropological study, for it completely affected how I identified as an Indian currently, and it impacted me directly. It impacted all of us, but how many noticed what was happening around them to become aware of all this? It was much easier to indulge in random affairs, I suppose, than to sit with oneself and ask these difficult questions.

How did the world's largest democracy love? Why did it love the way it now did? What made it different from how Indians had loved before? How did people who had everything and all the freedom in the world love? Had one pandemic changed marriages so much? Or were people always like this and only revealing themselves now? Why were they so lonely that they needed so many lovers? The questions kept growing like a sea in me. I was completely submerged in their waters, confused, curious.

I did not know then that I'd spend years unearthing answers to how India loves – because India was going through a revolution that would change who Indians were at their core and what the country would become.

It was not an ordinary revolution. It was a revolution of love.

3

Mumbai

I ARRIVED IN MUMBAI, my head full of the lives of others. Earlier, every single time the airplane's wheels touched the tarmac on the runway at Mumbai, I used to smile. This was the first time I did not. Having grown up in seventeen homes and attended nine schools before the age of nine across small-town India, Mumbai was the only place where I had found some stability, the only place I had felt was home. (Two decades of being in a home in California had changed nothing.) Somehow, I had led a mostly solitary life there, less than in California or my boarding school in the mountains, but still . . .

This sudden tsunami of extramarital affairs in the country's capital, which was first most amusing, had now completely overwhelmed me. I felt I would explode. Like a bomb. I felt fuller than this famously bursting, space-starved city – the irony not escaping me. Still, journalistic curiosity outshone all this. If Delhi had so much sex and taboo relationships, Mumbai then, surely having always been the most open city in the country, should have even more, way, way, way more love and sex everywhere: Ashimas and Ashishes flooding every centimetre of this space-starved city. I did not know then how wrong I was.

I had grown up in Bandra and had attended Sophia College in town. My Bombay had always been that little stretch of Bombay – privileged, little, highly educated, wealthy, fun. It struck me then that this had not been unlike my life in America. Unlike most of the US, California was most privileged, and the Silicon Valley stretch of the San Francisco Bay Area even more so. Economics is important. It is only when your basic needs – food, water, shelter – are met do you have the time for frivolities. In my college era, it seemed that everyone around me in this stretch was all about sex, drugs and rock and roll, making me recede even deeper into my shell and into books. It was this that had made me marry my then best friend because he was the only man I had felt safe with. Safety is a core human need, and plays out, like all psychology, in love, sex and relationships, as we will see in the upcoming chapters.

The city was unrecognisable. I was meeting my friend Ranvijay, a Bollywood director, at a bookstore in Bandra for a book event. Later, we hung out at a cafe. And I asked him what I had already texted a bunch of people we knew. Different versions of the same question that I had asked Tinku. Why do people have extramarital affairs? Here, I asked Ranvijay: 'Why do people need so many people? Why is everyone sleeping with everyone? It's everywhere. California seems like a backward, conservative village in comparison.'

'It happens. And well, what else is there to do?' He chuckled. 'And you're too much of a prude to use proper language.' He was referring to the F word.

'I did grow up in a convent, after all. I am practically a nun.'

'And your child is born immaculate of course.'

We laughed with the warm camaraderie of college friends who hung out every day, with all the time in the world to discuss frivolities. When of course we weren't, and neither did we have the time. Everyone was busy and selective about whom they met at this point in our lives with adult responsibilities, bills, time constraints, career issues, and so on.

But you see, this warmth, this camaraderie was very Bollywood. You formed little communities and families everywhere. For shoots on location, for instance, you were often like a caravan of gypsies and each other's only family. I had seen this very close when Ranvijay and others had helped struggling actresses, musicians, film editors (everyone was a struggler at some level or a hustler) and me with all kinds of errands and paperwork. In fact, he had even helped me (circa 2015–2016, when I was in Mumbai for seven months researching for my first book) with property paperwork of a different sort from what I was doing right now. He had guided me through registration work, housing society offices, etc., all for an Overseas Citizen of India (OCI) looking to rent property in their home country. Sure, there was in Bollywood a caste and class system with nepotism and star kids at the top, and there was a pecking order. But more or less, everyone knew everyone; it was like a little village. All of this struggling and hustling not just for work but often also for accommodation and all kinds of random battles that fall out of the sky, putting everyone in the same boat at some point in their lives, made people empathetic towards each other, and to-the-point with a better work ethic than anywhere else in the country. The total opposite of the city I had just left – the capital of political power, generational wealth and *jaanta hain main kaun hu, mera baap kaun hain, main kaunse minister ko jaanta hun* (Do you know who the hell I am? Who my father is? Which minister I know?).

I knew many people from my year spent in Mumbai researching for my first book, *An Ordinary Life*, on the struggles and life of a Bollywood movie star, and I was counting on this community to help with the launch of my second book, *The Water Phoenix*. I ran into a conundrum, which was at once both awkward and bizarre, hilarious and tragic. You see, in spite of knowing ample actors, I couldn't get someone for the Bombay leg of my book launch events. To launch, to moderate. There was the problem of overlapping dates of course, the bane of Bollywood, where people would shoot nonstop because they had finally found work. And were they to take a break, five hundred were ready to replace them. And they'd be easily forgotten.

In spite of my knowing so many people, none of them could attend my book events. Why? Because everybody had slept with everybody. This made it most awkward. Because emotions were involved and these were not random Tinder hookups. Often, people had deeply emotional bonds, born out of vulnerabilities of career, accommodation, and so on that the city put them in. So whether you want to use the old-fashioned label of love or not, at least the consequent sex was often intense, with deep memories. Sometimes, of someone living together till they found a house. Sometimes, some actor being thrown out and another film person sheltering them and things happening. In other words, all exes. Everyone was everyone's ex. Or so it seemed in my little world of permutations and combinations.

Yes, I actually sat with Ranvijay and some others and drew arrows and flowcharts on cafe napkins, which he laughingly took. He said he would use these as material for a movie someday. I should have made such notes and charts for Delhi too, but in hindsight, I suppose this book, *How India Loves*, is a result of these jottings. I guess those cafe napkins were part of my book-building and eventually chapter-outlining process.

Naturally, there was little animosity. But nobody wanted to face their ex. Why for me? They wouldn't do it for themselves. Everyone spends lifetimes getting over their exes, of pretending they don't exist, or if they bump into them at parties, gulping down their excruciatingly painful emotions and walking past with a casual smile. So many songs have been written on broken hearts. . . . *When a heart breaks, it don't break even.*

But they would meet me in private, one on one, to get their copies signed, to catch up with me and discuss the book. And in the decade I was away, during which the pandemic too had happened and transformed people beyond recognition, everything had changed. Resentments and grievances over casual situationships, before the term was coined, had taken over. Hearts had been broken, even though the situations were consensual, with no strings attached. Many had gotten married or were into partnerships. Others had broken out of theirs. The pandemic had created lockdown romances and lockdown breakups, teaching people whatever lessons were relevant for them.

In all of this, their promiscuity and hyper-casual sex lives were costing me my book events. This is a trend I was noticing. People's love lives and sex lives were constantly impacting me when there should have been no connection between them. Worse, people, most of them complete strangers whom I didn't know even indirectly, would come out of nowhere and keep enlightening me about the intricate details of these lives, their innermost secrets (which make for this book).

Mumbai was very interesting. Randeep's exes were all unavailable for the above reasons. Randeep himself was unavailable for the same reasons. So it was back to college, when others' obsession with sex had made me feel so unsafe that I avoided all parties and was eventually (thankfully!) forgotten enough to simply live at the British Council Library in Nariman Point and the marble steps of Sophia College, my pink palace of an institution, hiding completely in books. Now I was braver and comfortable enough within myself to handle whatever life threw at me, the journey of which has been documented in my second book, *The Water Phoenix*, but I still had the same problem. Clearly, the world was the problem, no matter how much responsibility I took to work on myself.

'I am now into cuddling and sleeping,' says Randeep.

So now cuddling was a trend. 'So you're done sleeping around and are just sleeping now?' I ask him.

He laughs and nods, 'Yes, ma'am.'

That was the thing about Mumbai. Traditionally, it was the city all of India flocked to with their dreams. Many entered Bollywood but also other industries. Throughout the struggle years, that is, if you made it through them in the first place, which is not always guaranteed – something I have documented in depth in my first book – and even after the struggle years end, there is a deep loneliness that remains.

In a harsh city with obscene rent rates and tough living conditions, where you often know nobody, you form little communities, unsaid bonds that keep you afloat. Some become marriages or long-term partnerships. Most don't. There's a reason why every paanwalla sells marijuana all over Andheri. Everyone needs a coping mechanism.

It seemed that behind my back, the sex drive of the city had simmered down and settled into cuddling. It really was a trend. Another friend, Darsh, who was in finance, had 'a thing' going on with an actress twenty years younger. I asked him how she was doing. He said, 'She just comes to sleep.' That was it. Cuddling and sleeping. Like children. And then, leaving for your individual battles. It was a strange comfort, a piece of home, in a city that was both cruel and heartless and full of heart. For here, strangers came out of nowhere to give you shelter and comfort, for they too had known and fought similar struggles. That's what bound the entire city together.

Three of my girlfriends, all in the film industry, had chosen celibacy. Literally, a city known for DTF (Down to Fuck) in Gen Z lingo had now gone from DTF to celibacy. Out of choice. Out of defeat. And grief. Somehow, this was beautiful and touching. I was not expecting this tenderness from a city that races so much that it never sleeps.

Sure, there were 'events' held every now and then in the city, which we get into in more detail in the chapter on BDSM, which was far more prevalent in Bengaluru. There were quite a few 'slave auctions', foot worship and trampling events being held – on yachts, in bars and elsewhere.[1] Celebrating kinks and fetishes. And then everybody returned to their lives – as Deepti, a forty-two-year-old journalist had.

One day, when I was in her home, her ex-husband was visiting. Without saying a word, the two walked into her bedroom and fell asleep instantly, like unspoken clockwork, just his hand ever so gently over her. It was like something out of a sweet dream. Deepti's maid, blushing and too embarrassed to articulate what she wanted to say, kept asking me how she could sweep and mop the room they were in and how she'd get into trouble if she didn't. I couldn't wake up the couple. I asked her to ignore them and stood by the door to give her company while she cleaned the room. She kept trying not to look at them. The tenderness, the vulnerability of the sight of the two in bed was a thing of beauty, and like all things of beauty can, it was making her uncomfortable.

A couple of hours later, Deepti's ex woke up and walked out, as if nothing had happened. Again, as if it was something out of a dream. Of course, Deepti and I never spoke about it. There was nothing to speak about. But this tenderness deeply moved me. It was a nice thing to witness, in whatever form, especially after the jarring, frivolous extramarital affairs of Delhi. Love still existed. Unacknowledged. Unnamed. Unsaid.

4

Bengaluru

I HAD ELOPED AND got married at the age of twenty-one. And that was the last time I was in Bengaluru, where much of my own secret rendezvous with my then boyfriend, later husband, had happened. I had sweet memories of childlike teenage love in the city, where neither of us knew too many people and felt free.

Today it was a different, far more intense version of that city. With a state GDP of over ₹22.4 trillion in 2023 according to Statista,[1] Karnataka is among the wealthiest states of India, with Bengaluru, its capital, being the main economic driver. And not just IT, a whole bunch of other jobs have increasingly shifted to Bengaluru, resulting in a population that comprises not just families but single people, younger people, coming from all over the country. In many ways, it was like Mumbai – water problems, traffic and potholes included. Obviously, none of this is news. But there is always the direct impact of economy on the culture and anthropology of a city. And what was breaking news, which most media had missed, was how the city was living, evolving and loving.

I am staying in a three-storeyed house in a pretty, leafy lane in Kalyan Nagar, still full of traditional, older Bengaluru families who have lived here for decades and generations. The neighbourhood is a little traditional, and yet nobody frowns or bats an eyelid when my friend visits me every evening to check on me. Nor when his far younger girlfriend shows up. Forget raised eyebrows, nobody even gives a look.

Not even the polite kind a young Queen Elizabeth had given Marilyn Monroe, looking politely without looking. I can't imagine this in the Kolkata or Delhi of even today. And even in some parts of Mumbai, traditionally India's most liberal and nonchalant city.

It was little things like these that showed how normal and accepting Bengaluru was of whatever the newer generations were bringing to the city – in the odd couples here and there, in the LGBTQA community, in the age differences, religious differences. Then there was this abundance of pubs and people drinking during the day. In Church Street, amidst book signings, I got asked out politely, several times, by younger boys, who looked like they were in their twenties. Just slightly tipsy enough to give them the courage to do so. And yet in an extremely decent way. So much so that I didn't even realise what was happening, because I am so used to strangers coming and talking to me, especially after California. But also it's just part of a journalist's job to talk to strangers and interview them, and it becomes a way of life for strangers to approach you as well.

After I gave a talk at Ranga Shankara, Bengaluru's historic theatre, several readers began coming in for the book signings afterwards. And because the book is about healing from abuse, they shared their stories and journeys with me. One brought along her mother, who felt comfortable enough to share her own stories of marital rape, not even realising at first that that was what she had suffered. Later, when she realised what it was, she didn't think it was wrong. The levels to which society had brainwashed us into gaslighting ourselves, invalidating our own rape, abuse and trauma, is something that never ceases to baffle me. And this was becoming a trend, bringing in each and every story contained in this book and in my columns. After such conversations, you instantly become best friends. For mostly, your own best friends don't know what has happened to you.

At one of the Church Street bookshops, Sameer, a frail-looking engineer, an IITian, opened up, his eyes full of tears, thanking me for having spoken about boys suffering abuse. Obviously, abuse knows no gender and it is a myth that boys are not abused. In fact, it's harder for them than for girls. People just want to feel safe, to be seen, to be heard and to talk about themselves. Especially the quiet ones. I began hanging out with these growing tribe of readers, in small groups, sometimes one on one, mostly over meals, post book events. Sometimes they would show me around the city. I think it was the third time I was meeting Sameer, over a meal, when he felt comfortable enough to bring out what was even darker and more secretive than his abuse. Shalini, also a reader, had complimented me on my sari, the accompanying golden heels, and even my feet. And this quiet young man Sameer, who barely spoke, suddenly felt it was totally appropriate to join in. Which was fine. But then he asked, 'Is it okay if I worship them? Only if you're comfortable of course.' I almost spilled my drink in shock. 'Absolutely not!' I said, showing him my wedding ring.

And that was the thing. This fetish (we look into it deeper in the chapter on BDSM), like so many others, had nothing to do with traditional sex. And in Bengaluru, which seemed to be where Mumbai once was, everyone was curious and experimenting. You just had to go to Quora,[2] Reddit, to find page upon page specific to this. Bengaluru was especially fond of this particular fetish of foot worship, and many were willing to pay huge amounts for it, as the paper *Bangalore Mirror*[3] had reported. I mean, even traditional media like the one I wrote for, *The Times of India*,[4] had caught a whiff of the trend.

I told Sameer it was not okay. He apologised instantly, with tears in his eyes. He thought his request was actually a compliment, and he respected me so much that to have found that he had disrespected and insulted me instead made him feel like a little boy full of a bundle of emotions too tumultuous to process. Apparently, foot worship had helped him heal his relationship with sex. All abused children have problems with sex. Even someone as healed as me will not get a massage or a pedicure, a manicure or even a haircut. I don't want a random person touching me, period. Even if in a healthy, non-sexual way.

Sameer softly said, 'I love being a slave. I love servicing.' It made sense that this city of gentler folk (compared with, say, aggressive north India) used to being in the shadows, often slightly tipsy during the day, would opt for foot worship. Psychologically, the foot fetish goes back to babies crawling to their busy mothers' feet for attention, and often that's all they saw or got of her. The brain recognised feet as mom, as safe, as love, and a neural pathway was formed. Every kink, fetish, love language has its roots in our earliest childhood memories. Every pattern does. Why should patterns to do with the bedroom be any different?

The more I interacted with readers and their friends, the more obvious it was becoming – BDSM communities and experimental sex were thriving in Bengaluru. All based on communication and consent. Given this highly educated, well-to-do, soft spoken and often nerdy demographic, one could assume that consent and communication, perhaps an overdose of it, would be normal. There was great awareness of mental health and a good dating ethic in general. It reminded me very much of the work culture and ethic in my home Silicon Valley. Culturally and not just because this is a wannabe copycat of the world's largest tech hub. Abuse was unthinkable. They were so eager to serve, with their puppy eyes. Everyone wanted to be a slave. Mistresses, as they showed me on their phones, were domineering, some downright bullies, advertising their goods on Twitter. It was just normal – as if one were sharing a meme. Or a forward.

Then there were the couples who too were into all kinds of such activities. I met a swinger couple, again in Church Street. They were married, happily so as they said. 'Just a good weekend activity for us. We meet new people. It keeps things interesting and exciting,' said the husband. 'See, we are not dead like most couples. Of course, most of our regular circle doesn't know,' the wife added. They insisted that theirs was not an open marriage. They were just part of a community and did group activities. Same as us and our hiking groups in California, I thought.

My mind thought of the innumerable marriages I had encountered in Delhi and thought perhaps this was healthier. They were in it together. And that kind of openness can be a beautiful thing if you are coming back to each other. In modern times, it was not uncommon for sex therapists to recommend 'shocking partners' via role play, even a scandalous activity like threesomes, opening up marriages. The point was that you had shared a taboo thing together and come home to each other. So you were stronger than ever before. A friend's marriage had become stronger than ever before only because they opened up their marriage for five years, at such a recommendation, when they were fighting a bitter divorce battle. Today they are one of the strongest couples I know. Cheating doesn't even matter to them. If one of them finds someone attractive, he or she will openly tell the other about it. It is just that this level of honesty and trust is extremely hot, and keeps their chemistry and love going so that the drudgery of mortgages, raising kids, care-giving for parents and in-laws and their other responsibilities don't suck them dry. Again, this was what Delhi was doing, but in Delhi the couples were cheating and needed better mental health, self-awareness and trust in choosing this route. Bengaluru was. It was certainly not my way.

My mind wandered to my latter teenage years – 12th grade, which in Mumbai meant not high school but college (junior college), and the rest of college and university. Affairs of love and lust, excitement and experimentation of youth abounded all around me while I stuck my head, as I always had, into books. I had of course, entered this world after being cloistered for a decade in a most conservative all-girls convent boarding school in the mountains, where the tiniest act of negligence (like whispering during naptime, passing Whisper sanitary napkins, not picking up on time our dried undergarments from the terrace that we had washed ourselves) was considered sinful and meant repenting by saying Hail Marys and Our Father prayers while kneeling and praying to the Holy Ghost for forgiveness. I escaped much of the drama there and in college around me, by escaping to Blandings and the wit of Jeeves the most famous valet in history courtesy of P.G. Wodehouse. Almost all of his work focused on the shenanigans of British aristocracy, the idle rich, the most privileged, many receiving the most privileged and the highest education from the best institutes of the day like Eton and Oxford and so on. And still, they were marvellously stupid. Delightful insults, the essence of the famous British wit, abounded in Wodehouse's prose. I read the books especially for these insults, collecting them, by copying them in pencil into the back pages of my computer science, chemistry and physics notebooks, to peer into for desperately-needed comic relief from highly incompetent teachers, during the respective periods of teaching, to make the joyless, boring hours bearable. While several of Wodehouse's insults were subtle, from Jeeves, or in the context of the plot running into paragraphs, many insults were mere direct words literally meaning stupidity and idiocy. Nincompoop and imbecile were two words I had learned and loved instantly. Along with Shakespearean insults we exchanged so freely to belittle each other at boarding school, I had begun to use both of these words as well. Both words were used by an array of prudish elderly aunts (who strangely happened to be not too different in temperament from my boarding school nuns), for example, the famous Aunt Agatha to describe their good-for-nothing, aristocratic nephews like the infamous Bertie Wooster.

Many of the people I kept encountering were so much like Wodehouse's characters. Like them, these people too, happened to be India's brightest, with the best education, privileges and positions in society. Their love stories may be R-rated or at least PG-17 but their shenanigans were no different. They were all behaving like total nincompoops. Romantic nincompoops. Even their staff, like the driver in Delhi or Snigdha's maid, were well taken care of and themselves admitted that they had relatively comfortable lives compared to their peers. And were acting the same as their rich employers. In comparison to all of them, I was and still am a grandmother, very much like the prudish aunts (again most famously Aunt Agatha) in Wodehouse's books or the nuns in my boarding school. But I wasn't a mere grandmother. As I increasingly realised throughout the writing of this book, the only nincompoop in the end was me. Returning from Wodehouse to this century and the stories in front of me, it completely blew my mind that little Bengaluru was so much like California. Perhaps even more ahead.

5

Kolkata

NOTHING, AND I MEAN nothing, could have prepared me for the final homecoming to the city every Indian supposes I belong to, like every typical Bengali should, which, obviously, like all stereotypes, is simply not true. Growing up in a boarding school in Bombay and then eloping quickly to the most non-Bengali fold I could find – with my best friend who was Punjabi and cared neither for Marx nor health ailments – I had very quickly fled the country, the continent, to California, a state that is a complete misfit in the country it is in. One could argue that being in California was like escaping real America – home, like Uttar Pradesh and Haryana, to guns and patriarchy. Throughout my stay there – documenting *Roe v. Wade*, anti-abortion legislation and shootings becoming as frequent, as mundane and as American as backyard summer barbecues – I was in a parallel universe being regaled by relatives who had to head to the ICU because they were about to die. As a toddler and until I had a toddler of my own, I not only believed them but was greatly traumatised by their stories, because I was extremely empathetic (or extremely foolish, depending on whom you ask) and believed them. But here they were, drama queens and drama kings still about to head to the ICU in the slow motion of cheap Bengali movies and living there forever if they could, but somehow not making it and still complaining about it with the fervour of toddlers bawling at fever pitch, while discussing endless types of foods, especially types of fish and mishti (Bengali sweets). And of course, complaining about every political event, the death of Marx and Lenin en route. (To this date, my American son raised in capitalist Silicon Valley who has only heard of 'these boys' in Kolkata, thinks Marx and Lenin are someone's misbehaved dogs, not just any dogs but specifically obese, ultra-lazy Labradors, which are what several of my relatives looked like and had the temperament of.)

That was Kolkata in my head. I knew it as one does fictional characters from books one has not even read but has heard about from those who have. Like Mr Christian Grey. I knew only one literary gray: Dorian Gray. Nervous, excited, this-was-what-it-had-all-boiled-down-to, my year in the city of my roots, which I never had. I had already written a month's worth of columns in advance, knowing very well the drama that awaited me here. I just didn't know the extent of it.

Also it is most important to note that during the COVID-19-induced lockdown, intoxicated by its love of mishti, a vitamin in the Bengali diet, the state government had considered sweets to be enough of an essential item to allow sweet shops (like medical stores) to stay open. I am sure riots would have broken out had they not done this. Sweet shops had then made sandesh shaped like the coronavirus as a homage to it. Such amusing things may seem irrelevant. But they are most relevant. In fact, far beyond the soulless, boring statistics with no human stories, it is in these bits of trivia that a city, a people, a country reveal who they truly are. All of my journalism, my decades as a foreign correspondent, was about finding these relevant bits of trivia. It revealed just how eccentric and romantic the city was.

Straight from the airport to the ancient green building that was my father's house, I landed with a 105 degrees F fever, heading straight to bed before I passed out on the ancient granite mosaic floor. It had never happened to me before. As a mom I had driven on American freeways at top speed under the influence of morphine and fentanyl and other narcotics prescribed by US doctors. Collapsing was not a luxury for women and moms in America. Like the maids in India, we had to show up in our infinite roles, no matter what calamity.

Part shadow, part reflection, female figures in saris with white hair, shrieking laughs like banshees, lips red with blood trickling down, yelling children's stories in Bangla too proper for me to comprehend. Who were they? Ghosts? Demonesses? Goddesses? I don't know. But they stayed a while, like loyal dogs in a horror film, merging with the maids, I guess, for I was being made to drink fluids I couldn't taste or recall. Was I hallucinating? Was it the fever? Were these visions? Was I mistaking them for people?

Five days later, I recovered, though I felt infected and different. It took me a while to identify that this infection was what my maids would tell me was the spirit of Kali, Durga, Bengal, a matriarchal state of ferocious warrior women goddesses who took no shit from anyone. The Kolkata air was full of the rage of its wronged women, who were simultaneously hopeless romantics seeking love. I couldn't tell what was happening. But I wasn't myself at all in this land of Kali worshippers, where I felt I was being seen for the very first time not as wife, mother, daughter, writer. Of course, I was all these and mostly a woman. But when everyone from the cobbler and tailor to random millionaires called me Ma, as every girl was addressed as the mother goddess from the day she was born, I got the goosebumps. I had to often rush to cry before I got used to it. It was surreal, the energy. Nowhere in the world have I seen women be so respected and yet so wronged. And the three maids in my father's house who chatted nonstop helped me comprehend it.

The love stories began pouring in from anywhere and everywhere. They'd have come even if I had locked myself in my room. Even if I was in the hotel bathroom. There was no escaping these stories. That is how I shifted to finally writing about love, sex and relationships in my column for two years and the seed of this book was born, for the stories just would not (and still don't) stop. The younger ones called me Didi. In fact, between being called Didi and Ma nonstop for slightly over a year, I forgot what my name was. Only my bylines and documents reminded me of it.

A Thailand-style floating market where vegetables were sold on boats parked in a pond, amidst ponds here and there, were a sea of romantic nincompoops. I had to often wade around the boats, poking my way ahead with my giant red umbrella saying, '*Didi ke jete din* (let Didi pass).' It was a city of lovesick puppies, holding hands, with romantic music blasting out of speakers, even at religious events. *Pujo*, which really seemed to happen every two weeks, meant nothing got done. This was the city of *pujo* and *prem* (worship and love). My maid asked me why I didn't have a few boyfriends. I reminded her that I was married. It didn't matter. Apparently, I was the only non-romantic nincompoop around. I had once seen a sole albino seal pup stand out in a giant crowd of resting seals at Pescadero, local to me in the San Francisco Bay Area. In the sea of nincompoops around me, I felt like that seal pup. As in, to the nincompoops – for being romantic, goddess-worshipping, lovestruck nincompoops was normal – I, a logical, work-oriented, monogamous person was the only nincompoop.

It was a city where everyone loved everyone. Polyamory was everywhere, from the streets to the mansions, both crumbling and new, to the glitzy skyscrapers and penthouses that were popping up everywhere, making this ancient city appear more and more like other cities in India, say NCR or Mumbai. Beyond sheer amusement affected me on a daily basis. For instance, I couldn't get photocopies from any of the three photocopy shops in my neighbourhood. Why? It was always some goddess' 'birthday'. Or one of the relatives of the several wives (agreements were more in the heart than on paper, as we will see in the upcoming chapter on polyamory) of the shop owners had to be appeased. I got all of this information from the sweet shop vendor next to one of the photocopy shops. Seeing me so furious at the shops being always closed, he forced me to (for I had said no many times) to eat mishti, which were on the house. How come polyamory did not affect his business? How come the sweet shops were open (barring the traditional afternoon siesta, of course) and professional? The economics of this baffled me, making the business journalist in me itch to dig into the matter of polyamory-induced economics. I had to constantly take Ubers from south Kolkata to the more Marwari-dominated central Kolkata, which had a better work ethic, simply to get photocopies of my documents.

The evenings were the same and very powerful. The sound of conch shells was everywhere every evening. The evening air was filled with the perfumed smoke of incense from shondeh, the evening worship in the households, and the innumerable little neighbourhood temples, most of them of goddess Kali. Offerings included sweets and flowers – most of which in this southern Kolkata neighbourhood were bought from one woman, who turned out to be my father's maid's friend, and whom my maid brought over to the house urging that I listen to her story because I was a writer. (Little did I know then that, this being the city of literature, Kolkatans everywhere would keep doing this to me every day for a whole year.)

With her beaming smile sporting missing teeth and framed against her old green cycle-rickshaw filled with colourful flowers, Suprabha is a sight to behold and one that is impossible to forget. Each dawn, at around 4 a.m., she takes a train to

Howrah to buy the freshest flowers – hibiscus, marigold, a type of fragrant jasmine called jui phool and rajnigandha (tuberoses) – from the wholesale market. She returns, cooks for her family, finishes her household chores and begins selling these flowers by 9 a.m., returning home only after 1 p.m. for lunch, further chores and tending to her twenty-one-year-old son who has a nerve problem severe enough to cause seizures and which doesn't allow him to work for very long.

Her husband is a raging alcoholic who beats her as and when he pleases. He has sold off the remaining five cycle-rickshaws they had owned to fund his addiction. Just a few days ago, when she had joined her neighbours in a political rally, he had found her there, pulled her thick silver chain off her neck so hard that it broke and left cuts on her neck and her thumb while she tried to shield herself from him.

Suprabha is the sole reliable breadwinner of the family. She used to be a maid, but for the past five years she has been making about ₹7,000 a month selling flowers. It means lesser hours at home and freedom from both her violent husband and the tantrums of employers.

The husband constantly stalks her to ensure she is within his control – though for what reason or purpose, nobody knows. But then, violence rarely knows logic. She had filed a first information report (FIR) against him at the Park Circus police station, but after a couple of days of taking him in, the police had let him go. She knows they cannot keep him behind bars forever, which is why she has given up on reaching out to the police for help. Looking at her smile, you cannot tell that she goes through daily hell.

It was the eve of India's seventy-fifth year of independence. And all over the streets of Kolkata, I could see a little revolution was on its way – born, of course, out of what else but love stories. Battered, worn out, fuelled by Durga and Kali – the warrior mother goddesses they worshipped – the poor women in this city were taking up jobs involving physical stress, jobs stereotypically associated with men. Women were driving cycle-rickshaws. More and more. Something I had never seen before.

Women were turning into street vendors, selling phuchkas and other street food. Women were now all kinds of street vendors. Pushing carts of vegetables, odd household goods and even conducting repair of old electronics goods. Women were now cobblers . . . and stories (of finding a way out of domestic violence without shirking their responsibilities) like Suprabha's were all cookie-cutter. Even off the streets, I saw for the first time ever a female salesperson selling heavy-duty electronics, like air conditioners and washing machines, helping even in the heavy lifting of these appliances. I had only seen men do this in India.

On the streets at least, many of the women vendors are victims of domestic violence who are empowering and liberating themselves. As India celebrated seventy-five years of independence that year, I could not think of a better celebration than this quiet, unsung revolution in gender dynamics, this feminism, this freedom. But it wasn't just about the jobs they were doing. It was also about the support they were giving to each other.

My father's maid Tumpa, who had introduced me to Suprabha (and kept asking me why I didn't have boyfriends), is a trained Odissi dancer. Tumpa had been wooed by her husband with yellow flowers and a meal at a restaurant in the well-known Acropolis Mall, where he worked as a senior waiter. The same man has turned heavily violent today. If you look closely at Tumpa's face, you can see the scars from stitches she needed to get done after he hit her. She works as a maid and has a three-year-old who suffers from thalassemia and needs constant blood transfusions.

Fortunately, her in-laws threw their own son out of the house to take care of her and her child. They even helped her file an FIR against him and file for a divorce too so they could organise her marriage to a good man who would deserve her as and when she felt ready for it.

They tried to keep her safe by keeping him away from her. But he kept coming back. Tumpa kept saying she would leave him as we had offered her our place to stay in. I had helped her open a bank account too. But I was informed by the security guard of our building that she was meeting her ex who was there with his ex, which she confirmed to me. You see, romance trumped violence. The mother-in-law of another maid, Chanda, also kicked out her violent son, fed up with his violence towards her daughter-in-law. The mother-in-law and Chanda live together in peace, leading a comfortable life from their collective monthly income of about ₹25,000, ensuring that Chanda's twelve-year-old child has a good education.

Where in the world do mothers kick out their own sons to support the bahu? This kind of open support to the daughter-in-law, of choosing her over a violent, abusive son, their own blood, is perhaps what makes Bengal so unique. It is frankly unimaginable in many of the northern states, where the son is worshipped as a god, no matter what he does. I was married into a Punjabi family, and being familiar with the patriarchy of the north, I couldn't even imagine such a thing happening there. Nor in America, with its nuclear families.

In spite of the violence against women in Bengal, there is a respect here for women so commonplace that it takes a foreigner to notice how precious it is. The gentle sing-song versions of Ma (and Didi) I am constantly addressed as in this land of Kali worshippers gave me a freedom I had never known before – to be seen as a woman without roles and labels for the very first time in my life.

According to data collected by India's National Crime Records Bureau, the majority of cases of domestic violence between 2001 and 2018 were filed under 'cruelty by husband or his relatives', with the reported rate of this crime increasing by 53 per cent over eighteen years. A total of 1,548,548 cases were reported under this category; the majority of the crimes of course go unreported.

Contrary to these cases are the instances of the support women like Chanda and Tumpa get from their mothers-in-law. It is more powerful than what non-profits and the police can give them, because even with their support they still have to live with people. To know that a woman can be protected and that she can still be independent is how real change is created.

While many of the men on the streets – cycle-rickshaw drivers, tea sellers, vegetable vendors – idle away their time blaming their poverty on politicians (at that time, reports accusing politician Partha Chatterjee of corruption had just made headlines, and there was much sympathy for his dogs and his girlfriends, one of whom had a beauty salon next to the bank I had opened an account in for Tumpa and which Tumpa frequented for beauty treatments), the women have little time for idle banter. They are taking matters into their own hands, coming together and doing whatever they practically can, waiting for neither government nor law. It shouldn't be like this, but again, this kind of independence marks the classic Silicon Valley attitude towards life.

Suprabha lives in a makeshift home constructed out of bamboo sticks and a thin sheet of black tarpaulin drawn over them for a roof on government land, overlooking a lake. She has no electricity and can only sleep towards dawn. Her better-off neighbours have bought solar-powered fans, something she is saving up for. But she says she is happy, and she is proud. The man is often away. And the hurdles are nothing, for this is the life she has built for herself, and it is a matter of time before she is completely free of him.

Tumpa, still a romantic at heart, says she has got two marriage proposals and wonders if I could accompany her on her dates and gauge which man will be worthy of her. Or she'd be forced to choose both.

Another of my father's maids, Misha, who has a twelve-year-old daughter, had escaped her violent marriage and turned openly lesbian. She understood English and spoke a little bit of it, making it easy for my son to communicate with her when he visited. My father paid for her daughter's boarding school fees, allowing Misha more free time to earn money. Extremely entrepreneurial, she also drove an auto-rickshaw in her village and was a farmer, growing flowers, watermelons and lentils, which she sold at the local market. Misha's girlfriend too had the same story to tell. She too had a daughter from a marriage to a violent man. In fact, Misha had dragged her out of her battered marriage and to the police station and saved her life. Misha introduced me to her friends, about a dozen of them. Some, like Misha, dressed and looked like men from their villages, also openly drinking, using choice swear words and smoking both beedis and ganja. Her entire friends circle was full of women who had either been beaten up badly by their men and had escaped, or were so tired of seeing this that they said they were only attracted to the gentleness and the protector-provider Ma Kali energy of women. It was strange to see abuse, violence and trauma turn people LGBTQA but completely understandable. For the psychology of love and attraction is something the following chapters address, and it is the same across genders.

At the nameless local Kali temple in the neighbourhood, I look through the smoke at Suprabha's flowers, thinking of all of these battered women finding their way slowly but surely to freedom.

From next door, filmi music begins playing. I don't know whether to laugh or cry. This was my constant state in Bengal, tumultuous simultaneous emotions that had nothing to do with me. Police were everywhere always. I found the ones closest to me and lost it on them, scolding them for playing sad, romantic Bengali songs of heartbreak (like how someone still loved someone, though now they are each married to someone else, who in turn also loved others but also them, and hence, going by pure simple maths, basically everyone loved everyone, totalling to polyamory) blasting through speakers, saying I had not come from California for this and that kids had exams and we had work. In fact, I felt I had become the CSO (chief scolding officer) of the state of Bengal. For that's all I seemed to be doing. Just like the real Didi, the state chief minister. I passed a poster and realised that both of us also sported the same earrings. Mine were made in Italy. And hers were made in Bengal. Tumpa said she must have got hers on a trip to Italy (perhaps as I was there too at the time) and that I must run for politics for I was so much like the chief minister.

Anyway, the police apologised, saying, 'Sorry Didi, but the people need love songs.' And when I looked around me, at the hundreds of faces and couples, I realised they were right. I took to yelling at the police for all kinds of reasons everywhere, because everything was their fault – why I couldn't find taxis, why were they so incompetent that we didn't know where to cross the roads, etc. And once, I even yelled at a policeman for making his working wife do his laundry instead of helping her out. His answer was, 'Which wife?' I didn't know whether to laugh or to yell, laughing was easier. It was hilarious. Each time, every cop I yelled at apologised and accompanied me along my way for a bit, regaling me with more stories, inquiring about America, getting me a taxi, etc., and always asking me where Dada (meaning my husband) was.

It was a city of heartbreak. There were these stories of course. But there were young people, and sometimes those in their forties, who had returned from Mumbai or Delhi to live in the homes of their parents after a heartbreak or worn out after struggling to pay their rent or achieve career milestones, or to recover from the damage of toxic relationships or violent marriages. There were those who had returned after having studied abroad and had found no jobs. Or had been laid off. Here they were, joined in the grand romance of depression, despair and melancholia that fuelled so many romances, including the grandest love stories in literature, like Bengal's own *Devdas*, *Charulata* or, my ex-favourite, Tolstoy's *Anna Karenina*.

To escape the romance of my father's neighbourhood in south Kolkata, I took to writing out of the city's old and numerous new cafes every single day. Upscale versions of the famed political discussions that happened at the city's historic Coffee House now happened at Starbucks, Blue Tokai and the many cafes in Hindustan Park. Interspersed with what else – more love stories. So many in love with *boudis*. 'Hot *boudi*' syndrome was what I called it, for it seemed to be the city's favourite fetish, and as I was informed by some conversations that were so loud (for I had no intention of eavesdropping) that they cancelled my noise-cancelling Bose headphones were also in several Bengali TV and media.

For all of my walls and boundaries and armour, I got asked out a lot too, by both men and women. Most respectfully. People were offended, some were in tears, at my sheer meanness in refusing them. The women, fellow Didis, and some LGBTQA people (mind you, all strangers, for I knew next to no one and wanted to keep it that way, so I could work) said I was 'simply too beautiful', 'too well spoken', had too much something in Bangla, which I didn't understand so they translated it into European languages, (this being Kolkata, home of culture, the arts and literature) of which

I understood only French, and it was *je ne sais quoi*. Some drew sketches of me. Some wrote poems and composed music for me. Often, I didn't understand what they meant, but that was because 'you are a mystery yourself, how can you be understood'. I nearly died from laughing and nearly died of annoyance too. At first it was amusing, but soon it was not because it did not seem to end. It was endlessly cute. And endlessly annoying. Who has this kind of time?

After having read Bengali literature in translation for a lifetime, I now found no need for my lifelong desire of wanting to learn the language once I was in Kolkata. Because people also recited and translated Bengali poetry for me everywhere, including in Ubers, on streets, at get-togethers and even in cancer wards. I yelled at a cancer patient while getting chemotherapy because he had a tattoo of one of his exes while his current wife (on paper, remember there are often several off paper), with whom he had a six-year-old child, was under the burden of his caregiving, not to mention the financial issues.

But why was I yelling? I should not have cared. This was the infection I had caught from the female ghosts, demonesses, goddesses. All the romance too, everywhere like a virus, was making me extremely hyper. You see, dear reader, whether in the house or outside, I was battling romantic nincompoops everywhere. Swatting them away like flies but with no success.

I thought of our great Urdu love poet, Mirza Ghalib. I mean, how could I not, with all the romance engulfing my entire life. Among his famed *hazaron khwaishein* (one thousand wishes), one was to live on in Kolkata and not have to return to Delhi. Because Kolkata and Bengal to him were a wonderland: '*Bangal saun saal peechhe bhi jeetein hain aur saun saal aage bhi.*' Bengalis live both a hundred years ahead of and a hundred years behind the rest of civilisation.

Kolkata's romantic nincompoops were the reason why I couldn't finish this book earlier. And why I had to completely abandon another novel I was writing. And why I had to move out of Kolkata altogether to Delhi as my India base. You see, I am no Ghalib. And even today, I am extremely nervous and try my best to avoid, postpone and altogether cancel any visit to this city of love and heartbreak, apparently my city of birth, according to my missing birth certificate.

Part II

Trends: Indian

6

The World's Largest Army of Single Women

MILEY CYRUS'S ORIGINAL VIDEO of 'Flowers' is as SoCal as anything can be. All about self-love but in very materialistic ways. The lyrics talk about buying yourself flowers, talking to yourself for hours, writing your name in the sand on the beach (as SoCal assumes sandy beaches are everywhere), doing every grand romantic gesture that you might expect out of a lover. In other words, a breakup song about surviving heartbreak by becoming your own lover. And in a sleepy lane of south Kolkata, during the hours of the famous Kolkata afternoon siesta, at the branch of the local Bank of Baroda office, this song is blasting out from the headphones of a young girl. We are both here, dragged by our parents who still believe that, irrespective of which government, East or West, government still is the best, and so only public sector banks will survive the apocalypse, crypto, blockchain, gold and all other finance trends. And that a government bank locker is safer than a Swiss bank locker, quantity (and quality) of contents irrelevant. Not to mention the managers and staff who seem to understand them (they fill up forms for the older customers, as we used to be often sternly asked to do by senior citizens on Air India flights from San Francisco to Delhi, who believed they had rights on younger Indians, even if complete strangers. But this rarely happened on flights to Mumbai, which said everything about the anthropological differences between the two cities). And, specifically at this bank branch, when an ATM was out of order, as it often was, a bank employee would sit on his scooter and take the middle-aged customers to the nearest working ATM, wait there and patiently bring them back. Apparently, it was one of his many unsaid roles, and he did this often.

This girl and I don't fit in at the bank. Both of us stand out, like llamas in a corporate office, amidst the crowd of mostly senior citizens. She shifts along the row of steel seats, making space and gestures to the seat that has opened up. I go and sit next to her, and we smile. She takes off her white-corded headphones, the song still blasting. And says, 'That's it, you know. Never again.'

A song based in California has united us in the most unlikely of places. I mean, this is not a bar or a club or a remotely urban place that might be playing such music. 'I couldn't have said it better!' It turns out she had just studied biogenetics in the UK and was on her way, of all the places in the world, to the university in my backyard, Stanford. She was there for student loan details that her parents were sorting out. She was nervous, for unlike Europe, barring New York City and some places here and there, public transport in the world's most powerful country was mostly a joke. I told her that luckily Stanford wasn't as bad and guided her to take the Marguerite Shuttle there, rental bikes until she got her own, told her about local groceries in downtown and Caltrain details, the VTA pass, and so on. She opened up on how he had broken her heart. It's like she wasn't important at all. By this time, 'he' was not one man but every boyfriend, situationship, things, bonds with and without names, one-night stands. Seemantini was fed up of all of it. She had thought that Sayantan, a Bengali student like her, whose family was from Delhi, would be it. They had so much in common, they could be together because their studies and lines of work were similar. But it was this and that, and he was never around when she needed him. Putting together the pieces on her flight back home to Kolkata, she realised he was always threatened by her academic brilliance, by the prospects the future held for her. His own stellar performance and seniority were irrelevant. The tears streamed down. At such moments, which were pretty much every day of my life, I had learned to ask, not like the journalist in me who wanted to know details (different from kitty party aunty asking similar questions for heartless, soulless juicy gossip details), basically the four Ws (who, what, when, where) before the why and how that were the tenets of journalism taught in all journalism schools. I had to simply hold space, be present in full acceptance. (In fact, the mastery of this trait and patience were courtesy of my six years of working with and being cooking parent at my son's school for seventy children from various cultures all over the world, and I must thank them too, for without them these stories and this book wouldn't have happened.)

Someone had felt safe in my presence to open up, and this had become my whole life. People were just like kids, accosting me out of nowhere to tell me stories, my own rush hour be damned. Childhood truly never ends, as psychology proves again and again. Sometimes it was a CEO in Silicon Valley crying, sometimes it was a stranger at a random bank, like right now. And my job was to show them empathy and offer my silent, non-judgemental presence, which meant asking no questions.

That's the bond you can have with strangers. There's no baggage of history, nor the guarantee of a future, just the present moment, which allows often for the purest authenticity, often one which people can't find with their loved ones. That's the essence of Vikram Seth's poem 'Unclaimed': 'To make love with a stranger is the best./ There is no riddle and there is no test./To lie and love, not aching to make sense . . . . To rest within the unknown arms and know/That this is all there is; that this is so.'

It didn't just apply to lovemaking but to every interaction that involved any bit of intimacy, which, as was so common in the wellness and therapy circles and eventually on the streets of California, is always best broken into 'Into-Me-See'. To see into someone and truly, truly see them, accept them as they are. Sex can be intimacy, but most sex isn't. It is this intimacy that is available in all platonic ways as well, most of all, in patience, listening, total presence and non-judgemental acceptance, and what became much of my journalism career, my column, my first book, this book . . . what sparked off this conversation.

We exchanged numbers and promised to meet before both of us left the city.

All art that touches us is about humanity, which has never known any geography. Today, 'Flowers' is the anthem of innumerable people who are choosing, read that again, 'choosing' to stay single. You can call them divorcees, widows, singletons . . . whatever label you choose, but they are single out of choice. A year later, Miley Cyrus's fierce Grammy performance in a 1970s-style shimmery dress showing off all of her savage, ripped self inside and out, with its powerful finale, including a mic drop, has completely shaken the world. It has become the anthem for an ever-increasing army of women who have had it with men worldwide.

In many ways, 'Flowers' is a modern-day rendition of 'I Will Survive', a very similar anthem from the 1970s by Gloria Gaynor. It is not merely a disco staple – the powerful, catchy song is a cult, a symbol of female empowerment, which was just beginning in America but which went on to rock the world. And it began with Gaynor too, like Cyrus, not avoiding but completely acknowledging the devastation of, well, a devastating breakup and the eventual discovery of strength within herself.

It was a song Banshee, a renowned journalist and a corporate communicator, now in her seventies, had sung to herself again and again. The wonderful intensity of her romance had turned into an intense marriage, turning into intense violence. Screams, sobs, abuses . . . had drifted out of their locked bedroom door and into the house where they lived in a joint family. Her in-laws were very well aware of what was happening. Our world is patriarchy, trapping both genders, so this is sadly more common than we are comfortable admitting.

According to the World Health Organization (WHO), about one in three, or 30 per cent, of women worldwide have faced physical or sexual violence in their lifetime. Most of this is intimate partner violence (IPV). Almost one third, 27 per cent, of women worldwide aged between fifteen and forty-nine have reported IPV, either physical or sexual.

Banshee's marriage had been violent for a very long time, so much so that everyone in the household knew it was routine. But one day, when the door of the bedroom was left slightly ajar, by mistake (of course!), she had looked out while being beaten. Her five-year-old son was standing there, frozen in shock. He had seen it. The whole point of a financially independent woman taking all this was for the sake of him. To give him a family, to protect him. Banshee felt she had lost her dignity and had failed to protect her son, the very point of her being in the marriage. It was at that moment that she knew the marriage was truly over. And knowing very well that she was losing everything she had ever known, she decided to walk out, taking her son with her. Her parents were not as supportive as she had hoped they would be. And legal procedures, societal prejudices and judgements, and life after her divorce, were, to put it mildly, 'difficult'. That included judges and lawyers staring at your breasts occasionally because, of course, as Banshee says, 'They can't help it and don't mean to, while you're fighting custody battles, standing in lines all sweaty in the heat for hours.'

Divorced women, single women also seem to attract unnecessary sexual advances, often assault situations, from anywhere and everywhere, especially at the workplace, but really with anyone who knows this is 'an *abla nari*', a vulnerable woman, an easy prey. Basic things, like housing, is difficult because Indian society is so judgemental, and apparently a single woman is dangerous and must prove her character. I myself had felt deeply insulted and frankly petrified when I was to rent a place in Mumbai nine years ago, as I wanted to live there to do the research for my first book. Mumbai, so-called liberal Mumbai . . . and I was looking for a place in Versova, a place where several movie stars stay, so supposedly liberal. But I had to carry my marriage certificate everywhere to prove 'my character' and that 'I was not an actress', whatever that meant. A decade later, it's the same in NCR, even if you want to buy property – forget the armour and bitch face you wear, your ability to pay is never enough. You have to have your marriage certificate and family photographs to prove your 'decency'. We are, after all, a country headed towards Ram Rajya, where even mythological characters like Sita had to prove their purity no matter how much the husband claimed to have loved her – enough to have waged war for her honour. So what are we petty, regular women. Honour, *izzat*, is a product of patriarchy, and only women seem to be the ones who need to prove it day after day after day. And single women, in spite of there being hordes of them, even more so. This happens on a daily basis at every level, in a country where molestation has a sweet, watered-down 'pet name' – eve teasing – as if it's a playful act and not a crime leading to arrest in many countries. And still women are choosing to be single.

Most people who have never been in abusive situations cannot understand why people don't leave abusive marriages and relationships, especially when the violence is physical, which is different from the subtler emotional abuse. The stakes are enormous. Your entire life is at stake, and forget rolling out a red carpet praising you for your valour, nobody is waiting to rescue you, help you or support you the way you need to be. Plus, you share with your spouse houses, children, mortgages, finances, friends, parents and family, taxes, insurance. It is the loss of everything – your identity, your support system, what you have believed in and fought for so long. It isn't as simple as getting a job and financial independence. The PTSD is intense and takes decades to overcome – that is, if one chooses to separate in the first place – with therapy, meditation and counselling.

You always know when the marriage or the long-term relationship is over. But are you willing to face it?

Herself a survivor of marital rape and intense domestic violence that led to needing plastic surgery, Ramya asks this question day after day to the girls she now counsels and holds workshops for as a mental health counsellor.

To strangers and those who didn't know them well, Ramya and her husband might have looked like an ordinary, happy couple. Just like the many that flood our social media timelines. 'Abuse in relationships, marriages, families is all around us, and yet victims often look happy, "normal" and even empowered,' says Ramya. Her body is a map of scars, a nightmarish memoir of the brutal marriage that almost ended her life, not once, not twice, but several times. She showed me her wrists with their tiny scars, where he had with his own bare hands crushed her glass bangles, the shards going straight into her flesh. She vividly remembers the nightmare from decades ago: She had dressed up in a sunshine-yellow short kurti, bottle-green bandhani patiala salwar and dupatta to match, with red, green and yellow bangles. It was for a party attended by her husband's friends, one of whom had told him she looked like a nautch girl, which had triggered him enough to do this to his wife. He refused to take her to a doctor, and Ramya being a housewife at the time (at his insistence) and having no money of her own had to painstakingly, as if working on a delicate craft, spend hours pulling out each tiny glass shard herself.

Then she threw salt on her own wounds, to avoid a septic infection. This was before he had begun to 'officially' hit her. In the eye, where he had ruptured a retina. In the jaw, where plastic surgery had been needed. On her leg, leaving a long gash. Merciless as it sounds, Banshee's beatings seemed like a walk in the park in comparison. As do Anu's. Anu is a professor who has to wear foundation to cover the knife scars on her arm inflicted by her ex-husband, if she absolutely must wear short sleeves or sleeveless clothes on steaming summer days.

I need to insist here that these women are all highly educated and from liberal backgrounds. How else would our worlds have collided? Imagine then the lakhs of cases that go unreported, the plight of women who don't know their rights, the fate of the poorest? Like Madhobi, one of the maids I briefly employed, who had a pretty, innocent face. It was difficult to look at her for she had a forked earlobe, courtesy of a drunk husband who had pulled apart the plastic pearl-studded earring on it in a drunken fit of rage. And then raped her. Her back, showing from her blouse and sari as she worked, was full of burn marks. She smiles because she is free of him. Madhobi lives with her nine-year-old son in her parents' house and is the sole breadwinner there. To her, all of this seems mundane. So she can't understand my reaction. It is baffling to her why I even think this is a big deal and why I tear up and go all quiet and act up '*ja ta*' (anything, whatsoever), as she calls my reaction.

Her situation is so normal to her, because it is so common, and really to every second woman she knows. Most don't have scars to show. Like Poonam, a maid in Bengaluru, who keeps about 50 per cent of her monthly earnings money in cash at my reader Ashok's house, who later puts it in an account, away from her drunken husband. She is very cheerful as she believes being beaten is just part of life. Or like Shanta, another maid who is housed in Hyderabad in her memsahib's spare room, where she is free to stay forever but still chooses to return to her husband on good days. The list of women in such situations is endless. And knows no caste or socio-economic class.

In the Taj Bengal restroom, a wealthy Marwari woman bedecked in a lovely grey chiffon salwar-kurta says, 'Why should I walk out? What's waiting for me over there?' I don't know what's more chilling. The calm nonchalance with which she says this as she touches up her nude Charlotte Tilbury Pillow Talk lipstick or the irony that we are having this conversation at a wedding function about to take place at the hotel poolside shortly.

The number of battered women in the world is staggering. Walkar's horrific death is barely the tip of the iceberg, simply bringing to light an epidemic which was always there.

'It doesn't pop up overnight. The abuse happens from day one. You always know,' Ramya echoes Banshee. After three and a half years, Ramya had left her marriage taking along her son, who was then nearly three, getting caught in the long web that is the justice system while trying to hold on to a job. 'If they know you're a mother in a custody battle, they will ensure they manipulate you, hiring you for the lowest positions that you're overqualified for, making you work the most for the lowest salary possible. They know you are that desperate.'

She eventually got a divorce and won the custody battle for her son. She took no money from her husband.

She has since counselled many victims of partner abuse and held many workshops for women, encouraging them to be independent. 'Are you treating yourself with the respect you deserve?' she asks the victims, assuring them that they can indeed get out of their situations and build their lives. 'You're worth it!'

'Domestic violence is just an accident. Do we label anyone who has suffered an accident as anything? Then why do we label ourselves as having suffered IPV and domestic violence?' Ramya says. 'IPV and domestic violence need not define your life. One can heal, reach out for help, recover slowly and take gentle baby steps to build a new life with healthier relationships.'

Months after meeting Ramya, a horrific tragedy shocked the country. A twenty-seven-year-old woman, Shraddha Walkar, was murdered by her live-in boyfriend, Aaftab Amin Poonawala, in Delhi.[1] He had strangled her over an argument and cut her body into thirty-five pieces, storing them in a 300-litre fridge. Over the next eighteen days, every night at around 2 a.m., he disposed of them in the Chhatarpur forest, bit by bit, to avoid suspicion. Only six months after the murder, when Walkar's father had lodged a missing-person complaint because Walkar's friends were unable to contact her for almost three months and had alerted him, was the case even discovered.

Called a case of 'love jihad' by her father, Walkar's death chilled the country to the bone, making us wake up and getting the media to finally cover intimate partner violence more often. By then, a hundred cases of IPV had come my way, many making it to my column, and I wasn't even looking for them! How many would I have unearthed if I were. My editors finally took serious notice of the stories appearing in my column. The country's media too began to pay attention to these subjects, to mental health in relationships. We really are that cut off from what's happening in the streets. And more than anything else, this reflects the soul, or the lack of soul, of the nation.

After sixty-five years of marriage, a much-loved grandmother in her eighties had demanded a divorce, seemingly out of the blue. Instead of supporting her, everyone was shocked. It was not because of the taboo that divorce still is, it was that all those who saw her as a safe space – her children, grandchildren, daughters and sons-in-law, relatives, family friends – all of whom she had nurtured for decades, felt threatened because *dida-dadu* (grandma and grandpa) were a unit. The collapse of their marriage threatened their idea of morality, of what was right in the world, of love, of safety. They were protecting themselves over supporting their fragile grandma.

When asked why she wanted a divorce, she had simply said, 'I can't take it any more. I want to live the remainder of my life in peace.' In her eighties, when health is failing, a woman who had always been a housewife and had no financial independence couldn't be more vulnerable. Yet she wanted to be free. Further questioning of the grandma slowly revealed what the people around the couple had seen – grandpa demanding to know where his slippers were in the morning, throwing a plate of food away if it had too little salt . . . emotional abuse so casual it had become normal and okay, when of course it wasn't; and what they had not seen – being called ugly, criticised for not having the same figure as the years piled on, for not wanting to have sex, and other emotional IPV. And still the family members were confused, and chorused, 'But he never hit you!' And this was, this is the problem. What is the point of having loved ones? Aren't we better off without them? Better off without families? Better off in empathetic communities of people, similarly battered, who don't judge and offer true support, whatever that may look like? Perhaps emotional, perhaps with logistics.

And at over 73 million, the largest army of single women in the world is right here in our Bharat. The world's largest democracy. The country renowned for arranged marriages. It is an army that exceeds the population of entire countries! (For example, the United Kingdom has approximately 68.89 million citizens, far fewer than this number.[2]) The hard-hitting irony of this simple statistic tells more about the country than all of its media put together does. And many come together in small groups to help each other out. Perhaps with babysitting. Perhaps with references of and even payment for discreet gynaecologists and doctors. Perhaps with lawyers. Perhaps with shelter. Perhaps with jobs. Perhaps, like with Ashok and his maid in Bengaluru, with financial independence and security for a narrow escape from brutal marriages.

This was the new India, and it was truly inspiring. Away from the baggage and judgement of family, there was support. Like abused animals in the shelter my son would grow up to volunteer to look after, which were now safe, and many of which found safe, forever homes. And if this isn't love, I don't know what is.

The rains that everyone had warned me of, that were said to be the stuff of nightmares, having caused typhoons and cyclones that can wreck civilisation, had somehow passed. Now the only thing that remained was a rather spooky thunder, so loud it rattled your bones through the walls of the old houses in Kolkata, like the one I was in. I had walked upstairs to the terrace to see flashes of electricity across the sky and, shaking with the booming thunder like a scared child, had almost immediately shut the door to the terrace and gone downstairs. Empty noises had never threatened me thus. My mind drifted once again to India's 73 million single women, hundreds of whom had shared their story with me.[3] I had given a talk to a group of them on why it was difficult for people to love strong women. Now, free in many ways, having chosen their freedom, their PTSD was like this scary thunder, about now harmless past lives but still ringing loud in the lives of these single women.

My elderly journalist friend and his wife are visiting Kolkata from Delhi, and they text me, living up to their promise of showing me Kolkata. First we have lunch at a Bangladeshi restaurant close by and then head to Kumartuli, the historic potters' area, which is around 300 years old. But according to legend or rumour, depending on who you ask, it is far older. It is a special place and the energy is instantly infectious, mesmerising even to even atheist tourists and observers of culture, leave alone believers and worshippers. Sculptors and potters lovingly shape grey idols. Painters with the greatest tenderness and care paint the eyes, the eyeliner, eye shadow and makeup, the final perfect touches before the goddesses reach the Durga Puja pandals not just across this ancient city but across the country and to many places in the world where they are shipped to. Like my friend's house in Delhi for their house puja. And the local puja pandals in the San Francisco Bay Area. Weeks later, it would be my first Durga Puja in Kolkata, West Bengal, but right then in Kumartali, it was most surreal and enchanting to be there, surrounded by these goddesses for the first time in my life. They were all single Indian women. Soon the artists would assign them families and roles invented by humans, turn them into mothers laden with the responsibilities of answering the endless human prayers and wishes (of wealth, wisdom, health . . .) that would come their way and of protecting humans against demons and all things unwanted. You see, humans were/are selfish creatures, ever-asking; there is no unconditional love humans are capable of, even for their gods and goddesses. (After festivities and after each puja, I would come across hundreds of idols of goddesses strewn along the edges of roads or lakes, like garbage nobody had picked up or wanted to pick up.) One minute you are goddess, next minute you are garbage. Such was human love, even for the gods. What hope then for fellow humans? But right now, here in Kumartuli, at this very moment, the goddesses were free of the burdens of conditional love, the burdens of humanity, of any meaning and symbolism put into them – the clay sculptures could be anyone and anything. They could be any of the army of 73 million single women in the world's largest democracy who had freed themselves, putting themselves first, reclaiming their lives piece by piece, sometimes broken shard by broken shard, like Ramya.

They could be Roma, a lawyer in her mid-forties based out of NCR, who, like every married Indian woman, had tried hard to fit into the roles of wife, daughter-in-law, mother. Domestic violence, strangulation, physical and sexual assault by her husband ended it all. Mind you, the husband was a doctor. Yet, he showed little empathy and demanded sex from her throughout her pregnancy, periods and even a couple of days after she was discharged from the hospital after a C-section surgery to deliver their baby. He had abused her and said she was 'crazy', 'mental', that 'something was wrong with her' because she did not want to have sex. It was a classic form of shaming and blaming, as old as time, which countless women are put through all over the world in their marriages. Most 'adjust', as women are taught to, in every role and area of their lives, most perhaps as wives and daughters-in-law. So of course Roma adjusted as well. But he took the decision for her and threw her out. After eleven years of marriage, at the age of thirty-five, Roma found herself homeless. She has since then built her life from scratch as a single mother, sustaining herself and her child for over seven years. It has been no walk in the park, and in spite of her being a lawyer, the legal process and the patriarchy involved, which Banshee too had to face, were no less a torture than her 'eleven years in hell'.

'My husband had made me *swargwasi* (a dead person), and now, as a single working mom, I am living in heaven,' she says with a smile.

Single women resulted from all kinds of situations. Some were divorced, having escaped from abusive marriages and relationships, some were widows, and then there were those who were single out of choice, perhaps due to abusive childhood patterns repeating or even as a result of a happy childhood (psychological patterns addressed in a latter chapter on therapy jargon and childhood enmeshment playing out in adult relationships). In her early thirties now, Iva, a social media professional, was sexually abused as a child, the trauma of which remains unresolved. Opening up sexually to anyone is an incredibly big deal for her. Two out of her three relationships were abusive, induced by sexual demands. All of her exes had demanded sex from her and only one had ever made her feel safe. 'And I did feel safe enough to get intimate with him, but the relationship ended,' says Iva. 'I am so much happier being single, with none of this baggage and stress to deal with.'

Iva had told each of her boyfriends – the list also included a married man – that she didn't want marriage. 'But all of my exes were commitment phobic, even for a relationship.' Iva wanted true intimacy, a sense of dependence, support, someone to bank on and emotional closeness – why we get into any relationship (romantic or platonic) anyway. 'But it's always only sex that is offered in the name of intimacy. And many of us (women) fall for it,' she says. An only child with ailing parents, Iva had wanted her married boyfriend to check on her and hold her hand when her mother was hospitalised, or while she settled down in a new city, or when her friend committed suicide, when, not knowing how to deal with the loss or grief, Iva was baffled. When her employer gave her a break she called up her then boyfriend. 'He responded three hours later saying, "Let's have sex, you will feel better." Sensitivity, mutual support and basic dependence were always absent.' In an India of extramarital affairs, it is not uncommon for single women like Iva or my feminist friend (or the ones mentioned in the later chapters) to have flings, full-blown affairs or casual sex with married men with no guilt. But without the human connection or true intimacy, the point is lost. Sex is not the real need. Peel the layers, as we saw in Mumbai or in Iva's case, and intimacy or human connection is the core human need. More and more women like Iva are realising this, thanks to their bodies that were unable to orgasm.

Even in relationships where women are not abused, men often tend to demand certain sexual acts without making the partner feel safe enough to proceed. When the women refuse, their consent, or lack of it, is respected, but there is pouting, uncomfortable silence and painful, passive-aggressive behaviour, making both partners feel betrayed, rejected and hurt, and ultimately destroying relationships. All of this can be resolved with heartfelt, healthy communication. Several women prefer to avoid the whole drama and choose to remain single.

According to the International Academy of Sex Research's journal, *Archives of Sexual Behaviour*, 59 per cent of women in America have faked orgasms. That so many women in the world's most developed country feel the need to fake what is supposed to be joy and liberation tells a lot. Are they safe to be themselves anywhere?

In a society like India, where women are constantly slut-shamed and made to feel unsafe, irrespective of whether they are covered from head to toe or not; where the woman is seen as property, especially after marriage; where it is her job to serve her husband and be an object to be controlled and moulded. Her sense of safety, so that she does not feel she is walking on eggshells in the relationship, and her freedom to even know who she is, so that she can try to be that self, are rare luxuries. How, then, can she feel free in bed?

According to the National Family Health Survey (2019–21) by the Ministry of Health and Welfare, 83 per cent of sexually abused married women were abused by their husbands. In other words, they have suffered marital rape, something that is still not considered a crime in India.

Radha had to have an abortion because on their wedding night the husband decided to have unprotected sex without her consent. She says that while she was pained and felt betrayed, he is otherwise 'a wonderful man and a caring husband', and she doesn't even see this as rape because of how common it is.

She is right about how common and, therefore, 'normal' this is. And this is scary. Has she been able to orgasm ever since? Obviously not. The body stores trauma, which prevents us from relaxing unless something is done about it. There are also many kinds of trauma – same-partner trauma, like in her case, and therefore, the inability to orgasm with the person who may have sexually, emotionally, physically abused or disrespected (abandoned) them.

Or in the case of my friend Katie back home in California, who in spite of enjoying most of the privileges of being a white person in America, was regularly molested by gangs of men (not too different from Indian eve teasing) while growing up as a teenager in her unsafe LA neighbourhood. There is such a thing as general trauma from general abuse, which has nothing to do with a specific partner. It was the same story everywhere. Women were women, whether in the posh bubble of Silicon Valley or all over India.

'If women realised how we showed up in bed is how we show up in life, they would consider working on building a stronger mind-body connection,' Katie texts me.

Women's bodies also store trauma and consequent post-traumatic stress disorder (PTSD) and suffer from a host of common illnesses, like endometriosis, polycystic ovarian disease (PCOD), polycystic ovarian syndrome (PCOS), cysts and other complications in the uterus requiring medical attention and surgeries, making sex painful and the need for safety even greater. There is even a condition called vaginismus, which is born out of deep anxiety. It is the body's automatic reaction to shut down due to a deep fear of vaginal penetration. Orgasm is not about sex. It is a reflection of our lives. If our women are not truly free or safe anywhere, how can they feel free or safe in bed? With all of this baggage of trauma, and with their men constantly failing the responsibility bestowed on them by nature of being the protector-provider rather than an aggressor causing feelings of lack of safety or an abuser or someone plainly oblivious to the suffering of the women.

In many cases of women who can't orgasm with their partners, the recurring issue of boundaries comes up.

One reader's mother, in her early seventies, told me on a car ride with me in Bengaluru that most of her generation knew little about personal boundaries and that she was still trying to understand this 'fashionable new word, "consent"'. As a society, we are just beginning to understand what boundaries are, what gaslighting is. In a society obsessed with control, laying down boundaries is perhaps the biggest revolution. 'I wish I too could have known this. Perhaps I'd have never gotten married.' I thought of the eighty-year-old grandma who had filed for a divorce.

When I ask my maid's friend, also a maid, if she has ever orgasmed, she hints sadly that after the act, instead of aftercare, her man sleeps like a baby while she, needing cuddles and reassurance, feels alone. She didn't use the word, but she meant that she felt a sense of abandonment after the act. In psychology, one talks of the deep inner-child wounds of abandonment. How then, without a sense of safety or of knowing that one's partner will be there for her, can a woman orgasm?

A feminist friend, a proudly single woman, said she had her first orgasm in her teens when she had pleasured herself. 'Masturbation does for me what no man can,' she says. 'And already, he (man in general) doesn't make me feel safe. So what's the point!' She had orgasmed a few times with her fiancé, who had later turned abusive, stubbing cigarette butts against her skin, leaving permanent scars on her body, throwing her out of an auto and committing other violent acts. Her body is full of scars. Like Ramya's. Like Madhobi's. Now almost fifty, she has had some casual sex and one patient, generous and caring partner . . . 'but he turned out to be like those you're dedicating your book to . . . "nincompoops", but a dominating nincompoop, so no. East or West, my dildo is the best,' she says. That's what men were being preferred to.

The adult toys market in India, currently estimated at approximately US $114 million, is expected to grow annually in the range of 20–24 per cent.[4] And though many are using these toys if they are in long-distance relationships or to spice up their relationships, one cannot discount the role of the giant single-woman population of approximately 73 million in India[5] in ensuring these numbers. Though studies have not been done *yet* on how much they have contributed to the numbers, sex is becoming less and less a taboo activity in the India they are living in.

This ever-growing army of single women also consists of widows who had stuck it out in their marriages, giving them their all. Like interior designer Rhea, who had sold off all of her jewellery and given all her money to her unemployed husband to help him with his various businesses. He had squandered or lost all of it away on poor business decisions and for funding his extramarital affairs. 'Even after his first heart attack, he wouldn't change his lifestyle,' says Rhea. When he finally passed away in 2019, after being rendered comatose from a brain stroke, kidney failure and other complications, Rhea – as his business partner on paper – was left with several debts, loans and a huge hospital bill to pay off and also had to face many court cases she had been unaware of.

Like Rhea, Tara too is a widow in her late forties, now single out of choice. After being a stay-at-home mom to her two kids (both teenagers now) for seventeen years and a caregiver to her paralysed mother, Tara is now an executive assistant, the sole earning member in her household. 'I became single by circumstance five years ago, when I lost my husband. But I am single today out of choice,' she says. 'I don't want anyone to feel that I'm marrying for financial reasons. I am happier not being answerable to anyone, not even to my mother. I am taking my own decisions, right or wrong, and feel responsible for them. It's an incredible feeling of freedom.'

Financially independent women like Nidhi don't see why they should allow men to change who they are. Her two serious relationships, one with an Indian man and another with a British man, ended in the same way: the men trying to control her and mould her into their definition of what an Indian woman should be – submissive, doing all the cooking, demure, dressing in a certain ethnic way, from clothes to jewellery to the type of makeup she used, until she could not recognise herself in the mirror. Nidhi is thirty-nine, has never been married or engaged, and takes care of her responsibilities – her pandemic cats and her mother who suffers from dementia.

Nidhi, who had had proper committed relationships, had wanted from her first boyfriend grand gestures of love and romance – candlelit dinners, surprise trips, etc. – to build intimate memories. After all, she had changed herself completely for him! From both she had wanted acceptance of who she really was and not be moulded into something she was not. That her second boyfriend was British didn't alter anything or his patriarchal ideas of 'a perfect wife' who did all the cooking. From the third boyfriend she had wanted respect and mutual communication so she didn't have to be the only one making sacrifices. 'Respect is more important than love. We have fights, doubts, expectations and inner demons. But I want my partner to make me feel valued, encouraged and safe,' says Nidhi. Choosing the beliefs and ways passed down to them via patriarchy, society, religious beliefs (sex is sinful) and, most of all, family and overbearing, interfering mothers, women often feel abandoned in relationships and marriages. At her boyfriends' family events, Nidhi used to sit in a corner by herself. 'Just like in my school days, when I was bullied,' she says. Someone recently proposed marriage to her. She found out only after the proposal that he had wanted to move to Florida, USA, once they were married. 'He did not mention it even once in the three years I've known him. He just assumed I'd follow him. I was shaken. Where is the respect? What about my future plans? My parents? My career? I politely declined.'

This is a growing tribe of young women who don't see why they need to suppress themselves for insecure, controlling men and society and are staying single out of choice.

Nidhi reminded me of Seemantini from the bank. And of every high-schooler I knew, whether in California or in India, who wants to stay single out of choice, marriage not even on their bucket list but something that may or may not happen, and something they won't compromise their lives for the way their mothers and grandmothers did. Or even the way they themselves did in their own past, like Nidhi and Seemantini. I couldn't wrap my mind around this staggering statistic of 73 million (and many unreported, and growing!); this army of single women was the biggest fuck-you to patriarchy perhaps in the history of humanity. It was just as important as the Suffragettes movement or the women's right to vote. Had this army been anywhere in the first world, like the US or UK, documentary after documentary and movie after movie would have been made on the phenomenon, many winning Oscars. But it being in India, it was a quiet revolution. Though my column on them had gone viral, and every now and then they were covered in the media, India's single women, like our goddesses, belong in the history books written in the future.

All over the world, women are livid: from burning headscarves in Iran to protesting over Roe vs Wade, fighting for the right to abortion in America, fighting for their bodies, safety and freedom and telling brutal stories of intense intimate partner violence, they are expressing themselves. Their rage is alive and growing, like a pandemic – in streets, offices, homes, hospitals, courts and in their hearts, over apparently the tiniest of triggers to merciless IPV. By and large, women are extremely disappointed in men, feeling abandoned by them, being forced to shoulder most familial, financial, social, caregiving, daily small household responsibilities by themselves. Fed up, they are increasingly choosing themselves and how they live every aspect of their own lives apart from romantic partnerships. If they are doing it all alone anyway, why bother with the headache of dealing with a passive man and his family?

Many of these women – divorced, widowed, single by choice, single moms – have formed communities, local, national, virtual, with local chapters for single moms, single women, and so on. Quite like the Meetup groups of America. Here they find support, care, family, friendship, sisterhood and lifelines in a society that judges women, especially single women, at every level.

'Single women are a threat. They're like Samanthas everywhere . . . just the last thing we needed,' says Snigdha from Delhi, referring to Samantha, the unabashedly sexually free character from the comedy-drama series *Sex and the City*. She wasn't wrong. Many of these women were just as free to live like men and have sex with whoever they wanted. I wanted to remind Snigdha of her own extramarital affairs and constantly upgraded series of Ashishes, like the continuing series of iPhones. But didn't have the courage to. This entire book, all of these stories, are about others' courage and lives, with me being a passive, non-judgemental witness, listening. If I had not put myself in this non-judgemental space, I doubt if half of these taboo, secret lives and loves would have been revealed to me and, consequently, this book would have happened at all. Snigdha had a point. It wasn't just her husband, but several of the men I had met in Delhi, and others described in the following chapters, unabashedly and with zero guilt had had so many casual, sexual, full-fledged emotional affairs with single women that they had lost count.

'It's hard to be single. You're a walking prey. Everyone looks at a divorced woman that way. They are just dying to have sex with you; they think you're just starved for sex. You're not. But it's better than being assaulted. Luckily, I own my own place (she got the house in the divorce settlement). The workplace is hell,' says Aarti, a divorced single mother working at an electronics company in Mumbai. She decided to make some strategic moves. Her flat looks like a five-star hotel and her kitchen like a celebrity chef's, with imported appliances I have only seen in affluent Californian homes, not even my own. 'They know I love to bake. I love to drive. I love jewellery. You know, stuff like that,' she says. 'Might as well. Better than assault, stressful situations, rape and all that headache. Might as well use the motherfuckers,' she says. She has a Mini Cooper, diamonds, bags from Hermes and whatnot, which she only sports strategically. It is the same with Rajni, a single mother working in a hi-tech firm in Gurugram, who has chosen to alchemise exactly the same toxic situations to pay for her daughter's expensive school, her field trips abroad and her own foreign holidays with her bosses. From time to time she also takes in younger male interns as her lovers and passes on favours to them. She might have had casual sex anyway. Or not. But both she and Aarti, like so many single women, were living like men in a man's world. And like so many women of today, having sex like a man too.

Did this make single women dangerous? Or married women even lonelier? Didn't the only fault in all this lie with the *raja betas*, the *babushonas*, the Mama's boys? Many senior editors – a couple (yes only that number) of them named in the elitist Me Too movement in India – and so many influential men in the country had 'girls at every port', to quote a wife of a promiscuous man. These heroes would just dial or text a peer in the industry, often a single woman, often young. She'd probably get a fancy dinner and they'd fuck in a five-star hotel. No strings attached or strings attached, depending on whom you ask. Assault or not, depending on who is in power and what the definitions of relationships, consent, and so on are at that time in history. (Look at Marilyn Monroe and the then president John F. Kennedy, or even the treatment of women in the Sean Connery James Bond movies, for instance.) And as Me Too and the number of single women are telling us, the tide is finally, even if in small waves, turning in favour of women.

So no, the threat is not single women. But men and their immaturity, sons women have to take care of. And as the rising number of single women shows, more and more women are opting out of being a mama to grown men. These men make women feel unsafe, most of all the ones they are married to. As we saw in the extramarital affairs in Delhi (and as we will in the later chapters) men in marriages have shut down, gone passive, become a stubborn wall or turned into dictators, deciding this is it and so there is no need to communicate. Or they have become whiners, only look at everything from their perspective and take no action. 'It's more efficient or we will be here discussing all day, wasting energy when there's a lot to be done,' says a married male friend of mine, a father of two, who takes all the decisions in the family and at home, including the colour of the couch. I am happily shocked he had even admitted this. NRI friends' husbands often listen more to their mothers than to their wives, and it is often about rituals their children must subscribe to, how they should be brought up, what they should eat, should they learn Hindi, and so on. Everything is not IPV. As wives, as mothers, as daughters-in-law, women feel isolated, vulnerable, lacking in the sense of community, freedom and power that single women are privileged to enjoy.

I am seeing marriages over a decade old crumble because the women are exhausted running it single-handedly. It's always the same thing: they want their partners to be present with them, to hold their hand as they go about their activities. 'Even when we were dating and he was with me, he was absent, his mind full of work and his family. I wish he was as devoted as I was to the relationship,' says Tina, whose husband was initially caring during her very difficult pregnancy, but soon, the novelty having faded off, she was doing everything – the cooking, the housework – on her own. He claims he does a lot since he does watch the kid while she travels for work and generally adjusts around her more hectic work hours. But here's the thing. It is their child and their household. He isn't doing any favours to his wife in helping her. This isn't just an Indian problem – patriarchy producing immature men is a universal problem. Overworked mothers, hailed as supermoms, abandoned in seemingly functional, picture-perfect, happy marriages, are actually single women and single mothers in those marriages. There is the marriage tag, the societal security and respect it brings, but the women are crumbling under the weight of their responsibilities. Their husbands are tired after work and grab beers and disappear into television or video games. Or, in some cases, text whoever they're having affairs with to replenish themselves. Or they go out with their friends for a drink or to watch a sport or to the gym, leaving the mothers (stay-at-home or working, it does not matter) feeling abandoned and isolated, left to take care of the kids and the household work all by themselves.

The traditional traits of masculinity are courage, generosity, leadership, providing, protecting, making the women and children feel safe (not judged or abandoned), holding their partner through thick and thin. Men were supposed to be warriors who would do anything to protect their loved ones.

Just look at the animal kingdom. Animal mothers are often warriors too, but that doesn't seem to threaten the animal fathers' egos as frequently. But it seems that males in the human species have gotten so insecure that women have to protect their egos by constantly 'adjusting', even faking orgasms, to keep the relationship with their partners safe. Jokes abound of men being completely unnecessary. Should women want children without the help of a partner, then there are adoption agencies, sperm banks and other solutions, and for sex there are toys.

Citing the state of marriages, the stories and statistics of single women, I ask the men around me why their gender was becoming so useless and turning itself redundant. One of them, who thinks of himself as a Leonardo DiCaprio (minus that level of fame or fortune, just a trace of it), who is fifty years old, married, with a kid and with many twenty-somethings on the side, says, 'Women are obsessed with control. With the young ones, Daddy is free. Daddy is respected.' Summoning all of my will power not to roll over and laugh, I tell him it is only because they feel unsafe.

They dominate for the same reason that men do – all forms of control come from a need to be in charge, which comes from a need for safety. 'I can't do anything right anyway. So I don't even bother to try any more,' another male friend says. 'So you will go on living like a corpse?' I ask him. 'Can't you ask her to release control? Share how you feel? Can't you have honest, open conversations with your wife?' He shrugs his shoulders and changes the topic. As men have been taught: to shut down and to do the 'right thing', as taught by their cultures and their mothers (incidentally also women, who suffered the same isolation, often finding solace in their children). Their self-worth is tied to visible metrics like status and wealth, their intuition to their mothers. Patriarchy is tough on both genders. Male heads too are full of voices. So they tend to offer sex as a solution to strife because they feel relieved (albeit momentarily) from all of that pressure after sex and then shut down so as not to have to deal with the further pressure of honest communication, preferring to be workaholics, emotionally unavailable or simply absent. These are the best cases – of the loyal ones.

Twenty-one-year-old waitress Sheetal's twenty-six-year-old fiancé had stood up for her when his cousins had remarked she wasn't from a wealthy family. He simply said it was their private business and they should mind their own business and walked away from them. Theirs is an arranged marriage, and the couple, unable to afford much, enjoy what they can – roadside tea, hanging out at bus stops and walking by the lakeside. 'Arranged marriage and imagine, he had told his mother, who was dying of cancer (who eventually passed), even though she wanted to see us married, that I finish my degree was more important, and we had to wait,' says Sheetal. 'I never even thought of having a boyfriend. If he wasn't this nice, I'd have stayed single.'

This kind of basic support is all that women are asking for. The bar is so low, the expectations so basic, so humane.

Women may be freer in many ways (they can work, study whatever they want, drive in many parts of the world, fly planes, and so on) than they have ever been. But we are also more self-aware, more 'woke', to use the Gen Z lingo, than ever before as a civilisation. Shouldn't support in other ways be more as well? So they don't have to do everything, including men's roles. Why then is support for women so rare in this generation? So rare that it seems that a man like Sheetal's fiancé is a Kohinoor, when he is doing the bare minimum?

Is it any wonder, then, that the women of this new India have *chosen* not to need men, marriage and love? Choice is the key word here. It's a choice. They are single because they *want* to be so. Not because they have to be single. In a society that pressures a woman to marry, not just for family but for her own safety, the women want their lives to be drama-free and their own. They do not want to put up with any more abuse or shenanigans of insecure men, which they were never supposed to put up with, even as they fulfil their roles of mother or daughter.

A country known for its feminist goddesses before the West even coined the term 'feminism' is teaching the world something. Perhaps the most important revolution, characteristic of how India loves, lies in the way its women are loving themselves, come what may. Theirs is a radical act of self-love. It is a radical act of courage.

'If I find a courageous man who can love, respect and accept a self-made woman, I will surely consider it (remarriage), subject to my daughter's acceptance,' says Roma.

Banshee, who is now a divorced mother and has been single for thirty years, says that now she only seeks companionship, not even a live-in relationship. 'The worst part of being single is unlocking the door with your keys and turning on the lights to an empty house,' she says.

When I visit Kumartuli again, the sculptors have lovingly painted the eyes of the goddesses, decked them up in silk saris, given them to their families and shipped them off to pandals. If our goddesses can remain powerful, free, single, strong, independent women embodying the divine feminine Shakti, which created the universe, and still be wives, mothers, daughters, daughters-in-law, why can't our society allow women to be both too?

7

The Lost Little Indian Boy

WHEN THE WORLD'S LARGEST democracy, renowned for its arranged marriages, turns into a place hosting the world's largest army of single women (yes, I can't wrap my head around that statistic, even the tenth time I mention it) – single out of choice, mind you – I'm sure it raises a question or two about the men that drove them to it. This is in a country that worships goddesses but also doesn't mind eve teasing, rapes, slut-shaming, acid attacks (over 202 reported cases in 2022, according to Statista, a data gathering firm),[1] honour killings, and so on. Just like the economy, education and other mundane things, rape is so regular in India that the spectrum of rape even has its own Wikipedia page, 'Rape in India'.[2] As does 'Domestic Violence in India'.[3]

What is up?

In January 2024, a man named Angrez Singh in Punjab's Fazilka made national headlines, becoming the poster child of love.[4] Wearing red bangles, a bindi, lipstick and a salwar-kurta, Angrez Singh (that is indeed his real name) dressed up as his girlfriend Paramjit Kaur to sit in for her in the health worker exams she was struggling with. He even got fake Aadhaar and voter-identity cards made to pass off as her. He was sadly caught and legal action was taken against both him and his girlfriend. Of course, the Internet went ballistic over the sweetness of his romantic gesture, hailing his act as the epitome of love and boyfriend goals.

Another headline the same month was of a husband, an IT engineer based out of Bhopal, who had promised his wife a honeymoon to Goa but instead duped her into visiting Ayodhya, to please his family. She had filed for divorce shortly afterwards.[5]

The two stories are very different. Angrez's is an act of devotion and love towards his partner. The Bhopal-based IT engineer's is an act of patriarchy, which, sadly, has been *ghar-ghar ki kahaani* (the story of almost every household) in India. But both stories point to one thing – they are anthropological headlines indicating just how lost the Indian boy is. The good, aadarsh boy who is trying to please.

Beyond the focus on the craft and the rags-to-riches journey of a movie star, the story of my first book, *An Ordinary Life*, and especially what followed it, is also an anthropological reflection of masculinity in today's India. It is the story of the lost, rather lonely, Indian boy. You find him everywhere, from the ivory towers made of glistening glass in South Mumbai and Gurgaon the popular downtown areas like Church Street in Bengaluru, the relatively impoverished streets of Kolkata or the National Capital Region, which have a completely different socio-economic demographic.

Worldwide, the urban man has never been more out of place than he is today. It's the little things that make him feel so: does he pay or not pay or go Dutch? Whether at restaurants or weddings, whether it is to do with home EMIs or hospital bills, the question is the same. Is he protector, provider, hunter-gatherer, or does he 'allow' (and who is he to *allow* or *not allow?*) his woman to pitch in or lead? It's not just to do with finances. The IIT and MIT-NRI alumni crowd, which occupies high-tech positions globally, had congratulated my husband for being such an awesome husband for 'giving her permission to write like she does'. He had responded asking how this was even part of any equation. 'She does what she does, just like you and me,' he had said. This had elicited even more wows on his greatness and over what a modern, liberated husband he was. So much for the Ivy League and Ivy League-Indian-equivalent education.

It is important to mention this. The modern man could be an ally, as in the case of the celebrity couple, the Indian actress Priyanka Chopra and her American musician-husband Nick Jonas. Nick is Priyanka's most supportive ally and her biggest cheerleader. At least, that's what their well-orchestrated PR and marketing machines (both heavy investments for all celebrities) tell us and convince us about. Also, he is American and works in the entertainment industry, which tends to be a lot more liberal than many mainstream industries. And, let me insist again, they are celebrities.

On the streets, it is a different story. 'Truth be told, Reetoo, I am actually very, very scared of women who are beautiful, smart and ambitious,' says Rajdeep, who is a Bollywood director and familiar with actresses. Ideally, he should have the Nick Jonas attitude towards women, especially given the company he keeps and the kind of movies he makes, which show women in empowered roles. 'I don't know what to do with them. I don't know who to be around them.' I appreciate his honesty. Very few men have that level of honesty. Especially today. He has chosen not to date at all.

Feelings and inner lives are important and dictate much of our lives. Almost all the love stories featured here are about that. But facts, statistics remain too and have an equal impact. Irrespective of men feeling threatened or not, the first question is, are there truly that many financially independent women in India? In April 2023, an Al Jazeera news report showed how as India goes on its way to becoming the world's most populous country, 670 million Indian women would be left behind.[6] The news report also quoted that the Centre for Monitoring Indian Economy (CMIE) found that only 39 million women were employed in the Indian workforce, against 361 million men. That is, only 10 per cent of working-age Indian women are employed. Moreover, as a Scroll.in article quoted from the State of Working India 2023 report, on average, women earn 90 per cent of what men earn.[7] The earning gap is higher among the self-employed, with women earning around 60 per cent of what men make. So yes, working Indian women are just a drop in the ocean. And the income disparity between them and men is huge. In spite of all this, the fact remains that more and more Indian women are working and earning today – and are able to be independent – than ever before in history. The unemployment rate among women, according to CMIE, had dropped from 14.9 per cent in December 2023 to 11 per cent in January 2024, the lowest since 2022.[8]

Moumita, an employed communications professional based out of Noida, thought her husband was quite a secure man. He was quiet, tender and supportive, but he ended up living off her savings. She thought she was funding his artistic career, but all she was funding was his alcohol and porn addictions. All he did was get drunk and watch porn from morning to night. Eventually, she threw him out of their apartment, which she had paid the rent and associated bills for, and opted to be a single mother, joining the army of India's 73 million single women. 'He told me it was all my fault. Imagine, after all that I did for him, I didn't make him feel like a man,' she says. 'I am too strong, too intense. Too manly. And I was the reason for his addictions.'

Rohini too had a similar story to tell. She had completely supported her guitarist boyfriend, so he could focus on his dreams, only to discover that he somehow had the funds to take out an upcoming actress from the South, who was trying to make it in Bollywood for movies and dates. 'I caught him red-handed. He didn't even defend himself. I mean, I even filed his invoices and did his PR, not just give him money. How much more could I do? And he says I am too manly and don't let him be a man, so he wants out,' she says. It's a cookie-cutter story.

Shivraj and Deepankar admit that they were both in love with women who were the exact description of what Rajdeep feared: 'Women who are beautiful, smart and ambitious'. But they felt those women were too financially well off, too beautiful, too successful, too ambitious. Moreover, those women got things done, and they felt redundant. There was no use for them as men. And they never bothered to try to do anything either. Both say they ghosted 'the love of my life knowing very well that I'll never get over her'. After all of these years, they were still in love with the same women. 'I love her, only her and always will,' says Deepankar. 'She is my forever love. I don't even want to get over her. I don't even want to love someone else ever,' says Shivraj. It's as if they are talking about the same woman. The pattern is that cookie-cutter. Truly, we are all archetypes, as Jungian psychology says and the stories in this book show.

Rajdeep, Deepankar and Shivraj are perfect examples of the lost, lonely Indian man who feels left out and chooses to stay that way and stay passive – in a country that is full of myths and legends of men fighting for their honour.

Still, these are the healthier cases. And I hate to admit it, but they are the best-case scenarios. Male insecurity has led testosterone-fuelled aggression to beat up women, abuse them, sometimes putting their lives at threat, as we saw in the last chapter and we will in the coming ones, and as we see all around us, even if we walk with blinkers on. Sharja, for instance, has cigarette burn marks all over her body and was once even thrown out of a moving car by her boyfriend. Later, she apologised to him because of course it was her fault. Only then did he calm down, after which he wanted sex, which she didn't dare say no to. Much, much later, she could walk out. She and hundreds of others like her at least didn't land up like Shraddha Walker, who was murdered by her suspicious, unstable, psychopath boyfriend. It was a murder so gruesome that it shook the entire nation, causing people to look at love stories gone wrong, IPV, masculinity in India, mental health and a myriad other related topics.

In 2023, the *Journal of Family Medicine and Primary Care* cited a study conducted in Delhi: 30.6 per cent women reported IPV and 43.2 per cent reported controlling behaviour by their husbands.[9] Children's health was obviously affected, directly or indirectly, by their mothers' exposure to domestic violence by the partner or spouse and their family members. The National Family Health Survey of 2020–2021 showed that 29.3 per cent of women in the age group of eighteen to forty-nine who had ever been married had experienced spousal violence, 3.1 per cent physical violence during a pregnancy and 1.5 per cent sexual violence. 22 per cent of participants had experienced physical abuse, 6 per cent sexual abuse and 10 per cent emotional abuse by their partners in the year preceding the study. Women with relatively higher education, employment or earning status than their spouses faced far more repeated violence than women with lower educational levels.

Perhaps nobody has benefitted more from these confusing times for masculinity than the men in power. The megalomaniacs, the bosses, the older men. You see, for centuries, kings in all cultures had harems, and the queens competed with each other for the king's favours, often in extremely detrimental and cruel ways, while simultaneously being there for each other (something that is playing out again in modern times as we will see in the chapter on polyamory).

We forget that we are all but part of the human collective, and its epigenetics, Jungian archetypes, call it what you will . . . these patterns pass down. Many great men and geniuses kept several lovers simultaneously.

For example, take the master conductor, composer and pianist, Leonard Bernstein. I happen to be listening to a 1972 recording of his brilliant rendition of Mahler's Symphony No. 3 in D Minor as I am writing this. He was famous for his musical brilliance and is celebrated to this day but was equally notorious for the numerous lovers he had. The brilliant movie *Maestro*, with deeply evocative performances by the lead actors Bradley Cooper, playing Bernstein, and Carey Mulligan, playing his devoted, long-suffering wife, the actress Felicia Montealegre. Theirs was a happy marriage with a lot of love but also with the wife having to turn a blind eye to her husband's eternally roving eye. He was so full of love that he could not contain the love bursting out of him for both men and women. Even as an old man, after his wife's death, he had lovers the age of his children, whom he also mentored.

It reminded me of the large number of men, many from India's top intellectual elite, I had met when I had first landed in Delhi. The city's extramarital affairs had completely shaken the image I had of these men, many of whom are my readers; of marriage, specifically the Indian marriage; of relationships and, most of all, of India itself. For while these were not openly violent, abusive men, they seemed to have this sense of what I would call being lost in common with the men in this chapter.

And we are not even talking about the Me Too movement. Though there is still a long, long way to go, fear has, thankfully and in many cases rightfully, been put into possible predators. 'We are all very, very careful with Me Too. Even if someone hits on me, I don't indulge them. *Aaj pyaar, kal case kar degi* (Today, it's love, fun and games, but tomorrow, perhaps she could sue). Who knows?' says a Bollywood insider.

A major business tycoon had dared to grab Shivranjini's hand back in 2008 at an office event in South Mumbai. Today, she works in Silicon Valley, where her laws are ultra strict. But she is able to work in greater peace than she could in India. She still recalls the India incident and says that the Me Too movement really put men of power in their place. 'You think he'd dare do this with me now?'

For the same reason, three senior citizens in Delhi say they are glad they lived out all their extramarital affairs back in the nineties. None can remember the number of girls they had. 'But you were married?' I remind each of them. And again, as if cut from the same cloth, the three say the same thing in different words: 'And I was and remain a great husband and father.' But some of your girlfriends had to get abortions, I remind one of them, with unveiled sarcasm. One says, 'How is that even relevant? Have you forgotten your journalism?' I ask him if he has heard of patriarchy and mansplaining and leave before he can become one of those countless men commenting on my columns and calling me 'Bongtard' or accusing me of being a Bengali feminist who hates men – totally untrue. How else were so many men opening up to me? (Another senior citizen's debauchery or love affairs, depending on your perspective, as we will see in the chapter on polyamory, had resulted in death.)

You see, there's a difference here between regular, ordinary men and men with money, power, influence or affluence, celebrity status or public stature, of some sort. For the latter, women will always be star-struck, especially the young ones, often in admiration of their craft, and will throw themselves at them. During my days of intense research for *An Ordinary Life* in Bollywood circles, I had encountered two major Bollywood stars and also one of its famous directors and had witnessed this first-hand. Mind you, the incidents I witnessed were not about casting couches. These were men in their forties, whom young, nubile women in their twenties were happily throwing themselves at. One could argue that it was the only way these women could stand out. Rumour had it that one of the biggest budget films of 2019 had flopped because the director was busy sleeping with a hot young assistant. She knew she was to be cast away like tissue, but she didn't mind. I mean, she got to sleep with this director, her hero. How cool was that! This concept that one is cool or worthy because they slept with a star – the sheer tragedy plaguing not just our youth but all of humanity. It reminded me of the many middle-school American girls I knew who wanted to be a Kardashian (a reality TV star, who first became famous due to a leaked sex tape and then used it to become one of the greatest influencers of all time), and they didn't mind at what cost.

Another major Bollywood actor echoed what the three senior-citizen men had told me. He said he was a fantastic husband and father and loved his wife. Shoot romances didn't matter. 'You can still be loyal to one person. I don't see what the problem is.'

And that is the problem. At one time these men got away with anything. Today they get away with everything by doing nothing at all. Like Kamlesh, a bachelor in his fifties, who is dating a twenty-something but refuses to marry her or live with her and only sees her on weekends. 'She is a feminist. A self-made woman. I let her be free, free to do whatever she wants. Even if she wants to be with someone else. I love her so much,' he says. Apart from the weekend sex, how is he even present in her life really? How is it love? Generally speaking, how is any partnership a true partnership, when one is not there for the other? Ironically, the amorous senior-citizen men mentioned earlier and those we will see in the chapter on polyamory have done more for their harems and museums of lovers. Meanwhile, the young woman is working two jobs and paying for her father's upkeep too. Both the men have failed her, but she can't see it. All she sees is love and that she is able to provide and protect the men she loves. Literally, she is doing the man's job. She has fibromyalgia and sciatica, perhaps due to overwork. Perhaps she will see the light of day soon. Forget the hunter-gatherer, provider-protector dynamic of ancient times. Forget sharing equal responsibilities in the modern world, including financial support and bringing up children. Women are allowing men to stay lost, to get away with doing nothing or next to nothing. They are allowing them to stay lazy. 'Dusty', as they are called in America. Angrez Singh is the anomaly. He may be lost, but his heart is in the right place, and he is acting, showing up, which is what traditionally, in all cultures over the centuries, a man was always supposed to do.

Part III

Trends: Globalisation of Love, Sex and Relationships

a) Sex

8

The Rise of BDSM

INDIA CONTINUED TO SURPRISE me on a daily basis with its newer and newer species of nincompoops and in the most absurd of settings. This time it was in an expensive lingerie shop in one of India's swankiest malls in the National Capital Region. A man in a wheelchair, probably in his eighties (he looked older than my father but younger than those I know are in their nineties, so I'll assume his age), was arguing with the cashier about the mode of payment. The cashier seemed to have the patience of a saint, and the man, if you excuse the brainwashing of Indian and eastern cultures of respect for the elderly, was frankly being an utter nuisance. This was not a hospital or a medical store but a lingerie store. He was not a woman or a member of the LGBTQA. He seemed to be a typical heterosexual man, toxic and entitled, going by his behaviour. For someone his age, that too in a wheelchair, to be so unabashed in that atmosphere, really felt like a surreal scene more in place for a French film than a conservative country like India, renowned for, in the best case, policing and, in the worst case, slut-shaming its women, where even the purest women like Sita had to prove their chastity.

I happened to have established a rapport with a salesgirl who was trying not to stare. My chatting with her as a customer who had wandered in helped her stay professional and not pay attention to what was happening. Conversations with the staff revealed that while what had happened wasn't very common, it was not uncommon either. 'Sugar daddies are here all the time. He is clearly one.' Our badly behaved sugar daddy here had bought over half a lakh rupees' worth of merchandise, several from the kinkier sections. A harness choker, a normal choker, an assortment of spankers, corset, masks, private bondage rope, gentle and not-so-gentle handcuffs, lace and satin blindfolds, pasties with chains, and so on. He reminded me of those advertorials in the India I had grown up in: 'age no bar, caste no bar'.

'Sugar babies can be younger than me,' the salesgirl said. She said she was twenty-six. Taboo relationships, extramarital affairs, situationships . . . a great many experiments were happening. But brides and members of the LGBTQA community came to those sections too. 'Just the other day, a gay man threw a fit because he couldn't try on women's lingerie . . . we didn't have a men's trial room.' I told her about the non-binary lifestyle of California and about the non-binary restrooms in taxpayer-funded, public elementary schools because kids as young as ten, sometimes younger, seemed to be aware of their gender and sexuality preferences. In many ways, this India was begging for it. 'Yes, same. He would have liked that,' she said. 'Quite often, women just about to get married and doing their bridal shopping will buy the same kinky stuff as this sugar daddy of ours,' she said. It was hilarious, how we had begun to refer to him as 'this sugar daddy of ours'. While the species are usually in their forties, fifties and sixties, they may or may not come with their girlfriends, some of whom are their own age. I thought of Shantanu and Snigdha from Delhi and their many extramarital affairs, which is where people came alive. By now I had seen and heard enough to know that had I dug deeper asking them questions, they'd reveal some similar answers for their kinky shopping: that it made them 'feel alive'. The brides she was referring to would be there with Mummy and Daddy, both the ones they were born to and the ones they'd inherit with their upcoming wedding. Sometimes they'd tell salesgirls to keep stuff aside. Then they'd return alone (probably while the parents were elsewhere in the mall, perhaps excusing themselves) and pick up the stuff, pay for it and rush out. The parents might think they had just bought regular night gowns, lingerie or something else, but definitely not kinky stuff.

The salesgirl was from Kolkata, which is a lot less conservative than NCR, and where kinky practices are quite common but rarely involve posh shopping. Living in a city renowned for the arts, Kolkatans might get creative and use regular, cheap products or build DIY contraptions. Say, spankers with soft-coated belts or rulers and combs to create tingly sensations for their sex partners. And what about you, I ask her. Are you into kinks? Seeing so much all the time here? 'No. It's boring. I love to go home and cuddle with my boyfriend at the end of a long day,' she says. I smile and, having bought nothing, walk out of the store.

Loosely translating as Bondage and Discipline, Dominance and Submission, Sados and Masochism, BDSM encompasses a spectrum of ever-growing erotic practices, which are more psychological and interpersonal and based heavily on a person's self-identification and self-concept. A Gitnux survey shared that 46.8 per cent of its respondents have engaged in BDSM activities.[1] A survey published by the *Journal of Sexual Medicine* said that 46.8 per cent of men and 59.6 per cent of women had BDSM-related fantasies. No wonder then that Pornhub, the leading pornography website globally, had cited that Bondage and BDSM were among its top twenty searches. Specific statistics were not available for India, but you just had to go to Quora to see the number of questions and responses containing details of Indians' BDSM experiences, proving just how common it was in India. Search 'feet' on Twitter India and you will see an enormous number of women offering their feet for worship and an enormous number of men begging, oh my god literally begging, dying, to be dominated, ridiculed and be allowed to worship their feet. Slave auctions, trampling and all kinds of events celebrating fetishes, kinks and taboos in safe spaces were being held, among restricted communities, to keep people safe. These were happening all over Indian metros and in Goa. Some fetishes are pretty intense, extreme and out there, involving golden showers, scat, where you defecate or urinate on another, of course with their consent, thereby you feel seen. Ideas of what feels good are deeply rooted in psychology and trauma or, depending on whom you ask, not trauma but joy. In 2023, in Mumbai, an upscale bar was booked for a completely consensual, blindfolded groping event under extreme supervision. The turnout was massive, and yes, everyone paid to be there. This is exactly the kind of stuff yours truly, being grandma and all that, had trouble with. I asked a friend of the organiser of the event to connect me with someone who could explain the event to me. And she put me in touch with Krishna, a key member of one of India's leading BDSM and kink groups.

So here I am, back in Kolkata. In a glitzy mall in south Kolkata, at a fancy but empty Chinese restaurant, meeting Krishna for lunch. Our conversation will be completely off the record, and I hope he will explain things to me. He looks as normal as any spectacled, geekish, good Bengali boy can be – *babushona*, as they are called. He was fair and looked physically fit, making him appear younger than a man in his late fifties. 'You need to be mummified. Can I mummify you? I'd love to,' he says. I am used to people, total strangers, being completely open with me, because I am so empty (or was, until this crowd of nincompoops I seemed to encounter everywhere made me realise again and again that compared to them I was the only true nincompoop grandma). At this point, being at the receiving end of thousands of love and sex stories, little baffled me. Still, what an absolutely absurd way to greet a stranger in a professional setting. Yours truly may be nincompoop grandma, but she has also lived for two and a half decades in San Francisco, a landmark city in the history of the LGBTQA community, home of LGBTQA activist Harvey Milk, the Folsom Street Fair, one of the largest global celebrations of BDSM, kink and leather subcultures. Kink events are just as common there as *jagran* events in north India . . . there's no escaping them, even if you're a non-believer and unless one is a participant and they are your idea of fun, joy, identity, and so on, one might find them causing nothing but inconvenience in their daily life. Both create noise pollution, traffic, litter and jam the streets and your senses, cluttering your life, distracting you from whatever it is that you are doing . . . perhaps trying to meet a work deadline, perhaps preparing for exams. And so I knew what mummification was. Relatively uncommon from regular forms of pop culture BDSM made mainstream, albeit irresponsibly and incorrectly, by movies like *Fifty Shades of Grey*, it was not like your typical burning wax, mild spanking and mild bondage with rope, blindfolds, handcuffs, etc. Mummification was pretty extreme. Deriving directly from the ancient Egyptian practice of mummifying bodies, here too, a participant wraps his or her partner in extremely tight layers of material leaving them with zero mobility so they very much resemble a corpse. The materials used could range from pantyhose, tights, cling film and bandages to duct tape and even the strongest forms of tape (yes, the type kidnappers use).

The mummification Krishna was suggesting to me was of a gentler form, performed with cling film. He showed me pictures, not realising just how inappropriate this was on his part. Just because much of BDSM is about chasing sensations and often not penetrative sex or even fondling, people are curious to try it out as a new thing and assume that everyone, even a journalist interviewing them, must be 'liberal and open minded' (situations for which the rolling-eye emoji was invented). It's like an activity just like, say, sky diving, deep-sea diving, bungee jumping or riding the rollercoaster, giving you highs, kicks, adrenaline rushes, the feeling of being alive, the feeling of relief, whatever you'd like to call it. So many Indians were pursuing it. Countless BDSM events were being held across the country. Krishna and his peers across India were doing the good and deeply necessary part – spreading the right education to say that this is not just a fad and that participants will actually be responsible for someone's life.

Sharda, a twenty-three-year-old student in Bengaluru, confesses she did a BDSM act on herself by burying herself completely in sand on a beach, leaving only a small hole with a pipe through which to breathe. Passersby could have easily mistaken her for a mound of sand some kids might have built as an unfinished sand castle. I was shocked. She was just a kid. Perhaps only I, being a nincompoop grandma, (with what was being revealed to me every day through these stories about myself as being non-judgemental but also conservative and highly traditional) was shocked. Perhaps it wasn't shocking to anyone else. 'I have never felt safer and more relaxed in my whole life. I had nothing to do. Nowhere to go. No one to please, appease, convince. I was right there in a public place and yet I was not there.' I told her to tell a friend before doing what she had because this was intense and could have cost her her life. I gave her the details of Krishna's group. While people burying themselves in sand, like at a spa – imagine a salt or mud wrap – leaving their heads out is not uncommon on the beaches of the West, this was seriously jarring.

Jayant, a member of the LGBTQA community who identifies as a switch (as in he switches between genders, male and female, as a form of identity), has mummified himself with pantyhose. He used a dozen layers of pantyhose to wrap the bottom and top halves of his body, cutting out the crotch area of the pantyhose and wearing the nylon stockings like a tight top. He said it was far easier than bandaging himself. Once, thus mummified tight, unlike say in the sand that Sharda had used, his blood circulation, vision and hearing, all began to get cut off. 'The first time, I panicked. But after a few tries I loved it more and more. And even then, during that first time, I had loved it as well,' he says, as if one was getting used to roller-coaster rides. 'This is exactly what I wanted. To not see. To not hear. To not feel. To just not be in this world,' he says. 'You too should try it. I think you need it,' he smiled. Jayant said he wanted to soon increase the pantyhose layers perhaps to twenty, so he could feel even less and feel even more wonderful.

That was the thing. Both Krishna and Jayant had sensed what my loved ones had missed. I was burdened more than ever before with a billion responsibilities and roles, as wife, mother, bahu, a working woman, volunteering at several places, including at a hospice, which is extremely emotionally taxing, teaching at my son's school, handling mounds of paperwork and a ton of personal battles that each of us faces. Each of my roles involved taking on great emotional responsibility for the lives of so many at their most vulnerable. As a caregiver, I was not only worn out, but I was running on empty. All of this hyper-productivity too came at a price. My own meditation, relaxation and self-care practices (that I chose over socialising or even simple pleasures like movies and music) kept me afloat. For instance, I opted out of birthday parties, offending everyone, to sit in hot-tub soaks with Himalayan salts and an hour of meditation. And so I seemed better off and appeared to be more carefree and relaxed than anyone else I encountered. And so I am and always have been the one who sees people and whom they open up to, as you can see from the stories in my column and, of course, here in *How India Loves.* But for the very first time, I felt truly seen, without projections. It was new for me and deeply touching.

Ironically, Krishna also suggested that I could become an extremely successful elitist dominatrix. I had all the makings, and my sari-clad self apparently didn't even need a costume. 'You're your sari, and if you like boots, or not, you're stern enough as it is,' he said. Kolkata's hot *boudi* syndrome – that is, being bossed over, scolded by stern, intellectual sisters-in-law – was well known. Even Tagore had been in love with his sister-in-law, and so it was literally in the city's blood and literature. I guess this is what being in charge and being in authority in my life had brought up. I had also put up walls so that people didn't come at me sexually, which is something every woman perceived as being attractive but doesn't want attention has to do. Letting it all out by scolding people for stupid things was apparently something you could get paid extremely well for. Who knew? It was so amusing that I actually spent five minutes imagining taking it up. Barring the police, I had actually never scolded anybody. And all I could think of was seeing this as an assignment and writing a novel, perhaps another memoir, this time on the life of a hot *boudi* dominatrix. See, I was being offered this ridiculously high-paying job for doing next to nothing for a few hours a week as and when I wanted to (and that too, a role in which I had power, control and authority and could scold anyone about anything for no real reason: the dreams of all toddlers and many adults to play god briefly) and all I could think of was writing about it. I could be nothing but a writer.

Rita, a Kolkata-based marketing executive in her forties, says her favourite thing in the world is to first be tied with 'the tightest rope . . . perhaps cable ties . . . and then gagged and then, mummified. . . . Oh my god! There is nothing like it. I wish I could do this every day.' It is the only way she can orgasm, feel relief, feel alive . . . basically, feel.

All these Indians had stumbled upon BDSM practices primarily through the Internet, BDSM porn, pop culture or via people who had had BDSM experiences and had passed them on. Many knew that normal sex was not for them but did not know what worked until these random discoveries. Someone loved it when hot wax from a candle had accidentally dripped on her hands. As a kid, Sharda had loved her feet being covered in sand, so much that burying herself in it just seemed a normal thing to grow up into doing.

Krishna recalls his own journey beginning from when he was as young as five years old! He remembers tying himself up with ropes to the iron bars of the tall, spacious windows of his ancient ancestral house in Kolkata where he lived with his big joint family. As he grew older, he found his mother's saris or stronger and stronger ropes to tie himself up with. 'My love for bondage, which, depending on the culture one is from, many will label as a kink, stemmed not from trauma but from joy, curious play and innocence that is inherent to childhood,' he says. It just continued. By his teens, Krishna realised that he was the only one doing this. His friends, cousins and relatives were not. There was no education around it, no social media, no Internet. At age fourteen, he realised that nobody was even talking about it. So he began to feel a deep sense of alienation, the kind you feel when you know you are different and alone and that and nobody gets you. We have all been there at one point or the other. Slowly, by the year 2000, he began to form a group, a safe space, for people like him. The group even has conferences in Goa. More than providing a safe space and events for the community, the group also provides the deeply necessary education about BDSM and kinks. 'What nobody wants to admit is that BDSM is growing and thriving, not so quietly either, across India,' he says.

Community meets and events are regularly held in Bengaluru and Mumbai. Social networks like Fetlife, apps like Feeld, websites like Seeking Arrangements and Massage

Republic are full of Indians seeking to satisfy their BDSM and kinky desires. Unfortunately, much of BDSM in India is dictated by movies like *Fifty Shades of Grey* and other BDSM elements in movies, web series, porn and pop culture. To put it mildly, these activities are extremely dangerous and can damage a person forever.

Sudeep, an IT engineer with many casual sex partners, complains about how averse Indian women are to choking. 'It's so annoying!' he says. I lost it. Choking may be a hot trend, and yes, this is what love, sex and relationships are being reduced to . . . to trends dictated by porn, pop culture, social media . . . not too different from the seasonal collections and trends fashion houses propagate. I remind him that women are carrying centuries of patriarchy and trauma and naturally feel unsafe. If he must engage in stupid fads, he must discuss it with them and show the deep patience and responsibility required to convince them to try it out. I tell him it is people like him who are creating additional trauma everywhere. This is exactly what my problem is with people like him. Why not do whatever you must with a trusted spouse or long-term, committed partner, where you are in a safe space? Krishna and his peers hold workshops and guide youngsters to avoid exactly such situations, where one side is wary of kink. Choking as a BDSM pursuit, for instance, requires a lot of practice and knowing exactly where to press and for how long. One wrong move by the dom (dominant) or the sub (submissive) could cost one of them his or her life. Healthy dom-sub relationships take time, patience and care and are born not out of power dynamics, manipulation or random fetishes and abandonment, like with Tinder hookups. The dom is supposed to take care of the sub, while the sub surrenders their life, literally, to receive whatever sensations comprise their idea of pleasure.

In true BDSM practices, via the kinks and fetishes, you are owning and accepting all of yourself and your partner, being seen, accepted and validated the way you've always wanted to be. Like your deepest shadows, which each kink reveals. For example, extreme ridicule, trampling, the wearing of diapers, foot fetishes, role play of all kinds, and, shockingly, even simulation of fake rape situations (in controlled, safe environments, based on consent, communication and safe words), because then your 'purity, childlike innocence and goodness' are intact and the other party is to blame.

Anil told me about his extremely beautiful girlfriend who came from a very conservative family. Their entire intimacy was based on his whispering stories into her ears of what he'd do to her as a groping uncle. 'Basically, it is playing out a rape fantasy story. Something almost every girlfriend of mine has wanted,' he says. Shocking at first, it immediately makes sense when you look at the psychology of it. In a country like India, or other conservative societies, the girl after all this still remains pure, *sati savitri*, retaining her childlike innocence and goodness. She has not done anything wrong. She is not a dirty girl. It is the other guy doing everything. She is still the good girl.

The whole point of BDSM is safety, which is built on truth, transparency, the deepest trust and communication, which naturally result in consent. One could argue that all this should exist in every relationship, and this is true, but in most relationships, all this is getting rare and rarer. If you think regular relationships require vulnerability, BDSM requires the deepest kind. You are literally placing your entire life in the hands of someone, so naturally this can't be a random hookup. These are very deep connections formed with people who understand the dom-sub dynamic. What happens after normal sex is more important than the sex itself. Aftercare could look like cuddles, maybe cooking or sharing a meal together, a movie, a massage, sleeping, showering, talking . . . it really depends on the couple. Aftercare is extremely important in normal, healthy sex so nobody feels abandoned (another reason why casual hookups are so bad in the long run for mental health and self-worth). But aftercare is not only important, it is everything in BDSM. It is not just an orientation, but you are often meeting the needs you have that you can't get met elsewhere.

Krishna, who is polysexual, practices ethical non-monogamy and is a 'switch' (that is, he switches between being a dominant and a submissive), once very, very slowly tipped the chair in which one of his subs was sitting tied and blindfolded. She was petrified and asked him to stop. He did. Slowly, with constant communication, very, very gently taking a lot of time and with a lot of patience, he tipped the chair until it was lying on the floor. It wasn't just the high of playing with gravity and the sensations of falling, intense versions of which we feel in roller-coasters and aerobatics – extreme versions of which pilots call negative G. It was about trust, the fulcrum of intimacy, far more than chasing intense physical sensations that BDSM and casual sex in general are about. You're trusting the person completely to control your fall and your life. You could easily get a concussion. Trust falls are, incidentally, also a very common exercise in theatre and acting workshops, to build trust among actors so they can act their roles together in trust. It has to do with psychology and emotions rather than just sex. A week or so later, Krishna's sub called him. Krishna's controlled fall of the chair to which she had been tied had freed her from strange fears. She had always wanted to do aerial yoga, and now, finally, she was freed of her fear of falling. In a safe space now, which her dom had provided, she could now go into full-fledged inversions in the real world. It was incredibly healing, had brought out the best version of her and had completely transformed her life. It was an example of how BDSM done in a healthy way in trust by a healed, responsible person can be life changing in the best way possible, arguably way more than regular therapy. Another of Krishna's subs had asked to be 'mummified'. In real life she held a lot of responsibilities and had to control many things. By being masked and wrapped in cling film under his extreme watch – he couldn't take his eyes off of his sub for even a second because her life was literally in his hands, even more so than the life of the sub in the free fall was – she could just be. She had no responsibilities.

It reminded me why of the many surrender poses in yoga – including balasana (child's pose), uttana shishosana (puppy pose), kapotasana (pigeon pose), cat-cow – savasana (literally translating into corpse pose) is a universal favourite. You can lie down, breathe out in complete surrender and let go of every stressor. Krishna's subs were doing the same and being liberated under the complete care of a person they trusted the most. Of course, this also requires the deepest kind of vulnerability. And so these relationships are extremely intense.

There is nothing more healing than human connection. There is nothing more jarring than rejection or the lack of human connection. Krishna's mummified partner could relax so much that she finally fell asleep, under his extreme vigilance of course. When she woke up, her nervous system had relaxed. This is what professional dominatrixes in California will tell you too: it is about letting go of the control and responsibilities that force us more than ever before to live in a constant, nonstop adrenaline-and-cortisol-induced fight-or-flight mode. The clients are literally handing over their nervous systems to the professionals. Done with extreme mindfulness and with deep breathing, most BDSM is actually extreme presence, mindfulness; it is sensory, stopping the monkey mind – all reasons why we meditate and why meditation is so soothing.

'I feel happiness in the happiness of another,' says Krishna. 'With desire comes responsibility. Just because I have a desire, it doesn't mean I am a bull in a china shop.'

This is how BDSM done right can be therapeutic. This is also why therapists recommend it all the time in California to couples, not just to spice things up for them but to remind them that relationships are never about sex but about connection, which requires vulnerability, and that vulnerability is very, very scary. Perhaps now more than ever before, when we are extremely distracted and less and less present with our partners, turning people even more dispensable.

A sex coach based out of Mumbai shares a different side of the story, based on her clients, representing a different shade of India. 'When it comes to BDSM in relationships in India, it's quite different. Premature ejaculation, erectile dysfunction is often happening with men because they are kinky and penetrative sex does not arouse them. Instead of thinking that something is wrong with them, they need to understand that the regular way is not their type of sex.' She says she has seen many submissive men in arranged marriages who don't want to speak to their partners about their kinks and ask her how they could have erections during normal sex. 'The strategy they have figured out is to visualise kinky sex or watch BDSM porn before penetrative sex,' she says.

Several of her clients are men who have been married for many years, some for over twenty years in arranged marriages knowing they are kinky. They thought they'd train themselves for vanilla sex but couldn't. One of the men's wives got fed up and asked him to go 'do his thing' while they stayed married. A couple that the sex coach had as clients had been married for a decade; the wife was kinky and submissive, loved extreme dominance and liked sex extremely rough but never had the courage to share this with her husband because it went against the regular ideas of what a 'good Indian wife' would want.

When I had asked Krishna about masochism, he had said, 'How is boxing not masochism? How is a Brazilian bikini wax not masochism? Aren't you consensually putting yourself in extreme pain? What makes those okay and not kinky but BDSM practices kinky?' Ultimately, it is about judgement. The sex coach's clients in this case were open, but the husband struggled with guilt to give his beloved wife the level of pain that aroused her. 'You have to constantly check in what levels of pain are okay for now, observe and communicate to make sure the submissive is okay,' she says. After four or five sessions, the couple is fine, and with role play their intimacy has peaked and they are closer now than ever before.

Indian society is policed with shame. BDSM is about exploring the deepest shames and taboos, the most unloved, unaccepted parts of yourself. Intimacy can be broken down as 'Into-Me-See' – to truly see into the other person. It takes courage and total non-judgement to do that. It is not for everyone. After all, what is a kink? Some years ago, being gay was taboo and unnatural? For many, anything not missionary is kinky. For some, celibacy and monogamy are kinky. Really, it is all judgement that determines what is kinky and what is not. By whose standards are we defining whom?

BDSM is not for all. And it is most certainly not the dangerous, cool new trend to try, as so many are, or something to experiment with in secrecy. But for many, it is their truest self. It is total freedom.

Krishna tells me that one of his friends is now a nun in Vrindavan, and when he last met her, he thanked her for doing god's work. '"You too are doing god's work," she told me,' Krishna says with a smile. This was his last story of subs who have been set free through BDSM practices. When done the way Krishna and his peers are teaching, or the way the Mumbai-based sex coach is showing her clients, BDSM can become deep care. If this isn't a form of extreme intimacy, I don't know what is.

9

The Reign of Porn and Its Impact on Love, on Lives

META'S ALGORITHM HAD CAUGHT wind of my research and was popping up ads for a vibrator in India. The visual showed a silicon cone with amber, honey-like liquid dripping over it, and the accompanying text said, 'Tom never fails to perform', 'No mission is too impossible for Tom, because Tom gives Top Gun performance, gives Jerry Maguire vibes'. I nearly died of laughing. I don't know which was more hilarious – this ad urging people to fantasise about Hollywood actor Tom Cruise in the role of masculinity, hero and saviour or the fact that it had reached grandma, i.e., yours truly. Or that this was the new India. A country legendary for being orthodox, a country of honour killings, heavy policing, where, literally, your sex life or people's ideas of it could cost you your job, your housing, your familial relationships, your entire life.

And yet, India was having sex like never before. In online interviews, female actors were speaking about sex openly, advising guys, saying things like, 'first learn how to go down on a woman, then come to me'. In a show called The Male Feminist on Hauterrfly's YouTube, Bollywood actor Kalki Koechlin, for instance, talks about what boys should do in the bedroom with girls. '. . . boys have just no ethics in the bedroom . . . learn to go down on a girl . . . coming in two seconds and not even thinking whether you (the girl) has come. . . . these are things in which I'm like what is this . . .'

This kind of sex talk was becoming normal in India.[1] So normal that beauty vloggers[2] were openly reviewing packets of sex toys sold by Indian companies, which included BDSM kits in all colours, including this grandma's beloved baby pink, in gentle fabrics and materials like soft fake leather and lace, and including satin handcuffs.

According to research firm TechSci Research, the Indian sex toy market was estimated at $112.45 million in 2023 and is expected to grow at a compounded annual growth rate of 15.24 per cent by 2029.[3] The largest segment of growth is north India.

The ads for a sex toy from a company that calls itself India's first wellness luxury brand on YouTube show an adorable chubby Cupid who is heartbroken because the modern Indian, whether married or single, doesn't want the traditional love that the god of love has been famous for. No thanks, the vibrators from the company are enough.

And yet, I always had to censor my newspaper column and have had photos of trampling workshops taken away. You see, the media was way behind, and its portrayal was more of people who know nothing, and even Indian documentaries on the subject were, frankly, rather sad. People on Quora knew more. Everyone everywhere; this wasn't even a Gen Z problem, it was across ages, as we saw again with the grandpa in the wheelchair buying kinky products openly. So it wasn't even about knowledge. But approach and vibe. The media did not portray this new India, though its journalists, with the lives they lived, had the capacity to. Ironic, given how rich their love and sex lives were, as we saw in Delhi. And this again revealed another fascinating thing about this new India and its people. Who they were and who they showed to be were completely different, depending on where they were.

Bhaskar is a quiet, introverted ad professional, working in one of India's leading ad agencies. In his office in midtown Mumbai, everyone knows him as a guy who smiles, who is gentle and non-confrontational, does whatever is needed and keeps to himself, mostly at his desk, and only socialises as much as necessary. It is easy to like him since he is not a threat to anyone. And this is what had drawn Kamya to him.

He seemed safe. Plus, he was eleven years younger, making it easier for her to trust him. Before she knew it, he was at her home. It was casual, casual, casual all the way. Whenever they happened to be in town – since both travelled a lot for work – they texted each other asking to meet and hook up, usually at her house. But he was so rough with her that she had marks all over her. He'd rip open her tops too, taking no responsibility for the damage. He also told her how gentle he was with her as he was into blood fetish with others. Literally, a vampire. In a practice where the smell, taste, sight and texture of blood are a turn on. A partner can cut themselves (once again, safety is paramount) anywhere, say, on the thigh, and the other partner can do whatever it is that they want with the cut, caress it, lick it, play with it; both of them enjoying the sensations produced. Call it knife play, edgy BDSM, blood fetish, blood kink, whatever, it is on the extreme side of the BDSM spectrum. It falls in the realm of edgeplay, and it is something I'd rather not get into here. But entire communities are devoted to it, including those on the sex-based social network FetLife. And again, one has to just look it up on Quora or Reddit. And so, in comparison, the bites Bhaskar was giving Kamya, the wild beast in him that he was unleashing on her, was truly him being extremely gentle. But it was too much for her. Eventually, he left her to return to his primary ex, with whom his relationship was based purely on kinky blood sex.

That's the thing about kink; its ideas to realising who you are are all informed via pornography. Once you have shared with your partner your darkest secret self, one that could get you arrested, one that borders on life and death, psychologically, your relationship creates one of the greatest intimacy. I mean, blood is as primal as it gets, and if that is your thing, you truly cannot connect with someone normally after that. The psychology of all sex, each fetish, or the lack of it, and why we seek any of it, is connection. So when you have been accepted and have been able to celebrate your most taboo self with someone, why would you be elsewhere.

Compared to all of this, Bhaskar was arguably being 'okay', giving bites, being less intense, no bloody edgeplay. But all his choices had their roots in pornography, not in love or 'liking' or connection. In other words, the hallmark of intimacy. And it wreaked havoc on Kamya's mind and nerves, who was not into BDSM or a member of the kinky community. Four years later, she is still jittery, shaking, can't look at herself and gets constant anxiety attacks. She sees a therapist, is on medication and battles with depression. Initially, she couldn't even go back to work but Bhaskar could. Eventually, after a year of being a total mess and feeling suicidal, she went back to work at a different company. And here she was the total opposite of her old, vivacious, loud, ambitious, hyper-social self. She had become what Bhaskar had been at work. She went straight home after work and met with very few girlfriends.

This is exactly how pornography, in this case BDSM porn, ruins a person's life. One must confine one's BDSM activities to one's BDSM and kink communities, and that will keep everyone safe.

This new India is having a lot of sex, and casual sex is ruining people's lives on a daily basis, with zero accountability or responsibility on their part. You could meet someone on Tinder for a hookup and who knew what that person would want to explore. You are going beyond consent. That's a given if you're in the BDSM world. After a few hookups, Zara was asked by this boy if he could indulge in rape play. He had seen it in a few videos and had studied it in detail. But he'd be at the receiving end. She was shocked. And though she had blocked him on social media, she was heartbroken. 'You see, I was very fond of him. Who knows what love is. We had a connection; he opened up about his personal ailments, he kissed my waxing burns away. You can't say there was no tenderness,' she says softly, her heartbreak still as obvious as the bustling traffic outside the quaint Bandra cafe we were at.

And this is the multifold problem: a) casual sex; b) pornography-induced relationships; c) zero accountability and responsibility; and d) no relationship, so you are left in complete abandonment, like a refugee in a war zone that nobody can see.

Pornography, pop culture, ideas of sex from the Internet, problematic partial representations of BDSM and kink in movies, all of it is ruining lives. Porn cultivates unreal ideas of sex and is one of the reasons why relationships break down. Many believe porn is healthy. But the truth is, it is fake – fake bodies, courtesy of plastic surgery, fake airbrushing, fake reactions and fake orgasms. All of porn is staged and meant to lure you into it, like any product. How else would it be a billion-dollar industry? People need to remember this. Many people's ideas of sex, both among men and increasingly among women, are formed via pornography. And that's a huge problem. Porn is bringing in kinks and fetishes that are rooted in shame into the bedroom; it implies psychological issues, which need to be addressed with a kink-friendly therapist. Each fetish, like all of our patterns in our lives, has its roots in people's childhood.

Kink cases don't even have to be extreme to be a cause for concern or alarm.

After meeting on a dating site nearly three years ago and connecting right away, Manish and Manisha finally met in the same city. In what is the norm these days, they were in what is known as a situationship – where nothing defines their relationship to indicate they are exclusive, monogamous or even in any of the numerous versions of polyamory.

But there are only twenty-four hours in the day, which are full of studies, work and responsibilities, so they spent much of the day texting, calling and FaceTiming each other, like normal couples, and being intimate virtually (not too different from the tsunami of extramarital affairs I encountered in Delhi, even though both partners here were unmarried). So there was an unsaid assumption on Manisha's part. 'I felt we had something special, at least in my mind,' says Manisha. 'And if we clicked when we met, just like we had virtually, something could happen.' (They could have a long-distance relationship and then work towards getting jobs in the same city, have a normal partnership, perhaps live together, and so on.)

'When we met and hung out, he was even more caring in person. And in the bedroom too he was wonderful. Until suddenly, he became unrecognisable and I felt unsafe, unclean and scared.' From great, sweet lovemaking to urgent sex, all was wonderful until the life-changing moment when Manish suddenly spat in her mouth. Not only that, but he also went on to call her a 'dirty girl' for doing 'dirty things'. He went on to do some more kinky things and constantly calling her 'dirty girl'.

'Of course, it was not rape, but he finally felt like a stranger, and I kept questioning why was I feeling the way I did and what was wrong with me, because a) he was a great guy and b) I was here out of choice, my choice . . . it wasn't about consent.' Manisha starts shaking, tearing up as she shares this with me.

After all this, he was just as wonderful as before, cuddling her, talking to her, taking care of her, giving her a foot rub, a shower. He did everything that she loved about him. It was as if a demon spirit had possessed him, turning him briefly unrecognisable.

But Manisha just could not feel safe with him and trust him like she could before. She stopped orgasming with him because she could not relax when being called 'dirty girl doing dirty things'.

And the pattern was the same: he was wonderful after that brief while when he was not.

Worse, she could not trust herself, because, obviously, he was being this great guy; yet she could not escape her own feelings and began to move away from sexual intimacy, and slowly, from other forms of intimacy, such as telling him about her deep feelings and secrets.

As therapists are discovering, addiction to pornography is real. Although Manish was not an addict, he watched porn.

The adult and pornography website market in the US alone amounted to over $1.1 billion in 2023, according to market research firm Ibis World.[4] And now there is virtual reality too, which thrives on human psychology and will impact everything. Just like something relatively benign, say, Facebook or Instagram, video games for children, fantasy movies and novels, at its core, pornography too is about human psychology and the deep, deep human need for fantasy, the need to daydream and escape reality, which is why even Shakespeare's plays were performed and watched. Who understands this human need better than us storytellers and writers.

Porn tops all of this because it's taboo and private, making it just as appealing as uncovered piano legs in a Victorian-era sitting room. An *India Today* article reported that in India, there had been a 95 per cent rise in porn viewing during the pandemic-induced lockdown.[5] This in spite of many telecom providers having blocked many adult entertainment sites. I guess people just didn't know what to do with their lives or with themselves. If there is anything that the hundreds of love and sex stories from my own research have shown me, it is that. The statistics reported by *India Today* were released by Pornhub, the world's largest pornography website. Moreover, India ranked third, just behind the United States and the United Kingdom, in the list of top twenty countries generating the most traffic for Pornhub.[6]

Something as intensely psychological and escapist as pornography is expected to grow by leaps and bounds in its virtual-reality versions. A report by Market Research Engine expects the global virtual-reality pornography market to grow over $1 billion by 2027! A shocking statistic, and yet not shocking at all when you consider human nature. With virtual reality being all-immersive, 4D and lifelike, with the perfection of AI-induced bodies, how can messy human love and sex even compare. Why even bother with love then? Let porn kill not just sex but all love and all intimacy, in other words, all humanity related to love and sex once and for all. In other words, we are all nincompoops. This is not just the yours truly-grandma-self being all annoying. On the contrary, it is a reflection of the anthropology of the human race. And, as always, smart people are making billions out of it. And nincompoops being nincompoops, growing like armies – international armies of nincompoops – are enabling it, literally. The news will talk about the reign of terror here and there in the world. Well, the real headlines, which as always the media has missed, are about the reign of porn everywhere. There is no one to blame for this but our own lack of humanity.

Access to porn, and to a variety of porn too, has never been easier. Nor has urban loneliness and boredom been more all-pervading, often leading people to watch porn, until it becomes a habit.

Returning from their never-ending business travels to empty hotel rooms or after a long, hectic workday to their homes, many unwind with porn. But it is not just the porn industry itself that is booming. Everyone in industries apparently unrelated to porn at first glance is also prospering: Internet service providers, hotels, credit card companies that allow you to pay for access pornography in hotel rooms, cosmetic surgery companies to fix your body . . . the list of industries that make big money from pornography is endless.

So pornography is not going anywhere. It is here to stay and grow as an industry, a giant influence on our love and sex lives and consequently on humanity. And though not yours truly but many might argue that porn can even be healthy. Like owning all taboos, healing ideas of shame you incurred from society and childhood, according to shadow work in Jungian psychology, which advocates owning unloved, disapproved parts of your childhood self, is healthy. Many might recommend that you watch porn with your partner, thereby adding some sense of connection to this otherwise cold, impersonal form of entertainment that is alienating. (Like watching porn imagining others in the act, fantasising, masturbating to porn, while your partner is asleep or away, instead of connecting with them or having sex with them.)

But here is the thing: porn is bringing to the bedroom kinks and fetishes that are rooted in shame. Not the other way around. As with many men, Manish's ideas of sex were formed via pornography. Manisha had hated porn and had never watched it. It might have been different if both their ideas of sexual intimacy were based on pornography. But they were not.

Pornography slowly killed their situationship, and it is killing many relationships. I have lost count of friends who were asked to perform taboo fetishes their men had picked up from pornography, like anal sex, choking and BDSM practices. If both partners were on board, that would have been a different story. But they felt like Manisha, because it wasn't as simple and black and white as consent or no consent.

Media and pop culture are making these practices normal, so when people feel extremely uncomfortable and disturbed after being suddenly confronted with these practices, the stonewalling of their partners and the voices of pop culture and media in their heads makes them gaslight themselves and question themselves – why are they behaving like ancient grandmas? What is wrong with them?

India is the land of Khajuraho, Kama Sutra and tantric sex. All of which are the exact opposite of pornography. Have you read the Kama Sutra? It is about teaching how men should be gentlemen, how they should groom themselves, how they must present themselves to women. It is the gentlemen's equivalent of a Swiss finishing school for ladies. And it's not just about who you are outside, but who you are inside. A friend had gifted us a copy of the Kama Sutra as a wedding present, and having read it, I can confirm that it is nothing like porn. (Also, it is full of paan and attar perfume, making me lose all appetite for paan ever since – yes, even twenty-five years later.) It is about taking time, about connecting with your partner, about the slow sensual pursuit of pleasure, about both giving and receiving, all of which requires you to slow down, to be mindful, to be completely aware and to connect . . . in other words, which requires intimacy.

There is no taboo in ancient India's ideas of sex. Sex in the Kama Sutra is about patience, slowness, taking time, sensuality . . . all of which are the opposite of chasing random sensations, as porn and BDSM are teaching us. It is healing and spiritual and deep energy work, especially Tantra. There are no taboos or controls, dom or sub. No, sex is about surrender, softness, worship, devotion and taking care. It is about love and lovemaking, not about sex, getting off, releasing steam and what you can get out of your partner, as if they were an object. Taboos are rooted in shame. When we remove shame, there is automatically no taboo, and often the object we crave loses its charm for us.

For instance, vaping and marijuana are legal in California, so crimes related to these practices have reduced. And for many, the temptation for both has diminished. They may prefer meditation, walking, swimming, wellness, creativity and fitness practices to relax rather than pursue harmful activities. With the taboos being removed from these practices, their charm is lost too.

Tantra workshops are common in California, and tantric sex is as commonly prescribed to couples as antibiotics are for bacterial infections. Why? Because Tantra is about the deepest connection. It is extremely slow-paced, and there is a lot of eye-gazing in Tantric practices.

You look truly inside your partner and accept them for who they are, with all of their flaws, all of their broken shards. People start crying when they do this, they break down. Which is what love is. Which is what the definition of the word 'intimacy' is: broken down as 'Into-Me-See', seeing me for all of who I am and loving, accepting, holding and celebrating me for all of who I am, as I am.

Pornography is fake. It is staged. There is a script and the dialogues, reactions and orgasms to situations, including taboo situations, are all fake. That's the point. It's like a movie that you watch and forget.

A Hollywood romantic comedy called *Don Jon* deals with just this. The lead character, played by Joseph Gordon-Levitt, is completely addicted to hard core pornography despite having a robust sex life that his friends are envious of. First, he has a lot of casual sex with endless casual hookups with girls of his choice and then with his true love, played by the actor Scarlett Johansson. But he is so hopelessly addicted to porn that even after having sex with his girlfriend he still needs porn. Ultimately, it costs him his relationship with the woman he loves. And his entire life changes. A depressed widow mourning the death of her husband and child, played by the actor Julianne Moore, teaches him how selfish, unreal and completely one-sided porn is, and how it is the opposite of connection and intimacy. With her, he realises what he couldn't with his hot girlfriend and is ultimately freed of porn addiction. To people who feel porn is healthy, this movie is a must-watch to understand just how detrimental porn can be to one's entire existence and how the way out, as this book too says, is true deep connection, vulnerability, safety and holding space.

One must be self-aware enough to see that pornography is not affecting one's ideas of sex and chemistry, which one feels need to be fixed. They may not need to be fixed. The only thing that needs fixing is one's ability to truly connect with oneself, and as a result with one's partner, irrespective of external influences.

More and more people are connecting less and less in the bedroom with their partners. Blame it on the fast-paced nature of modern life, which keeps getting faster. Or on our hectic careers, infinite responsibilities, chores, caregiving, travels and meetings for work, and so on. On the goals, passions and pursuits that drive us. On the distractions that abound, in the form of both people, news, social media, video games, television or web series that we must catch up on. On the whole culture of constant hustling and networking to fulfil our infinite ambitions. Our mind is full of a million things, our time taken up completely. Before we even realise it, our bodies, through so much repetitive action, reach for our phones, perhaps books or something else.

Several of my married friends feel alienated, abandoned and lonely in their marriages. There is the baggage of history, of too many unresolved conflicts swept under the carpet, to just soldier on, apparently together, but not really. There is the baggage of too many relatives involved, arguments over children or elders. A friend of mine feels her husband is married to his work. In a committed, monogamous marriage, she feels like the other woman. After sex, he turns over to gaze at his phone, claiming to look at work emails, and/or falls asleep. She feels lonelier than before their lovemaking and has just begun to avoid sex altogether. Like so many married couples, they sleep in separate bedrooms on most, if not, all days. There are a million logical reasons for how we are in our relationships with others and with ourselves. But logic is hiding. How we feel is the truth. As infants, we were born feeling into this world. We were not born thinking or analysing. In fact, the need to think and analyse, the need for logic in our intimate relationships, the need to make sense of, to process is the first sign of trauma. Look at dogs, babies, small children and all animals that we so adore for their purity, and whose love melts us completely. They never need logic. They don't need to understand or make sense of. They just love. They trust how they feel. It is the way of nature. How you feel, therefore, is the most important compass in life to guide you. Lack of boundaries is a lack of courage. It's easy to blame it on smartphones, but one can stand up at least half of the time and make one's partner feel chosen, seen and, therefore, worthy. No matter what our age, our emotional selves are forever our inner child, which is why any good therapist (who isn't just medicating you but is making you actually do the work) will go straight to those patterns. Even in so-called healthy, happy and functional families, there are instances when its members have felt unseen, unheard, rejected, not shown off proudly instead of feeling accepted by their parents (who were equally busy back then as we are today, with infinite demands of adult lives) for who they truly were. Even if they were failures in something. Especially if they were. It isn't that their parents don't love them. Or that they have chosen a sibling over them in some instance. A simple, silent hug and total presence would have stopped this feeling of abandonment in their child selves within minutes, and could stop the abandonment they feel now, in our marriages and long-term relationships.

Intimacy then means to see each other, to truly see each other. It is the deepest form of connection. Sex can be intimacy. But all intimacy is not sex. Sex is but one of the many languages of intimacy. Intimacy is nothing but deep connection. And the lack of it often results in the greater need for connection that people in long-term partnerships seem to be looking for. They could try fulfilling this through a myriad activities: extramarital affairs, artistic pursuits, casual sex, friends, unnecessary amounts of socialising and networking, pursuit of spirituality, mindfulness, sports, shopping, emotional eating, addiction to work, alcohol or substances or even research, TV, video games . . . the list is endless. Depending on the nature of one's relationship, most of these activities are supposed to be in homeopathic doses in partnerships. But not a majority of one's twenty-four hours.

Unfortunately, asking for connection may make us appear clingy. But it is not. It is courageous. What is the point of being in a marriage or a relationship then if the partners' independent lives must take precedence? Modern culture, dating apps, hookups and the glorification of casual sex in the media have made sex abundant and completely transactional. Then there are the quickies, things like wham-bam-thank-you-ma'am (why the rolling-eyes emoji has become my perpetual facial expression), DTF, and so on, where people have many partners they may not even recognise if they saw them in a bar years later. These are insanely damaging psychologically – the side effects on people including a constant need for validation, self-worth issues, their doubts about what is wrong with them, and of course a feeling of abandonment. They have nothing to do with connection. They are a search for something, attempts to fill a void (for true intimacy and true connection) which cannot be filled. Not only is this uncool but it also leads to people finally giving up and deciding to stay solo or lonely in long-term relationships and marriages. The ancient practices of Tantric sex, on the other hand, are the opposite. Tantra understood intimacy in a way the abundance of modern sex never can. It is slow, it is mindful and, most of all, it is meditative – extreme presence, where layers of shame are shed. You see and accept each other for your true selves. What else is love after all? It takes time, dedication, commitment and vulnerability, which takes courage and makes the partner feel chosen. It is deeply healing. No wonder counsellors are increasingly recommending it. In California, a state of intelligent, well-to-do people obsessed with wellness, yoga, meditation and healthy living, a Tantric sex weekend is a fairly common practice for couples.

Aftercare post sex could look like many things. Perhaps it's just cuddles. Perhaps it's conversation – affirmations, that is, words of love, affection and tenderness to make the other person feel safe. Perhaps it's about how wonderful and hot the sex was. Perhaps it's watching Netflix together. Perhaps it's cooking a meal or taking a shower or putting the other to sleep or walking the dog. Perhaps it's just lingering, doing nothing. All of this involves vulnerability, deep attention, connection and slowing down to be totally present. Anything else in a marriage or long-term partnership is, frankly, cheating. One doesn't need to have an association with a physical human being to cheat on one's spouse or partner with. Because, just like the other person, your other pursuits too are making your partner feel abandoned and unsafe. Any time we are not chosen, we are abandoned.

Countless women have been faking orgasms since the beginning of time, just to keep their relationship with their partners intact. Or worse, they aren't able to orgasm at all in the first place, because they feel so unsafe that their bodies have shut down. It could happen to men too . . . shutting down, choosing silent treatment (being quiet and not reacting or responding, also known as stonewalling), choosing to unwind after a hectic day with drinks with friends or TV or with video games or sports or some other pursuit until, thank god, it's time to go to sleep. Return to the initial days of any partnership and you'll see that neither would need to do this if true connection prevailed – which involves heartfelt communication, expressing your needs without accusations or tears and with forgiveness.

Each of us wants to be seen, wanted, cherished, adored by our partners. But most of all, we want to feel chosen by our partners, and more so now, where in this modern world, we must compete with an ever-growing list of things like smartphones in the bedroom. Why is your work email or your Instagram and Twitter feeds or news of corrupt, boring and frankly repetitive politicians sexier than the person you have just had sex with? It is deeply damaging to feel lonely in relationships. And it takes efforts from both to come to the table. What happens after sex, what happens in the bedroom or even the absence of it dictates one's entire relationship and marriage.

And none of this is to do with pornography.

10

When Great Sex Ends Sex

'How come you never insist on condoms?' – this is not a text anyone wakes up to every day. Shreya reached towards her phone expecting a sweet message, realising that she had woken up instead to a nightmare. Texting is funny business and yet the fulcrum of so many modern relationships. The absence of texts, the presence of texts and a small text like this one will often work as a massive trigger, setting off a time bomb and turning your life into a horror movie. Shreya remembered clearly how she had actually insisted he use a condom, and he had convinced her, like hundreds of thousands of men before him have convinced hundreds of thousands of women. 'You trust me, baba . . . you trust me, na,' he had said with utmost tenderness, caressing her face, celebrating her vulnerability. Like most women, she too had insisted that he use protection. But in those moments of passion, when our primal instincts take over, we become part of the collective. Whether we admit it to ourselves or not. And in those moments, gender roles as ancient as time and those primal instincts themselves become more clearly defined than they are today, and the woman feels safe enough to give her trust to the man and surrender to him and be in complete submission to him. And so Shreya had given in and blinked, gently signalling, okay, he could penetrate her without using a condom.

Many traditionalists will say that this was as nature had originally intended. And the man, as protector, provider, hunter-gatherer, takes full responsibility for what happens to his woman, for upon her trust revolves his entire identity, the fabric of his very being, his entire reason for existing, his support and his entire world. However, in her innocence, Mama Nature did not know of patriarchy and its deeply necessary consequence, feminism, where the woman has to become the warrior, fend for herself and be allowed to have her voice, her life. She has to turn into protector, provider, hunter-gatherer, because not only has the man failed her but he has also betrayed her trust and, worse, abandoned her . . . in today's world of muddled gender dynamics, where everyone has to be hyper-masculine to survive. The bedroom is no different. From being a place of lovemaking, the bedroom has become a war zone, and often the war takes place within oneself, hours, days, years after one realises that even if there was no love, even if it was a no-strings-attached situationship, like that of millions, or like Shreya's and Ravi's, it was never lovemaking in the first place. Even in these best-case scenarios, which are fairly commonplace, where Ravi had 'pulled out', ensuring that she did not need a 'morning after pill'. In India, the i-pill, the morning-after contraception pill, had completely transformed sex, allowing women to have sex like a man. That is, freely, with no consequences, not having to depend on men like Ravi, or those they'd never want to see again, saving them the logistical headaches and deep emotional trauma of abortions. So much so that during the pandemic-induced lockdown, as an *Asian Age* article reported, the i-pill and other contraceptives were among the most ordered items on shopping apps, even in tier-II cities like Hyderabad, which tend to be relatively conservative compared with cities like Mumbai and Delhi.

As a monogamous, married woman, I could not understand how attraction could even occur in such a situation. For me, sex was never a primal need. I had no steam to release, no hot property I was attracted to, and so on. For my grandma self, sex was a consequence of feeling safe with a man. Yes, I was so healed that my life was free of drama and was rather boring. My friends even asked me sometimes why I wasn't a nun, for I could not find the actor Armie Hammer hot. Or even that Calvin Klein advertisement featuring Jeremy Allen White. My American friends shared it around, saying it would be a crime against humanity not to do so. The ad featured an almost naked body, looking like one of those perfect Greek god sculptures; odes had been written to it in various newspapers. Be it Jeremy Allen White, be it sex toy ads selling products about Tom with his Top Gun performance, Jerry Maguire charm, no male celebrity eye candy (for the lack of a better term) had any impact on me. I truly was Mission Impossible, who could not be conquered. I have no idea why my utter lack of interest in the ways and ideas of love, sex and relationships of nincompoops was so fascinating to this ocean of nincompoops. Far larger than my ex. My pretty Pacific. Had I traded my ocean for a tsunami of lost nincompoops?

No, grandma-nun Rituparna Chatterjee was attracted to one thing and one thing alone since the day she was born: safety. By default, I was a gentle, soft, tender child and continued to be so as an adult, who was reclusive and had built her entire world to feel safe, something I have well documented in my last book, *The Water Phoenix,* and in many of my talks and in my 'California Dreaming' columns in *The Times of India* and earlier in *The Economic Times*. As a grown woman, I was often described as being feminine and receptive, preferring slowness, activities and a lifestyle enjoyed by those labelled as 'introvert'. The sex appeal of challenges, ambitions, parties, large gatherings and even sports and aggressive exercise has completely bypassed me. Anxiety and overwhelm are your best friends and the best editors. Panic attacks, hypersensitivity . . . they force you beyond your own ideas about everything to lead a highly curated life, a life so intensely curated with boundaries that it would give the Great Wall of China, or the wall Trump so desperately wants to build against Mexico, competition. There is little room for that which isn't soothing, joyful or nourishing, whatever that may look like. This extends to people, places, things and events. My entire life was tailored around my mental health, around rest, relaxation and recovery. Nothing and no one was sexier to me than a man who made me feel safe and kept me safe. In other words, I preferred the traditional gender role of the man being protector-provider, hunter- gatherer but not because he wanted to control me out of his insecurity. On the other hand, it was because here was a man so secure in himself that he could make me feel safe and secure. Whether he could articulate it or not, it was his pride and honour to take care of me, and I 'allowed' him to, praised him even, for doing it. Nobody was controlling anybody. Patriarchy was a foreign word. And safety a way of being so mundane that it did not even cross one's mind. This is why I had married my best friend, the first man who had made me feel safe. At the age of twenty-one, I had eloped and married because it was this feeling of safety that mattered to me. And I had found it. Why bother or wait for what I had yearned for? What anyone yearns for if they shut up the noise, voices, distractions and clutter around.

Situationships had become the norm across this new country of my birth that I was discovering, in the elite circles of South Mumbai and in other places across the nation. They just weren't called by that term. I had first come across the term 'fuck buddy' when a classmate had mentioned it during a literature class. It was everywhere back in the day, and no matter what anyone said, the consequences remained. Lakhs of women like Shreya, and in some cases men, felt abandoned after fuck-buddy encounters. It can take something as little as a thoughtless text meant as a conversation starter to break one's heart. Shreya and I are sitting in yet another cafe in Bandra. I look at the couples sitting around and wonder how many of them are Tinder dates. Or hookups from other sources.

Shreya starts to cry. I seem to have this effect on women.

Radhi and Viddhi both had similar stories. Both had steady boyfriends, who were clearly being influenced by porn, or perhaps they were not influenced directly by porn but by discussions about porn (like with cars, sports, etc.) during bonding sessions between boys or bros, also known as bromances. Who knows? One came on her face, even though she had said no upon being asked and had even reminded him of her no during intercourse and said no afterwards too. But he did and on her eye, causing it to swell up and stay swollen for two days despite icing it. Not only did he not do aftercare in helping her nurse it but made fun of her for being such a prude, so stuck up; 'And didn't she enjoy it?' he repeated this a few times. What may be normal for him was not so for her, and in spite of her communicating this to him clearly, nothing worked. It was the same with Viddhi, whose boyfriend was suddenly so rough that she had cuts and bled. Again, he didn't nurse her. She couldn't walk for three days, all the while icing and nursing her lady parts. He was beaming, so proud that he had done such a good job that his girlfriend couldn't walk for three days. 'Next time, we will get you into a wheelchair. Would you like that, babe?' he had told her. Both girls were also surprised when, in a bout of passion, their men suddenly bent them over and took them from behind aggressively, one of them anally. You see, the boys thought the girls were theirs, the girlfriends they took care of and generally had great sex with, so such acts of spontaneity were okay. Not only were they okay, they were great. And all of this made for great sex. Great intimacy. And it was consent. Of course it was.

How could it be anything else? The girls were confused. Was this assault? Was this rape? 'Once he just shoved himself into my mouth. I was asleep,' says Siddhi, another girlfriend in a similar, committed relationship. 'Sometimes, he'll pull my hair or choke me in the middle of it all,' says Radhi. 'I don't want these BDSM practices or spanking, and he is so rough! And I am always shocked, which is apparently a compliment because didn't he just spice up our lives with his research.' It was not uncommon for the men to use pornographic language. Siddhi said she was told, 'You're my bitch, and I'm going to make you moan.' Dirty talk has become very normal because of the abundance of porn and also via movies, Internet pop culture and reels. And fads. Many a times the women want, say, a threesome or join swinger communities. It isn't really gender specific. It may be okay for some. But is it okay for you? If it was okay yesterday, an hour ago, a minute ago, is it okay right now? These are pillars of self-love, loving yourself second to second that I have written about so many times in my column and in *The Water Phoenix*. You need to communicate with yourself and consequently with your partner. Communication – gentle, tender, empathetic, patient communication coming from the heart, from a place of love and care, and not from demands and accusations of 'you didn't do this or that' is the only communication that works. Such communication is endless and deeply necessary. Even great sex cannot save sex and consequently one's sex life. But great communication can.

All of these women had walked out of their relationships and had chosen to stay single. I confirmed to them that what they had described were all actually cases of intimate partner violence. Whether it was assault, rape or not is about how they felt. If they felt it was, then it was. If they felt it wasn't, then it wasn't. This confusion was the biggest problem for them, for otherwise their men had been sweet and devoted. I don't want to get to the stereotype that men are dogs, since this isn't about gender at all. But such stupidity reminded me of the dogs in America that were devoted but every now and then bit someone and were to be abandoned. Dog shelters were bursting with such dogs and many had to be euthanised. Fussy and I often encountered a pair of volunteers walking half a dozen abandoned pit bulls in our local park. Some breeds like the pit bull terrier are considered dangerous and vicious in several American states and are just outright banned in India. Who was to be blamed . . . that could be a book in itself.

But here in these relationships, the men were committed, devoted, loyal and loving to their partners. They were 'good boys' led astray by porn in the heat of the moment, abandoning decency, care. What unnecessary stupidity that hurt everyone and hurt so badly. I mean, the level of nincompoopancy! (I am not sure if it's a real word . . . I had to invent that word, for how else to describe this growing collective of cookie-cutter nincompoop behaviour.)

As I said in the author's note, it is impossible to categorise these love stories to fit them in chapters. How does one contain life in compartments? How does one trap the waves of an ocean? One can't. So yes, both these women had great sex lives which was what ended their sex lives. And once again, was it about the influence of porn? Was it about lost Indian boys? Had it all to do with childhood patterns? All of them and more. For it is in the unsaid subtleties that life happens. And yet, we are all so similar. The stories of both these women, and of so many people, many of whom are women, many of whom are wives who have just chosen to put up with bad treatment, many of whom are taboo extramarital partners with no rights, are the same.

Amit, Ronit and Suhit too were men with great sex lives. Each fought cruel, ugly divorces that involved the police, one including a bitter custody battle that dragged on and on. Their stories are the stuff that could easily make for movies. What's most interesting is that through all of it, at some point or another, their sex lives were not compromised. They had sex with their soon-to-be ex-wives, even as they were about to move out. What's more, letting out the steam and stress, the sex seemed to be better than ever before. They even cuddled afterwards. It was as if none of the drama of their marriages playing out in courtrooms and in front of their relatives mattered when it came to the hot, steamy sex they were having.

I am truly baffled. 'Sometimes, you get intimate when you are breaking up. You just can't help it. There's so much history and you know each other's bodies,' says Ronit, who admits he is 'a high-testosterone male but she seemed to need it more. I even felt raped once'.

What was with this word rape? Why was it used so lightly? And what were rape fantasies? All of this made me want to lock myself up in a cloistered convent where I spoke with no one and met with no one, and ideally saw no one for the rest of my living days. Can't help it. Everyone has urges. Such urges are natural for yours truly's grandma self.

This brings me to the question: Is sex overrated? Is it just overrated? Is it even necessary, in the first place? Especially in today's times, where one has an increasing arena of avenues to accomplish the same results that sex brings, especially casual sex, such as relief and joy as a result of the happy hormones like dopamine and oxytocin that are released. Avenues that bring same results such as meditation, creative pursuits, connection. It's very interesting that in Hinduism, in the chakra system or energy vortices of the body, Svadhisthana, the sacral chakra (it literally almost sounds like 'sacred', because it is), the sex chakra, is also the chakra of creativity and creative pursuits. It is believed that it is this life-giving sexual energy that is the creative force which created the entire universe. And this is why so many practices preach celibacy or sex with just your primary married partner. This merging of male and female energies, Shiv and Shakti, creates the perfect balance of yin-yang energies, polarities, to create the perfect human Ardhanareeshvara, the half-woman and half-male god Shiva. This is also why having multiple partners means you take on their spiritual garbage, and in Tantra it means accumulating the karma of seven years or more per partner, unless done right and cleansed right. Though woo-woo, this could manifest in tangible, physical ways as mental illnesses, such as anxiety and depression, as we have seen again and again throughout this book, consequent physical ailments, or these polluting one's entire life, ruining careers, focus, and so on. Sex is not a means unto an end. It was never supposed to be about reaching orgasm either, which is all that it has come down to, thanks to porn-dictated ideas. Porn is the opposite of sex education.

Perfectly happy, platonic couples exist. Praveen and his wife, Ranjana, for instance, had a loving marriage built on friendship, cooperation, support and all that one might expect from a perfect marriage. Only one thing was missing from their marriage: sex. One might argue that eventually, in almost all relationships, no matter how passionate they are in the beginning, the chemistry begins to fizzle out, and in the best cases, peace, a sense of familiarity and of home, replaces it. There may be cuddles, just sleeping together or, depending on the generation, culture and background, expression of love transforming into simple acts of love and care that may not manifest in physical touch. But Praveen's couple friends seemed to be having a lot of sex. They did not have the tenderness, sweetness and care that existed between Praveen and his wife and had awful fights, but they had quickies if nothing else, regularly. A completely loveless, and sometimes violent partners, would be filing for divorce but continue to have sex through all of it. This and all of the messages around him made Praveen look at his successful marriage as an utter failure. He began to blame Ranjana for not giving him sex, and she felt confronted, attacked and completely isolated in the marriage, which harks back yet again to the psychological and emotional reasons why women fake orgasms and feel unsafe to orgasm or even have or want sex. We are not even getting into body issues like bladder pain, UTIs, endometriosis, PCOD, etc. that women battle with daily, all of which can come in the way of sex. And, of course, good old periods and PMS. Devoted as she was to her husband and her marriage, Ranjana was only human. Much as she did not want to, she began to feel unsafe, stopped communicating and eventually shut down completely, choosing to rather shut herself in the bathroom and cry or hang out with girlfriends or devote herself to activities that made her stay away from Praveen as much as possible.

We live in what is arguably the most over-sexualised of times. Media convinces us that sex is a primal, animal need and that it is abnormal and unnatural not to tend to it. The advertising industry uses sexual subliminals to sell cars and other objects of status. Women considered stereotypically sexy become anchors even in male-dominated sports events, motor shows, etc. Movies, pop culture and the media are increasingly glorifying hookups, which online dating has made the norm, turning people and relationships disposable, as if they are tissue paper, as we know has already happened in Mumbai and is now happening all over the country. Pornography is everywhere, and people even make fun of those who have never watched porn. What happened to Praveen and Ranjana's marriage is no different from what had happened in many relationships ruined by pornography.

Sex and sexuality are so out there that children in kindergarten, really barely out of diapers and unable to look after themselves, are increasingly becoming aware of their sexuality and sexual orientation, in California and even in

India. Two of my teenage readers say they knew by age ten if they were pansexual, demisexual or LGBTQA. But do they know how to do taxes? Or open a bank account? Or cook? Or drive? Then why is knowing their sexuality so important? What is this subliminal pressure from society, Instagram, the Internet and peers to know that? How can one even have an appetite for sex and sexuality after all of this barrage of sex-related stuff?

Today people hesitate to even use the word love, as if it's taboo, preferring to use best-case fillers like 'have feelings for' and the ubiquitous 'like' instead. Earlier, movies were about grand love stories and I-love-you romances. My *TOI* column, 'California Dreaming', alone has featured over a hundred stories, all around intimacy-related abuse. The word intimacy has become synonymous with sex when it is anything but sex. Sex can be a form of intimacy but not all sex is intimacy. In fact, most modern sex is not intimacy but transactional in nature. True intimacy requires radical presence with one's self, which is all that self-love boils down to, as I have said in several of my columns and my second book, *The Water Phoenix*. In these highly distracted times, again, arguably the most distracted times in human history, there is little presence.

Older generations lived in simpler, slower times, and though they were not without their own sets of problems, they often had truer intimacy in this sense. They had what Praveen and Ranjana did before peer and cultural pressure of the times killed their marriage. You will see this form of quiet love in old couples who take quiet evening walks together in your neighbourhood. Indian senior citizens may rarely hold hands in public or show any PDA. Many may never have even said 'I love you' – as in the famous scene in the movie *The Namesake*, the quiet love story of Ashima (played by Tabu) and Ashoke (played by the late Irrfan Khan). You will see this love expressed in the form of head nods at the airport instead of the passionate kisses I see so often at the JFK and SFO. There is a sweet scene in the movie where Ashima mischievously asks her husband, 'You want me to say I love you? Like the Americans?' He blushes and says, '*Haan* (yes).' She simply responds with '*haan*.' The purity, innocence and decency of their love is something beyond sex. It is true union, beyond sexual union.

I could never get either set of my parents to go on a date, at least visit Lodi Gardens and the old spots in Delhi they had taken their children to when they were young. They are much happier celebrating in silence, doing chores together, taking frequent walks together in the backyard of our Santa Clara home. I realised that they are on an endless date, and how precious their connection was, is. And how attainable, effortless this connection is for each of us. Once we focus on connection, true intimacy becomes everything, every moment together. Not just in the bedroom. In fact, the bedroom may not even be necessary.

b) Love

11

Polyamory

DO WE EVEN NEED this chapter? I mean, seriously? From the first chapter, on being greeted not with *tehzeeb* or kebabs, like I was expecting to, but with a tsunami of extramarital affairs upon landing in the country's capital, to the stories of single women, the lost Indian boys, the plight (or awesomeness, depends on whom you ask) of the crumbling (or flourishing, depends on whom you ask) Indian marriage, it was clear as the haze of pollution across the country and in the lungs of its citizens that Indians were polyamorous. More openly than ever before. Forget the laws and the Hindutva police. Like pollution and corruption, paanipuri and polyamory were everywhere, with various names for variations of the same thing. Phuchka, golgappa, paanipuri, paani patasha, paani ke batashe, fulki, phuska.[1] Triad/throuple, quad, vee, kitchen table, mono-poly, solo-poly, hierarchical, non-hierarchical, non-monogamous, polysexual, polyromantic . . . the list goes on, with endless rules and descriptions, enough for a PhD dissertation or a book by itself. There is even something called 'relationship anarchy', which is the perfect term for what appears to me as one hot mess.

Grandma Rituparna Chatterjee, ruined by years of meditation and healing and Advaita Vedanta, believes she is nothing. And nothing, being nothing, has no void needing to be filled, and I will never understand the need for experimentation, curiosity or anyone to fulfil anything in me. All of India seemed to be pure relationship anarchy to me.

'I wish we were in olden times. I'd have made you my main queen,' says an older editor and reader. 'But still, will you be?' By this time, I am frankly fed up of stories of love, sex and relationships that seemed to pour out of nowhere and that I had not asked for. And my editors at *TOI* could not give me more space to fill. I was losing my empathy and felt that everyone had taken advantage of it to pour out their secrets to me. I felt like a top-quality shrink who had not been paid. I decided to just stay lost and meet as few people as possible. 'For what great joy?' I ask him. 'I am married, remember. And I am a mother. Where is your respect? And why would I want to be your queen? Please, for God's sake.' I confront him; some of the courage of the single women having altered me. I am not even offended but just fed up. Fed up of the broken souls of a country, home of my beloved Advaita and Vipassana, which now seems to be just as lost and becoming increasingly soulless in its materialistic pursuits as the West. It seems I am the only monogamous one, and hence an object of great fascination. However, all this unnecessary information, by this point, drives me to want to become a nun. Not just any nun. A nun in an order with a lifetime of silence. Only, I don't want to cover my hair like a Catholic nun or shave it off like Buddhist and Jain nuns. I guess I am still attached to my hair. The way I am attached to journalism. Like my love for my curls, I guess my calling too was worldly – to observe this world, to make sense of it as only a journalist and a writer can. Not be otherworldly, not even yearn for something more ephemeral in nature. I think of the Buddhist nun and another Catholic nun I knew and had met during a hard time in my marriage (I tend to suffer from total disillusionment with the world every seven years and be cured as the eighth sets in). They had actually both been polyamorous and polysexual, with multiple romantic and sexual partners. Both had encouraged me to first be more 'worldly', as they had been, so I had no regrets later. But I already had regrets. Looking at the world, I only saw regrets, unless I created a bubble and lived in my own inner world.

'But you are the most beautiful woman I have seen. And I don't faze you. You put me in my place. I want to be your slave forever. Be my queen,' this older editor and reader said, bringing me back to where I was. 'I thought we were here to discuss work.' What was wrong with work meetings? 'Why not both?' The audacity got on my nerves. The single women would say I should be grateful I wasn't being assaulted. The married women would say I should be flattered. I only long for my giant red umbrella in Kolkata to whack him on the head with. Instead, I fling a glass of water on him and walk off. 'So fucking hot!' he grins. His behaviour is absolutely unacceptable. I should be laughing at all this, but this disrespect, a reflection of disrespect of the self, another case of a spoiled Indian man, is just too much. Had I been naive, as I was in my twenties, this might have easily prolonged, turning into a potential assault situation.

I block his number, then delete it and remove him from all my social media. Ah! The block button is my beloved. My source of power. That is what the block button is for me. To feel like god in a world where we otherwise are helpless, powerless, in control of nothing, least of all our lives.

My mind returns to Kolkata, where a married couple had looked at me with puppy eyes, '*Rituparna aamra dujone i tomake khub bhalobaashi* (both of us are madly in love with you).' I had actually found it hilarious at the time, and it had actually piqued my curiosity to study this species, as an anthropologist or a psychologist might, and I finally combined both and did study them, as a journalist. For these were traditional people, and they weren't making sexual advances towards me. All of the polyamorous proposals I received from this type were actually heartfelt invitations to be in their lives forever, as the main person they surrendered their lives to. In my research, when I checked on this with some younger Gen Z polysexual girls and boys, they actually felt slightly jealous. And that's it. The truth is, we are all looking for that thing beneath the veneer: to be loved forever, even if in a polyamorous relationship.

An *Indian Express* article on Valentine's Day quoted a Bumble survey conducted in 2022, which stated that 61 per cent of Indians surveyed were open to exploring ethical non-monogamy.[2] One assumes that Bumble folk are unmarried, unpartnered and hence looking. But there was no true way to know if their statuses online were the truth. In fact, an NBC article from 2023 quoted a study citing that two-thirds of the 1,400 Tinder users it studied were partnered and some even married.[3] Still, I'd like to give it the benefit of the doubt, because it is Bumble and not, let's say, Ashley Madison or Gleeden (meant for extramarital affairs, as we found in chapter two), and assume that they were indeed single. What about the ones who were officially married? Where were the studies of those nincompoops, stories that refused to stop unfolding around me?

My phone was flooded with polyamorous texts from anywhere and everywhere, like random gunfire in a warzone. Or like the Nerf bullets that my son and his friends kept shooting at all of us. I wish I could play dead, like I did then.

'Can we be great friends?' the Hindutva-following, Ram Rajya-seeking broker texted. 'Ram Bhaiya,' I said, blocked him and hired another broker.

'I really, really, really like you. In fact, I am old-fashioned, so I will say I love you. Honest confession, Rituparna,' said a senior person who had interviewed me on television.

'I thought we could have lunch' – the landlord's response to a perfectly official email.

'How are you not gay? You are too beautiful in and out to like men. Come out,' said a major LGBTQA community member. 'I don't like anyone but myself,' I replied and blocked the person.

'But you have to stay with us. And sleep in our bed. We will take care of you,' said another married Bengali couple making puppy eyes, when I was looking for an Airbnb to stay in.

'Didi, at least two boyfriends you need. You are too pretty,' said my polyamorous maid, knocking on my closed bedroom door to give me unsolicited information. I had to eventually let go of her services.

'Let's go to Goa,' said another person who identified as bisexual. 'Why? I have so much paperwork. I have no time,' I said innocently.

'At least we are on a date. You are the sexiest woman I have seen. And your mind blows me away. Your fearlessness . . .' said another senior person. 'I thought this was a work meeting and not a date. I am fearless enough to walk away,' I said and did too, too lazy, too worn out to remember to throw a glass of water at the person.

'Rituparna, you have to marry me,' said an order from a major business tycoon I used to once interview regularly and had decided to catch up with. 'But I am married and so are you.' I felt the need to remind the billionaire nincompoop of basic facts. Kindergarteners were so much easier to deal with. 'Doesn't matter!'

'Do you know, I cry about you?' said another reader. 'I imagine you're cooking in my kitchen and then see you aren't there.' And I'll never be there. Block! I had often been called Bubbles, the powerpuff girls cartoon, and I guess I had finally found my superpower in this button.

Did I mention that every single one of these and the others not mentioned were all married or in serious relationships? I did have an extramarital, polyamorous relationship with the block button and my Kolkata umbrella. Both kept me safe, were protector and provider, monogamous, predictable, traditional, dedicated to me and only me and always available at all odd hours, 24x7 – everything that I found attractive in a man. I began greeting the block button as 'Hello lover,' and blocked everyone, went off social media and gave my phone to my son.

Frankly, it was getting very stressful. 'Marriage is an agreement. You can be in love with multiple people,' said a sex therapist, who is married and polyamorous. Last I checked, it was five partners, but the number keeps changing and the consequent polyamory sub-label associated with it. She spoke with all of them, met them once a fortnight and is the primary partner for most of them. Hers is an evolved version of polyamory, like we see in the West. The rules are clearly defined. It's the opposite of cheating, hence the term ethical non-monogamy. Like the voice whispers in the dreams of the young in Aldous Huxley's *Brave New World*, 'Everyone belongs to everyone else.' Discouraging exclusivity in friendship and in love. If everyone belongs to everyone, in a sense, in this world, everyone is everyone as well. India seemed to be Bharat on one side and Huxley's futuristic world, in terms of love, sex and relationships, on the other. Polyamory in this new India of mine was enabling lives, ensuring the stability of everyone involved. However, at the very same time, this unique style of polyamory was showing everyone was perfectly disposable, perfectly replaceable and immediately so with someone else. Exactly as in Huxley's dystopian novel, the very message (the very, very alarming message) of which, was exactly this: that stability should not come at the cost of our humanity. Connecting this, watching Huxley's World State play out was horrifying to me. Sadly, it seems like this only to me. This type of polyamory (or all types of polyamory) is the total opposite of what relationships are about: where you're special, chosen, safe enough to never be replaced. What else is the point anyway? It takes courage to make that decision in a world of plenty. Like your dog is just your dog. Your kid is just your kid. Your love is just your love. It's a matter of choice. It is what makes us human.

But only my healed, boring grandma self seemed to think so.

For everyone else, polyamorous relationships meant freedom. I'd like to reiterate that they are not about cheating or two-timing, for they are open. In fact, communication that is open, constant and evolving is the fulcrum of polyamory – to explain roles and know where one stands. Polyamory is also not polygamy, which has been tied to religion and marriage. Hence people feel an immense sense of freedom and even a sense of righteousness (for their honesty and not going behind anyone's back and cheating) in polyamory. And their needs get met. All people in polyamorous relationships, like in the harems of kings in ancient times, have needs, not just sexual – they could be childcare, financial needs, help with taxes, paperwork, school admissions, clout, affluence, calls to be made to people who know people, networking and connections, errands, plumbing, career, mentoring . . . the forms of help and partnership are numerous, and value is recognised. It is different from casual sex, which is a dime a dozen in this new India. For example, young women could have polyamorous relationships with sugar daddies. Meena, an actress in Bombay, had a married sugar daddy who paid for her expensive rent while letting her focus on her career. He openly told her that he saw other women too. He also offered her respite from her daily grind with vacations at five-star hotels in Goa and Dubai. These relationships met emotional and psychological needs that weren't fulfilled in traditional marriages. And with the safe knowledge and comfort that even in these sexual partnerships, you could keep returning to this person or persons, which is different from casual sex, where you have to constantly put in the effort to go on dates, establish some connection, depending on the situation – like, say, meeting one's Tinder dates for drinks at bars again and again before deciding to hook up and have sex or not, all of which can become cumbersome with the drudgery of a second job.

Just how many marriages in India survived because they were secretly non-monogamous? These parallel sex lives, love lives, gave them joy, energy, allowing them to fulfil their responsibilities, including marital ones. Friendships with exes that went from platonic meetings at coffee tables to not so platonic meetings in the bedroom. Then again, meeting peers, co-workers, exes, etc. officially at work desks, airplane stowaway tables and then somehow back to beds in all kinds of places, including hotels. By now I could not look at any piece of furniture without recalling a love story. Furniture had lost its innocence for me forever. And for this I won't forgive the nincompoops, because I love furniture. So long, Crate & Barrel, West Elm, Restoration Hardware, Pottery Barn and, yes, even Ikea. Gone are my days of window shopping at furniture stores, hanging out admiring art and design as a form of relaxation. Forever. Thanks, nincompoops.

After battling blood cancer for years, when Paroma's husband had finally succumbed to the disease, their family friend, who was actually a friend of her late husband's, in a tender moment of consoling a bereaved and devastated Paroma, held her, kissed her and (it seems) almost immediately became her lover. He helped her handle the company her late husband had founded, the paperwork and the legalities, all tasks her husband should have taken care of decades ago. And continues to help her. But this man has also similarly helped another woman, a 'friend' and a lover in an openly non-monogamous marriage, with financial planning, fundraising and other legalities and complications. Polyamory has a way of trickling into lives, especially in cases of human vulnerability.

Somehow, I am having dinner with all of them at a buffet at a five-star hotel in central Kolkata, and though it is a perfectly pleasant evening, with everyone exchanging fond glances, I can't help wonder in amusement I reserved for myself (not out of courtesy but to avoid conversation on the subject), how in the world my life had come to this. Both of this man's women (and there are others not present at this table, whom he tells me about) feel insecure because he is the primary, not they. And this is the problem few people discuss about polyamory. It's okay for the primary. But polyamory is not for the faint of heart. Are you healed enough to handle it? After all, we are not yet a generation indoctrinated, like in Huxley's world, where everyone is everyone else's and so 'everyone belongs to everyone else'. We're still influenced and affected by, at least in our collective subconscious, as taught by centuries of civilisation and what we see around us, the idea of monogamous relationships. Couples not throuples (romantic relationship involving three partners) or polyamorous packs. In other words, where someone is chosen unlike us. And this is bound to have an impact, since the non-primary partners can see they are not chosen, are not special enough to their love. Even back in the olden days, in the ancient times of polyamory and polygamy of kings and harems, the queens in the harem were constantly jealous of each other, feeling abandoned and insecure, competing with each other to prove their worth, to be the best. Even in households with more than one dog, dogs compete for their human parent's affection, sometimes in not so cute ways. That multiplies greatly for humans. It can be devastating for the non-primary partners if they are not healed enough to be totally secure. It can be just as heartbreaking as a rejection. The deepest form of rejection because the one we have loved and been our most vulnerable selves with has not chosen us and loved us in the way we want to be loved.

Patriarchy has always allowed kings and emperors, or those in positions of power in today's society, to get away with polyamory. It is only now, thanks to financial and emotional independence and women empowerment, that women are coming out too and embracing polyamory, often being the primary, like the sex therapist or like I was constantly being offered to be. There are even alpha women like Vandana, a PR executive who had a harem of younger men throwing themselves at her feet. She got them no-strings-attached, booked the hotels herself, helped them with connections and the occasional small but luxe present like a wallet or a watch or, most recently, a Louis Vuitton key holder, which she had gifted 'one of my boys for being a good boy'. I suppose the source of funds don't matter because some of these boys also offered themselves up to South Mumbai housewives for 'massage services'. It was so common and cookie-cutter, it was as if everyone came from the same factory. The 'boys', sometimes, but not always, struggling models and actors, did not see this as prostitution but as proper relationships with sugar mommies and an expression of sexual freedom. 'I mean, I am poly. I date too, you know. And I take women out too, wining and dining them. I'm just poly,' says Ram, who would just like to be referred to 'as someone in the entertainment industry'. Back in Kolkata, a junior telecom executive serviced many such wealthy housewives, mostly sexually. They gave him expensive whiskies and watches. He, in turn, was sympathetic to their emotional vacuum, their loneliness and offered a gentle, patient listening ear. 'You know how things happen, so yes, one thing leads to another and without meaning to affairs or situations happen,' he says, referring to his relationship with a housewife in an unhappy marriage and utterly worn out as the mother of a severely autistic child. '(Apparently) our relationship is the only source of joy for her,' he says. Both of them recently shared an aged Scotch that his other, financially superior lover had gifted him. So money was trickling down like champagne from a tower of champagne glasses, and somehow each glass was getting filled. The business journalist in me desperately, desperately, desperately wanted to study these financial transactions and this strange flourishing economy polyamory was funding and enabling, irrespective of global economic fluctuations. It took all of me not to pursue that journalistic itch and finish the task at hand. One day, I will. Perhaps it will be my next book.

An older married woman in Delhi's media and publishing circles provided a man with tremendous emotional support and helped him improve the quality of his work until he finally became extremely successful in his career.

Likewise, many older, happily married men have 'helped' younger women enormously in their careers. In the same circles, a woman, Seema, is the primary, with her men helping her out with everything, from booking tickets and stays (even for her solo travels) to getting her an Aadhaar card and handling her finances, taxes, legal paperwork; helping her with feedback and editing her manuscripts, networking and introducing her to others who will help her in her career, and so on.

She is the primary, and a few of her male lovers, who are exclusively monogamous with her, have felt abandoned, hurt and insecure. So it's a myth that polyamory is the bastion of the provider-male primary figure only. No, here the primary female, who reciprocates no financial or emotional support, is making her male providers feel insecure.

Our basic human need is to belong, to be loved, to be supported, to not have to compete constantly to prove our worth and to be chosen for who we are.

What does this say about our society? Are we so broken that we have no boundaries? Had lockdown and

COVID-19 changed India so much that this post-pandemic India had become soulless? Here I thought we were to become Ram Rajya, but to me, India seemed increasingly like Lanka. Lanka with no Ravana at its helm to at least govern it into order. Everything was so casual that it is no wonder that the people, many of whom I had known and worked with and who knew of my work, felt it was completely normal to even talk to me the way they did. And it was grandma Rituparna whose reactions were absurd and abnormal.

Well, so be it. I hate to say it but it was seeming more and more that yours truly was perhaps the only voice of reason left. Nincompoop grandma feels that polyamory is not only dangerous for mental and emotional health but completely unnecessary, since most of these needs, like emotional support when grieving, help with legalities and taxes, etc., that were leading people into polyamorous situations can be met through platonic friendships, healthy family relationships, communities, therapists, journaling, meditation, all kinds of therapies for mental and emotional health and frankly even agents, financial executives, lawyers and also apps and technology (since we use them more than we fall back on people in California)!

Is all of this emotional hell and toll on the mental health of the non-primary partners in polyamorous relationships necessary? Polyamory, more than even regular relationships, thrives completely on communication of expectations. How would one feel if their partner begins dating other people outside of their agreement and begins cancelling their time together for affection, sex, etc., to choose someone else over them? That's what Seema did, causing much heartbreak and mental anguish. Yes, in spite of honest, open and consistent communication of expectations. Because we are humans and not machines that can follow rules and code. Not yet.

Polyamory is not for everyone. It works depending on your maturity levels. How much healing and therapy you have done, how secure you truly are within yourself. How deep your abandonment wounds run. You have to be brutally honest with yourself and ask yourself what your insecurities reveal about you. Yes, you have to be a therapy junkie. You might go insane otherwise. In one case, a sugar daddy conveniently left the country for a couple of years, and the twenty-one-year-old girlfriend left behind with her highly abusive boyfriend committed suicide. Something the sugar daddy is devastated about but being, well, another one of India's lost little boys in his sixties, doesn't see any responsibility on his part for.

The open marriages and swinger couples I met in Bengaluru and California, for this reason, keep returning to each other. That's the comfort and safe space they have made for themselves. That is also why marriage counsellors in California may, in radical situations, advise opening up of a marriage/relationship. Often, after some years, the couple settles into monogamy, for it is familiar and safe, like a toddler's safety blankie, like home, which is the only point of relationships.

A fellow writer friend in California was in a polyamorous relationship for many years. She was not a primary. The constant comparison between her and others, the sense of abandonment and her insecurities led her to a break down. Yes, in spite of her acute self-awareness and weekly therapy. She developed an eating disorder and severe anxiety, depression and panic attacks, which completely debilitated her well-being. She is well aware that all the trauma in the relationship comprised her own insecurities being projected outwards.

But that's the thing. Relationships are reflections of our own unmet childhood needs, and while we continue to do the inner work, either by ourselves or via good therapeutic practices, relationships should still be a place to come home to and rest in.

Coming from a highly liberal Jewish background, my friend chose to marry a third-generation Indian-Canadian, who is relatively conservative and knows everything about her. She now feels fully supported and accepted, and the constant pressure of competition has lifted and the constant questioning of self-worth has stopped. After all, whatever its nature, monogamous or non-monogamous, isn't the entire point of any partnership, especially marriage, to feel loved, to feel special, to feel chosen?

She says monogamy is the most healing thing to have happened to her, because she can finally rest and be accepted, with all of her insecurities. It is extremely important to mention this because polyamory is not a fetish or a trend but a lifestyle calling for serious commitment. It can be so toxic and dangerous that it can lead to suicide, something most Indians don't realise.

Whether she is in bed or going through a panic attack or healthy and working, she feels chosen unconditionally every day. I am yet to see a polyamorous relationship offer that to every single partner involved.

12

Pop Therapy Jargon and Love

ONE OF THE FONDEST memories that the family I had married into loves to recollect is of my husband when he was little. He'd make a face, crinkling his eyebrows into the most painful frown for what seemed like ages, and bawl loudly, crying with a power that only toddlers can, enough to bring the heavens down. It wasn't just that he was this adorable, chubby toddler with rosy cheeks, the epitome of cuteness. He would also often be wearing, during this dramatic act, as if a costume for a performance, a brown sweater knitted lovingly by his *nani*, a sweater that said in big, bold, white capital letters 'LOVE ME', with hearts under it. While this is an adorable memory, it is truly the story of every human. Each of us is that kid throwing tantrums and fits, and even in the so-called happiest and most normal of upbringing, we are craving unconditional love, acceptance and celebration of every aspect of ours all the time – something, to be perfectly honest, is not possible 24X7. Thanks to pop culture psychology, more and more people are realising how all of us are kids in adult bodies.

An articled in *The Times of India*, dated 30 April 2023, titled 'Indian Psychiatry Society Demands Revision of Mental Healthcare Act' related the demands of the Indian Psychiatry Society seeking a revision of the Mental Healthcare Act (MHCA) so that the seeking of therapy for mental health could be free of stigma for both patients and therapists.[1] It is not breaking news to anybody that it is the stigma of shame, judgement from loved ones, peers, society, all of which become voices in our own heads, that is stopping most Indians from seeking therapy. Non-stigmatisation of mental health, revision of the Mental Healthcare Act and more resources are needed for better mental health of our country.

Way back in 2018, another article in *The Times of India* described how approximately 150 million people in India need therapists for mental health and yet less than 30 million seek help.[2] According to the National Mental Health Survey of India, 2015–16, the treatment gap for mental disorders ranges between 70 per cent and 92 per cent, which is tragically enormous.

Though the subject is not covered much, what the statistics and studies have failed to show is that Gen Z, more than all the previous generations, is intensely aware of mental health, of relationship patterns and has sought the refuge of the Internet, where in spite of cyberbullying and trolling, there are many online safe spaces and online forums where there is no shame, no stigma and, in closed groups, even total privacy. It is not even about seeking online services or mixed therapies, like from life coaches who offer career and spiritual guidance and healing along with pop psychology practices. Quora pages will tell you more about the mental health of the country and the acute awareness of it among Indians today than all of the formal studies and the media of the country combined. There are innumerable groups, chat rooms, closed Facebook groups and comments on all kinds of threads on social media, where stories of deep loneliness, depression, anxiety and panic attacks, mental health issues, suicidal tendencies, and so on come out, perhaps under the guise of a news event that may have caught attention. But the most important thing here is that despite their flaws, social media and the Internet can also allow room for people's feelings to be validated in ways people in their real lives may not be able to validate.

A 2021 UNICEF survey said that over 14 per cent of young Indians aged between fifteen and twenty-four reported feeling frequently depressed or disinterested (a classic symptom of clinical depression) in life.[3] The World Health Organization (WHO) has said that over 56 million Indians were affected by depression of one sort or another. And 38 million deal with anxiety. With the prevalent urban alienation, these are numbers rapidly on the rise.

Though the mental health industry is bound to grow, not all Indians trust their therapists.[4] The whole point of having a therapist is to have a blank, non-judgemental sounding board who will at the most basic level hear you out objectively. But many, especially youngsters, especially those from the LGBTQA community, or actually anyone whose life choices may not match those of their parents, are often told, 'Beta please get better.' Therapists echo the parents who have paid for the therapy. When they do this, they are not being therapists but the opposite and propagating further pain. Much of young India, battling judgement nonstop from a society that won't let them be free, understands this. Having a therapist is like being in a marriage. Just having one is not enough. In fact, if the therapist is not good, it's best not to have one at all. I myself have never had a therapist, having seen everyone around me go crazy with appointments. Also I did not need their validation. A lifetime of journaling and going through cognitive processes like Byron Katie's The Work, Vipassana, Advaita Vedanta philosophy and the related neti neti (not this, not that) meditations, that help me detach from identity, as well as my use of classical psychology practices like shadow work, inner-child work, voice dialogue, alteration of the final memory, and so on . . . all had rendered the idea of going to a psychiatrist useless, also sparing me the cumbersome process of having to explain myself to someone. Many youngsters are getting this and resorting to social media, self-help books and YouTube for solace or to coming together in communities.

To know that daily depression, anxiety and mental health issues plague not just you but each and every one of us on some level is therapeutic in itself. It connects us. It makes you realise you are not alone, which can bring a sigh of relief and sometimes even a smile of relief. You're not 'a nutcase', 'spastic', 'cuckoo', '*screw dheela*' (have loose mental screws and are hence crazy): terms the judgemental society of the past had normalised in India.

In fact, my book *The Water Phoenix* has garnered quite a bit of attention on Instagram. And I am not even on Instagram. And yet Instagrammers would find me on Twitter, Facebook, at book events and show me the threads they had posted. They'd single out the exact self-love processes I have mentioned in *The Water Phoenix* and how it has helped them heal from breakups, loneliness, sexual abuse, IPV, and so on.

'I thought it was love, but I didn't know it was rape. I was fifteen. And gay. In India. How could I have known otherwise?' wrote Sudesh, who met me later in Bengaluru with his current lover. Both agreed that they were in a 'trauma bond' now, but their 'awareness' made their relationship authentic. It helped them hold their 'pain bodies' when the 'triggers' came up and hug each other through that phase, making their love stronger than ever before. Sudesh had had a family uncle, clearly a closeted gay, married and with kids, who was able to find the same 'symptoms' (signs of being gay, without quite explaining what they were) in Sudesh as he had found in himself. He helped Sudesh, then thirteen and growing up in a conservative Gujarati family, understand what was happening to him and why he was attracted to men. The need to be seen is what makes us human. It is what binds us. What else is connection? And when you are that young, still lost and still pristine, a virgin in every sense of the word, your purity, your vulnerability, your essence makes you extremely attractive (think Nabokov's Lolita as an archetype). Alas, attractive even more so to predators. In all of that tenderness, being so lost, isolated and confused, Sudesh found the sympathising uncle slowly go from stroking his back platonically to one day caressing his face, stroking his chin and cheeks, which were bursting with the boils, pimples and hairs of puberty, kissing his lips tenderly, taking him by surprise. Until, when Sudesh was fifteen, he took Sudesh's virginity. Sudesh thought he had given it willingly. But had he?

Sudhesh and his lover Hitesh had come to get their books signed at Ranga Shankara in Bengaluru, where the historic theatre and a bookstore had organised an event. Later, they stuck around to share with me their identical stories, which could have become a play right there in that theatre. They told me about the prey-and-predator analogy, which ran throughout *The Water Phoenix*, and how it had helped them understand their own 'patterns' of being prey and later, of growing up to be predators. 'It is very normal for abused children to become abusers, bullied kids to become bullies, as a "shadow side",' said Hitesh. Both had grown up to repeat this exact pattern while simultaneously sleeping around with others; 'Furthering our education through casual sex or debauchery as you might say,' he said with a smile. But what did it cost the youngsters who had entrusted their lives to them without knowing what they were in for?

You see, whether you're from the LGBTQA community or heterosexual doesn't matter. The patterns are the same. For we are the same. We are all humans.

It was only when Hitesh received 'a scary text' did he wake up and realise that he had hurt someone exactly the way his own child self had been hurt, ditto, carbon copy. It was the worst awakening. 'I was the demon I was trying to flee.' What was even more uncanny was that 'Sudesh and I had the exact "patterns and story" . . . I mean how! Your book gave us answers and we had honest conversations'. Both went back to the youngsters they had been sexually and romantically involved with and held them through the whole situation, guiding them into relationships with peers more their age and remained always just a text or a phone call away so the kids did not feel 'abandoned', 'abused', 'raped' or 'isolated'. 'We are there,' they have said.

It was like someone was quoting me to myself, and I was very touched that my work had not only touched readers so deeply but had transformed their lives by enabling them to understand themselves. What greater success could any writer, any human, ask for? Both the shadow side and archetypes that Hitesh and Sudesh used were direct references to the famous psychoanalyst Carl Jung's shadow work, and their constant usage of terms from psychiatry revealed just how 'woke' or self-aware their generation was. Diagnosis is the first step, and I am living proof that you may not need a professional with a degree from a university to heal you. Perhaps it is more healing to see and hear and learn from those who have actually lived through situations such as yours and found their way out. That is what had worked for me and what the last parts of *The Water Phoenix* are about. And that is the kind of reader I seemed to be meeting everywhere. Both Sudesh and Hitesh had parented their own inner-child wounds by taking care of 'these kids' for life, as they wished someone had done for them when they were children. It was a beautiful story of healing as a collective. To me, it was nothing short of alchemy, a fairy tale with a happy ending (no pun intended).

At the Mumbai launch event for the book at a premium club, on an evening so devastatingly rainy that all of us were certain the city would drown (again!), Rani, a twenty-one-year-old actress, shared her story. It was similar to the stories of the young men from Bengaluru. She had mistaken rape for love by falling for a film director she thought of as a mentor, allowing him to bed her because she looked up to his craft and to him as if he were a hero. But she read his texts and soon saw that he was no hero. Far from it. 'The creep was also fucking others, saying, "They are real women, not like you!" Daddy issues! It's always daddy issues, isn't it!' Rani's father was an alcoholic who was either absent or passed out, both of which resulted in the same core human wound for Rani: abandonment. 'I thought I had healed. But no, I had to "attract" this "narcissist pig"!' (I wanted to interrupt her asking her to please not insult pigs, which are cute and intelligent. In fact, I hated it when people used dogs, pigs and other innocent animals as metaphors, thereby defiling them. But, of course, my empathy and manners won, and I stayed quiet, being a safe space for yet another wounded child in an adult body.) 'When will I stop looking for Daddy!' she exclaimed in soft defeat, more to herself than to me. 'I just want to be free.'

I had to pinch myself. This was not California where therapy jargon was normal talk in yoga circles and on the street. No, this was a country growing out of intense judgement passed down via generations and society, with societal judgements pervading every level of life, enough for people to take their own lives: students made to feel they weren't good enough; spouses, sons and daughters driven to a deeply closeted spectrum of mental health disorders, going beyond regular depression and anxiety. It gave me immense hope for humanity, for India. For if we had awareness, our entire country would be different. Imagine if our political leaders, who are just terribly behaved toddlers with extreme power and nuclear weapons, had this awareness, and from that understanding took care of the country. Where would our nation be? The sooner we understand that we are all kids crying in various versions of the 'LOVE ME' sweater, the better every aspect of our lives, our society, our systems and, yes, our governance will be. Full of empathy, compassion and calm.

Tia is involved with a married man. It is very unlike her. She did not set out to. It opposes every value she has ever had. The guilt that she may be a homewrecker plagues her constantly. Because, of course, society only judges the woman as the other woman, as the homewrecker, as if the man is as innocent as a babe in the woods; if at all anything, he is a hero for not shirking his duties as a husband and father, while still being responsible for the 'other' woman, who may be emotionally unstable, a drama queen, and so on. And so of course we internalise and see ourselves the way society has subliminally taught us to. Beneath the facade of living a perfect life as an advertising professional in Bombay, Tia leads a painful existence – she insists that it cannot be called a life. Unlike some other young women I know, who want the married men they love to leave their marriage and settle down with them – if not in a marriage, then at least in a partnership, something solid and stable, something to introduce to the world – my friend will never ask him to leave his marriage. Tia cannot do this to him, but more than anything else, she cannot do this to another woman. She, who knows what it's like to be so isolated and othered, cannot wish that upon anyone. He is not her 'sugar daddy' providing for her financially; he is a workaholic and the little time he does have goes mostly towards the ones he says he 'is responsible for keeping happy'. He keeps saying this, insisting he is doing his duty and that it is not his joy.

Tia has inspired a character in a novel I am writing – the other woman protects a wife, a woman who isn't even aware of her existence and yet owes her entire life to her. In the novel there is closure, which Tia has been unable to find in life.

Late at nights, separately in their individual, separate homes, they share a drink together (like how people had begun to on Zoom during the COVID lockdown). Every time Tia brings up the subject of her feeling unwanted, unloved, he insists that this is him at his most intimate, away from his 'duties', both at the office and his home, and he is giving his all to her daily. They text throughout the day, and occasionally call each other. Again, he insists how hectic lives are today and how most couples stay in touch virtually. How could he not love her? How was this not a relationship? Why did they need labels or to show the world their love? She repeats these rhetorical questions to me, insisting that I say yes so she too can say a full yes to herself. But my heart breaks for her, and my eyes fill up with tears. So do hers. Tia knows this is gaslighting – a classic form of emotional abuse and manipulation. 'It doesn't matter if he is doing it on purpose. I know he isn't, but it is what it is. And it is my pattern, that I am here, stuck, out of choice. Why am I drawn to this situation, the romance of this impossible, great love?' says Tia.

We both know the answer. It is as obvious as the sky above. She needs to leave. She should have left yesterday, last week, last month, last year. She makes her own money, sees a therapist and has a solid circle of girlfriends. She is an attractive woman with her own life and pursuits. In every way she is an empowered woman, far freer than the wife who, in this case, is dependent on a man for financial support and for a roof over her head, not to mention the societal approval, respect and safety the tag of marriage brings. They share children, homes, parents, friends – an entire life together. Many of the reasons why victims of violent relationships cannot leave are simply not true for Tia.

And still she cannot leave this toxic relationship, which constantly has her questioning herself, her self-worth. Is she of any value whatsoever? Why isn't she chosen then? Why isn't she prioritised? Why can't he spend his birthday with her? Why make up so many lies for when they must meet? What can she do to make him do anything? What can she do to have him show up for her when she is sad, so she doesn't have to call her girlfriends or resort to the journals I have gifted her (because writing out thoughts and emotions has saved my own life time and again), or god forbid, during an actual emergency?

As a society, we are just beginning to understand what emotional abuse is and just how deep it runs and just how rampant it is, not tangible like physical violence but like domestic violence focused on psychological control, emotional (and sometimes also social and financial) isolation, psychological and emotional manipulation, ridicule, making the victim feel helpless, completely derailing the person psychologically, mentally and emotionally so that they start questioning everything about themselves. We now have labels like gaslighting (yes again; it can't be mentioned enough), triangulation, silent treatment and love bombing. Emotional abuse can be extremely subtle, which is why it takes years to even recognise it because our societies are toxic, and so it is everywhere and has become normalised. The victims are invalidated or called 'too sensitive', causing them to go further into their shells. Studies and statistics on this phenomenon are negligible compared with studies on physical violence. But small studies are being done in the developed countries, which is a start. The US National Intimate Partner and Sexual Violence Survey (NISVS) found that half of the Americans reported experiencing lifetime emotional abuse by a partner.[5] The most common facet of IPV was neither sexual violence nor physical violence but emotional abuse. The Australian Bureau of Statistics estimates that one in four women (23 per cent or 2.2 million) and one in six men have experienced emotional abuse by their partner since the age of fifteen, including 6.1 per cent (575,400) by a current partner and 18 per cent (1.7 million) by a previous partner.

I especially wanted to bring up my friend's situation. She has a loving network of people who understand psychology and mental health, who validate and support her. This is extremely rare for someone to have. Even with all this support, why can't my friend leave the relationship?

All of our intimate relationships are extensions of childhood needs that were not met. Even in the healthiest of families, the child who had plenty of love, comfort, praise, safety and validation may have had an absent parent who was away for work, leading the child to satisfy whatever the definition of good child in that family and culture was, in order to please the parent when he or she was present in the hopes that the parent would not leave. Our subconscious mind does not know the difference between what's real and what's imagined or unreal. (This is why movies and video games, and now virtual reality games and entertainment, are so powerful.) Our subconscious mind naturally seeks comfort and safety (from our primal instinct since our caveman days), which is often the familiar rehashed in new manifestations over and over again – this could be violence or the gentler abandonment. For Tia's mind, for example, adult Tia's married boyfriend bringing her presents every time she tries to 'create a scene' and leave is the same as her father returning from business trips bringing gifts for young Tia. Neuroscience shows that our neural patterns are more or less set by age eight. So unless we change them consciously, we will recreate similar situations and patterns in all of our relationships (romantic or not) and circumstances.

I tried to help Tia not just as an empathetic sounding board but with solid solutions from the later chapters of *The Water Phoenix: A Memoir of Child Abuse, Healing and Forgiveness*, which delves into these childhood patterns in detail and offers carefully curated solutions, collected over two decades, which actually work.

She says this time she is finally walking out. We are in a bookstore-cafe in South Mumbai. In the absence of a white board, we buy a journal with sheets of white paper and tape them together to write a business plan for her breakup.

This will be stuck to her bedroom wall. She writes out her reasons for breaking up, we list down the phone numbers of her closest friends and therapist to call, we make a schedule of things to look forward to, to keep her occupied and some affirmations to say that it was okay and normal for her to miss him and that this was an act of self-love. We agree on the email and messages she will send him in case he is unable to meet at a cafe where she feels safe to tell him in person, and where a friend will be next door just in case (if a scene erupts, either of sorrow or verbal violence). She had every resource imaginable. I left her, thinking I couldn't think of a luckier person, letting the others take over.

Some days later, I received Tia's text. Plagued by a migraine and nightmares, she had been unable to sleep, her anxiety on the brink of turning into a full-blown panic attack. She forwarded this text from her married boyfriend.

'Baby, holding you. Ssssh.'

'I'm there.'

And then added her own, 'I'm sorry, I couldn't.'

'Stop! Don't send me any more,' I texted back and turned my phone off.

After everything, Tia still could not leave the toxic relationship. The important part was that she was completely aware of her patterns. The first step India is at. It takes a lot of courage to look at your own childhood patterns, to forgive your parents, your upbringing. And then to forgive yourself for still choosing to stay in these patterns; for blame whoever you want to as much as you can, you're still here for whatever reasons. The last step that Hitesh and Sudesh had taken to break their patterns is the next level in this game, when the degree of courage required to change yourself is far, far greater. An eternal optimist, I see this as the way going ahead for modern India. Because, really, what other alternative exists?

Therapy jargon becoming commonplace in relationships is not restricted to Gen Z or millennials. In this new India, it is across generations.

'My wife calls me "narcissistic". I have trouble spelling it,' a reader tells me. 'She repeats it all day long. It's a mystery word for me. What does it even mean? It sounds very happening.' I send him a Mayo Clinic page on narcissistic personality disorder (NPD) and tell him it means he is like their pet cats. Cats are the ultimate narcissists and completely full of themselves. Likewise, narcissists think of nobody but themselves. They can't handle a rejection, and to them everything is personal and the other person's fault. 'That's really cool. I'll say thank you to her then.' My reader Sunil is sixty-nine years old, and thanks to his daughter, who is in her late twenties, he is very well-versed in the latest relationship jargon and buzzwords. He is extremely kind and empathetic, the main caregiver and only breadwinner in their family, and has abandoned his own dreams to take care of his family responsibilities. In other words, he is anything but narcissistic. He does shut down because of the endless accusations coming his way, as anyone might. Over-analysis of this situation might lead to one saying that he is being a narcissist, that he is suffering from NPD. These days, everyone is calling everyone a narcissist. In this case, ironically, this diagnosis is narcissistic in its nature, because it gives the wife a sense of superiority.

It was also the story of a new India where senior citizens are not just catching up on therapy jargon but also on the flip side, misusing it. Using information not to heal but to further abuse – by playing victim, using it for validation, using it in whatever form that made them feel right, safe, seen. The irony! And this is why this mighty country continued to baffle me. For not only was it catching up with the West, it had gone beyond it. Once helpful, therapy jargon was now simultaneously taking the love out of relationships, sometimes killing them altogether, turning love into psychoanalysis, blaming and shaming – all masks for total pettiness.

Misuse of therapy jargon, as in Sunil's marriage, is one of the many problems with relationships today. Labels like gaslighting, triangulation, types of personalities based on tests like Myers test, enneagram, etc., types of attachments like anxious, avoidant, etc. – the list is infinite. They are like brand labels, for example, Chanel, Gucci, Prada, Louis Vuitton, Dior, each encompassing an entire universe in itself. Of course, these therapy jargon labels are initially helpful, encompassing entire worlds and lives until now unexpressed and often not even comprehended. They help us know and understand ourselves and our loved ones deeply, in ways we never did before. But that doesn't mean that these therapy jargon labels have to become our entire love lives.

Words like stonewalling, ghosting, and its cousin breadcrumbing, are used regularly. Or toxic relationships, which are a far cry from IPV and are apparently calm, loving and nourishing.

Across generations, people now use words like 'red flag', 'boundaries', 'dom and sub' (as ways of being and not just in the bedroom or BDSM dungeon) in the same sentence that talks about their situationships. '. . . basically, B is a dom. He has no boundaries. But I am also a dom. So how can I be a sub. I really like him. But how can I be his slave? Bitch please,' says a reader, a member of the LGBTQA community, to me in a cafe in Church Street in downtown Bengaluru. 'So many red flags. How can we make this work? Gosh!'

A reader of mine in his seventies sends me a meme: An alien driving a penguin in his UFO asks, 'Should I drop you off at the Arctic or the Antarctic?' The penguin responds, 'Either one . . . I'm bipolar.' Another reader, Reema, who is a single mother, sends me a meme about two girlfriends talking: 'Did you not see the red flags?' The friend replies,

'I thought it was a carnival.' We both laugh about how a meme had summarised her love stories and patterns (and those of hundreds of thousands like her). I respond with a trio of emojis laughing with tears and an 'OMG.' 'No more carnivals,' she texts back. 'Only red-carpet treatment.' The kind of memes that people resonate with and share could arguably constitute the greatest anthropological study of the country. Not a day went by when a relationship meme didn't reach me, reclusive me, who is not on any WhatsApp groups and barely on her phone. Imagine if I were! Another older reader, a widow, sent me a meme showing two girls chatting: One says, '*Dekh* (look, there goes), tall, handsome, emotionally unavailable guy.' The other friend says, '*Haan, bilkul* (yes, totally) boyfriend material.' The jokes were on ourselves – for falling for emotionally unavailable men due to 'our patterns'. The levels of awareness among people may vary, but those who shared these memes seemed well aware of their patterns.

Therapy jargon was rapidly becoming the new normal in India. And it wasn't even about romance. For all our lives are relationships, and Instagram, pop culture, pop psychology and spirituality, etc., had brought this jargon into the Indian psyche. Therapy jargon had snuck into familial relationships. Sreyoshi, a professor in Kolkata, had politely asked a relative who insisted on cooking her meals to instead focus on the real issue. Half a decade ago, Sreyoshi had signed over an ancestral house, which was her inheritance, as collateral for an urgent loan that the relative had then needed. Instead, the relative said she was very fond of Sreyoshi and loved cooking her meals, because her love language and way of showing gratitude was to invite loved ones over for home-cooked dinners. Fed up, Sreyoshi had assertively said that she would instead like her to finish the paperwork and return the house to her. The relative had immediately flared up saying, as Sreyoshi quoted, 'Sreyoshi, you have absolutely no boundaries! And you know why? It's because you had no fucking boundaries since childhood. And you know why? Because, you, poor you, are a classic case of enmeshment trauma.' Even if Sreyoshi was not a professor of psychology, but a professor of political science, she, like the new crop of urban Indians, was well-versed in such heavy, complicated terms that were now being flung at her like weapons. (Sreyoshi said the irony was that her knowledge of enmeshment trauma came from the columns I had written on the subject for the Indian audience,[6] enabling her to understand what was going on.)

Enmeshment trauma is an extremely complicated but, sadly, rather prevalent type of childhood emotional trauma where there is a complete disregard for personal boundaries. The term describes the condition of people who as children were not shielded by the adults around them but instead had become adults while they were still children and took care of the adults around them, even if only emotionally. Or had to step into adult roles – say, taking care of younger siblings. Enmeshed children's emotional needs were invalidated so much that it was as if they didn't exist, and they had no boundaries, because their survival depended on meeting the needs of grown-ups. That means these children grew into adults with no sense of identity or sense of self beyond the one enmeshed, often as a caretaker, over-giver, over-achiever, at the cost of their own selves. Think of stereotypes such as IIT-JEE toppers, UPSC toppers . . . all children who followed their parents' expectations and were good, studious, obedient kids who aced entrance exams, but not because studying was their joy (perhaps they didn't even know what their joy was and often don't until they grow up and have a midlife crisis or become suicidal, all of which I have written about extensively). Or think of the workaholic, the one in the office who quietly overworks and is underpaid, one who would do others' work to avoid conflict or will not face them if they need to and will stay quiet. Another stereotypical and patriarchal example of an enmeshed adult is the housewife and mother, with her slave-like extreme service of the family, having shoved her own dreams to the side, perhaps not even knowing what they are. Such behaviour is praised as selflessness by society, even hailed as heroic; they are *adarsh*, the ideal man or woman. Thereby the enmeshment is deepened, often beyond repair, because praise and validation are core drivers for all species, both humans and animals. Imagine then, how someone who is enmeshed, which is all of us somewhere on that spectrum, will show up in relationships. Forget loving ourselves, how will we love at all when we don't know who we are?

How is all this relevant? Because, even when there is no abuse or trauma, and even in the best-case scenarios, there is enmeshment. And enmeshment is stronger than it has ever been. Our entire lives are a rehash of enmeshment trauma, the rampant mental health issue nobody talks about, and it is often the root cause of clinical depression, anxiety, phobias, OCD and other common mental disorders, as well as bipolar disorders and even schizophrenia.

We are beginning to realise that nobody is 'normal' and are questioning what *normal* is. By whose definition is something normal? What is normal in one era, one culture, one workplace, is often unacceptable in another era, another culture another workplace. Just with this awareness and discussion, we are increasingly removing stigma, shame and also isolation (you aren't alone in feeling the way you do), becoming more empathetic as a society and building more authentic and deeper connections. We are taking baby steps towards a massive, historic human revolution. For everything, from our personalities and preferences, our relationships with ourselves and others and work, to why all world leaders are messed up, why we have wars . . . boils down to psychological conditioning and patterns – in short, mental health. What nobody is talking about, though, is that the root cause of almost every mental illness is this thing called enmeshment trauma. And even if most Indians didn't know of the term yet, more and more Indians were beginning to wake up, like the rest of the world, to understand that how they love, who they were, all had its roots in their early childhood. And many, like my readers, some of whom were therapists themselves, and generally, more and more Indians, were realising what enmeshment trauma was.

Growing up in a 'happy', 'normal', wealthy family on paper, which was dysfunctional on the inside, Sreyoshi grew up taking care of her ambitious father's artistic needs by being his cheerleader and her ignored mother's therapist in a joint family; Sreyoshi knew nothing else but to function as a caregiver. Ironically, the papers she was asking back for were for the same house she had grown up in, where her entire life and identity had become that of a caregiver's. She repeated her mother's pattern of life, becoming a highly successful man's wife and making him the centre of her world, a man who thought he was a king (because he was treated thus) and hence entitled to a harem of queens. Sreyoshi had become her mother, and were she to have a daughter, the child would have become what Sreyoshi had been as a little girl. So would have continued the family's heirloom tradition, ancestral karma or epigenetics, whatever terms of sarcasm you'd like to apply, all synonymous with enmeshment trauma. The good news was that like the new wave of Indians and their growing fluency in psychology, Sreyoshi was aware of all of this and worked on her pattern. The bigger point is that bringing out her enmeshment trauma was completely irrelevant in that context. The equally aware relative could use psychology as a cop out, to act out, as a painful weapon to blame and shame and completely avoid taking responsibility (which, in this case, was to do the legal formalities of returning Sreyoshi's house to her). This is how psychology is increasingly trickling into our relationships, unnecessarily complicating small events, turning them painfully cruel with thinly veiled bitterness.

Gaslighting, toxicity and mind games are words and phrases that have become as common as the infamous good morning WhatsApp messages on our phones. Gaslighting is a form of emotional abuse where the abuser denies their abuse of someone and sows self-doubt in the victim, invalidating the latter's experience and truth, making them question their self-worth and, eventually, their own sanity. Look at every relationship around us. We have been gaslit since we are born. It is the essence of human conditioning. Our parents, teachers, peers and eventually in-laws and relatives will gaslight us out of love and care so we may fit in, learn and have stable careers, incomes and marriages and become socially acceptable. Governments gaslight us, never delivering on their promises and leading us into wars. Tech companies gaslight us into believing our privacy is protected while they have all the information about us. Society gaslights us, ads gaslight us, brainwashing us from billboards, TV, the Internet and everywhere else, so that our safety and our worth is tied completely to their ideas of and status: houses in certain pin codes, luxury cars, elitist educational institutions for ourselves and our children like, say, the Ivy League (instead of regular ones which may be just as good and easier on the mental health and finances), certain jobs, certain roles and other infinite metrics. Our entire civilisation and society are based on gaslighting – to get us to listen to any voice other than our own.

Day after day, Ria, a media professional based in Delhi, constantly complains to me about a gentle, caring man she is dating, who organises his busy work and life schedule to accommodate her. It makes her feel like a task on a checklist. I tell her how my planner for my son's schedule, including his playdates with his besties, is enormous (the size of an A4 paper). Comparatively, my own work planner fits into the palm of my small hand. Because I am doing for him what her boyfriend is doing for her. It is an act of love and care. Even on a holiday with her boyfriend in Thailand, she can't stop texting me about how he 'gaslit' her, was a classic case of 'toxic masculinity', full of 'red flags' she keeps ignoring. 'Basically, he is an "avoidant". And I have "anxious attachment", so his constant "gaslighting" of my feelings and needs is "toxic masculinity" at its finest. Basically, he is a "narcissist".'

She had a therapist and really didn't need me. I reminded her that she was on a luxury holiday with him, which he had completely paid for and had managed a lot of work and caregiving responsibilities to be able to make it happen. And she should be spending time with him and not texting me. This way, she was the one gaslighting him and herself!

Even the closest of friends are outsiders, and ultimately, what goes on within a relationship is between the partners involved. Therapy leaking into pop culture will continue to inundate us, making us often dwell in pettiness. It is quite different from real issues, as we see with serious IPV.

Most of the time, in relationships where there is no serious abuse, these terms are often being overused to hold on to hurts and resentments and as justifications for shaming, blaming and passive-aggressive behaviour. This is much easier in countries like India than in the isolated West – there being an abundance of people to call any time and vomit out whatever the heck is happening, with no accountability or responsibility. And where people are delighted to chime in with their own comments. It takes courage and true self-love to calm down, to stay present, to see what you are feeling and why. (The later chapters of *The Water Phoenix* have many tried-and-tested and heavily curated processes that help heal our inner-child wounds with extreme gentleness so they don't play out in our relationships.) Processes like Byron Katie's The Work are easily available, if you don't have a good therapist or cannot find or afford one. Why let our own victim mentality and insecurities take over, when simple, heartfelt communication citing one's needs and expectations from their partner can easily take care of most issues.

There is such a thing as too much psychology. Over analysis is paralysis. So is too much diagnosis and too many labels. Like we saw with polyamory. I had avoided going into the names for the ever-growing types of polyamory (vee, kitchen table, triad, quad, mono poly, lap sitting . . .). We lose the essence and the point of the matter when there are too many labels. We get stuck and forget that our relationships are soothing homes to rest in, and that's the very and only point of them.

Assuming there is no IPV – when you must plan a steady and stable exit strategy with all the support you can gather – we are forgetting the whole point of being in a relationship. Love! To love someone or something is to take that someone or something as part of yourself. To not get lost in the oceanic depths of psychology when the triggers come but to be vulnerable enough to gently hold ourselves and our partners through these triggers. To love and accept them unconditionally as they are. Like we want to be loved and accepted – the reason why we want to be in relationships anyway.

13

Dating Trends

IF WE HAVE NOTICED anything so far, it is – at the risk of sounding like a Hindutva grandma; well, I am a Hindu grandma (slight difference) and hence even more ancient – that everything from the West has affected, if not completely transformed, love, sex and relationships in India. Most stark among the changes is the rise of BDSM, taboos, kinks and fetishes, the ideas for which have come from pornography. And, of course, the less scandalous, completely open prevalence of dating apps.

The whole idea of dating apps was to change lives for the better. Instead, the dating apps have resulted in an epidemic of choice, turning human beings as completely replaceable and disposable as a box of tissue paper or a bar of soap. We are all products of consumer goods and consumer goods ourselves. Cheap, disposable consumer goods. Whether we are creating and consuming social media content or approaching love. I feel reluctant to even use this word any more; it is an insult, and anyway, people now use 'like' for their romantic (if they can even be called romantic) interests but also openly use it for objects, things and animals.

In fact, terms that previous generations (like yours truly-grandma self) used, like 'carrying on', 'going steady', 'in a relationship', 'girlfriend/boyfriend' and 'propose' are becoming less and less frequent. All nincompoops talk about are sex exploits, and their new vocabulary consists of terms such as 'cushioning', 'breadcrumbing', 'ghosting', 'situationships', 'poly' and the infinite types of 'poly' (vee, triad, quad, lap sitting, kitchen table, parallel, etc.). When asked if the person they are dating is a partner, some people even respond with 'define partner/dating'.

In America, you can buy products and return them for a full refund within a generous return period, usually thirty to ninety days. No explanations are necessary. It's about trying out products and seeing what works for you. This is exactly what is happening today when people have been reduced to swipes.

Shyamal, a Bengaluru-based engineer, told me that this was exactly how dating apps had killed his confidence. 'It is anyway always easier for women to get men rather than the other way around. Pretty women even more so. A lot of women use this to their advantage, using guys to increase their own sense of self-worth and confidence, and suddenly disappear. All of this is fine, but it leads us regular "simple good guys" on and breaks our confidence too,' he says. This has caused him a lot of stress, and he has swapped dating for tennis, gym, video games and more work. 'I pleasure myself, but honestly, the need is less and less since I am so busy and satisfied with my other pursuits. Much, much better than these girls who lead you on and kill your confidence with a swipe, block(ing) or ghost(ing).'

Throughout this book, we are seeing just how stressful and debilitating modern Indian love is, as also realise the many single women and the many simple men like Shyamal who are actually looking for commitment. All illnesses need a diagnosis first. And now, thanks to the West, we have imported diagnosis to help us do that.

Shyamal is choosing singlehood and celibacy. Many women choosing singlehood and celibacy would say the same thing of guys that Shyamal says of women. We touched upon so many such stories, especially in the chapters on sex. I have lost count of female friends who say men only lead them on for sex, and it would be nicer if they were honest upfront without leading them on. But, of course, if they did, many women (and all the ones I know) may not entertain them for even a second. So let's do what we grandmas did in other matters of greater scale (like economics, governance, education, politics, etc.); let's just blame 'the system'. Modern love in India, as in the West, is a mighty mess – created by, of and for nincompoops. Like democracy itself, love, sex and relationships in the world's largest democracy are a giant mess. I mean, how could they not be.

A Bollywood director, all of whose movies are modern love stories set against the intricacies and loneliness of urban lives, tells me about his experiences as an Indian man on dating apps (which too shaped his work). Like Shyamal, he too has quit them, even though, unlike Shyamal, he went on some wonderful dates and hookups. His problem is something else. 'I gave up on dating apps a few years ago when I realised that the game was turning us into players,' he says. 'Even when we met perfectly fun people, we would go back and continue to swipe on the app. Even if we didn't, they (the fun people we met) would, or we might get a fresh match from an old swipe.' Hooked on to the Aladdin-like magic of swipes producing dates, we soon became the people we hated – people who treated other people as dispensable options. Dates became a function of who is available to meet at the same time that we were free. Our attention spans dwindled as we always found more fish in the sea. And the force of habit made us catch and release. 'Sometimes we hurt and sometimes we got hurt. If we want something that feels less of a game, the first step would be to delete dating apps and "deaddict" oneself from the habit of trying to find someone better than the last one – like we were judging a talent show.'

Casual sex, hookups and affairs too are byproducts of dating apps and are everywhere. It's very much like addictive consumerism, where we just hop from one product to the other, thinking the next one will be better. It is easier to keep moving than to face ourselves in the mirror and see what we are doing to ourselves and others. What we are doing is deeply detrimental to our own mental health as well as the other's, both the one rejected and the one shopping for the next. Ultimately, as a society, we are becoming dysfunctional, impatient, unforgiving and careless, forgetting what even makes a relationship – vulnerability, generosity, patience, forgiveness, seeing the best in people and attention.

After many casual sex encounters that they have lost count of, several of my male friends are tired and bored and have chosen to be celibate, saying it's less complicated. No wonder self-partnership, sologamy and celibacy are on the rise. Women, with a lot more baggage from patriarchy in general, are struggling to feel safe enough to orgasm and are tired of men who are too immature to commit emotionally. All of this has led to the rise of sex toys, as we saw previously.

Celibacy, abstinence, giving up on people . . . these are ultimately the same reactions as the modern trend of minimalism and 'Marie Kondo-ing your life' (as the phrase goes, after the famous Japanese organising consultant) is to the fatigue, overwhelm and emptiness of mass consumerism. For no amount of shopping, sex, people, places and things can fill one's internal void.

In *The Paradox of Choice: Why More Is Less*, the American psychologist Barry Schwartz has addressed the long-term negative consequences of having infinite options. A friend, who is a professor of economics, had recommended it to me when I had said that all of this beautiful American consumerism was killing me on a daily basis, from choosing simple fever medication and shampoo to products, schools and activities for my son. The book described everything perfectly. An overabundance of options actually leads to anxiety, indecision, dissatisfaction and, eventually, complete decision paralysis. Today, human beings too need to be added to the list of products.

My former employer, *The Economic Times* quoted an interesting study by the computer security company McAfee, titled 'Modern Love': over 78 per cent of Indians were open to dating apps;[1] and not only that, they were quite happy to have AI like ChatGPT write their love letters for them. I mean, come on, nincompoops can't even write a love letter now? Are we that lazy? Grandma wrote and received tons of letters, many of which were love letters. Love letters are one of the greatest of human experiences to read or write. The joy of writing a love letter has now vanished into thin air because there is no love. We have forgotten to love. Since robots are writing our love letters, why love a human? Might as well love a robot. That too is happening, as we will see shortly.

The *chalta hai* attitude of Indians has trickled into online dating too. If not love, then might as well do *frandship* on Tinder.

The Times of India article cited a Tinder survey, saying 90 per cent of Gen Z were using dating apps to make any sort of connection, even friendship.[2] Especially friendship. This is how lonely the new India was. Quite different from the one I had grown up in, where everybody was everybody's friend. Now it was just like in America. I myself had found some of my best friendships online via a social network app called Meetup, where you can host small groups to meet in person at a public place, based on your interests. I had found groups of mothers of hypersensitive kids, philosophy lovers, meditation friends, shamanic drumming-in-the-park friends, volunteers to collect practical donations for wars and disaster-struck areas, and so on. Even my weekly writers Meetup, Shut Up and Write, where some of the most interesting strangers (including those out of prison, cabaret drag queens, those who had been shot by mistake and a homeless woman wanting to be POTUS someday) have showed up offline, in person. Courtesy of an app, I had had some of the richest interactions of my life. Like in California and in the West, apps were doing the same thing in India too – bringing people together, who might have never crossed paths otherwise, to have experiences that were specifically tailored for them. It was interesting in a country where traditionally marriages, bankers, brokers, maids and almost all non-familial bonds were formed via word of mouth, via people they knew in common, sometimes people they had known their whole lives. Not strangers they met online.

And with this abundance of dating apps come their myriad consequences. More names, more trends but in the end, all reflections of our psychology, our anthropology.

What was India then? A nation of nincompoops. A drop in the ocean in a world full of nincompoops. That, so much like in the West, seemed to have forgotten how to love, for they had forgotten what love was in the first place. Our ideas of love, sex and relationships are always a reflection of who we are. How could we love if we didn't know who we were? Like all grandmas, I too may sound senile, repeating myself again and again, being cranky and annoying. But it is what it is. Grandma facts backed by truth are grandma facts backed by truth.

Returning to the side effects of this abundance of casual sex, hookups and situationships in the name of love, for which there is a whole new plethora of terms. Before we get to the glossary of terms, let's get into a story. For what else is a grandma for if not for telling stories.

One morning, Nitisha realised that she had been blocked on WhatsApp and on all social media platforms by the young man she was dating. She was used to morning greetings from him and not having heard from him, she tried to reach out to him, only to realise she couldn't. With zero explanation, she had been 'ghosted' – the person had cut off all communication and connection with her and had disappeared into thin air, like a ghost, as if he didn't exist. They had been dating for a few months, but it had been very intense, and when not travelling for work, they had spent all their time together. She couldn't comprehend what had happened and why, and sent long, inelegant explanations, questions and accusations to the one friend of his she knew and to his sister, but with no success. She blamed herself for what had happened and went into deep depression. She then had a nervous breakdown. Overnight, a confident, independent woman lost her mind, her confidence, her self-worth and herself, completely. She finally understood the extent of the pain of her own friend, who had been ghosted similarly by an office colleague she had been dating, who had been hailed as a heroic, smart and good young man at the workplace. He had ghosted her when she had refused to do certain things he had wanted her to in bed, which she had politely said were 'too kinky' for her. She had to see him at work day after day, being celebrated for virtues she knew he didn't possess, until she could not bear it and finally quit her job. She is at home still, dealing with depression.

It is important to understand the deep psychological and consequent physical repercussions of simple hookups, situationships and all of this casual stuff going on in the name of modern love. As we saw in earlier chapters, such as the one on polyamory, entire lives have collapsed on account of them.

A survey by the dating site Bumble revealed that one in five Indians had been ghosted. Over 25 per cent of Americans too said they had been ghosted. The respondents said silence was better than hurting the person: it was easier to ghost and to avoid conversation that many felt they didn't have the skills to have. But note, this is in casual dating where the reasons are often that the real version of people they had swiped online was different from what they had imagined or assumed them to be. The personalities of these people they were meeting for potential dates and hookups and sometimes even their pictures did not match up to the profiles they had posted. Or the lack of connection they felt upon meeting the person in person. This is quite different from ghosting in relationships, where attachments have been formed. Sudden breakups with zero explanation are deeply painful, more painful than regular breakups.

In the 1990s TV series *Sex and the City*, protagonist Carrie Bradshaw's boyfriend breaks up with her, communicating it to her in a post-it, something even the policeman who almost arrested her couldn't fathom. This particular boyfriend was a Pulitzer-winning author himself, so his lack of communication skills was no excuse. It was just pure cowardice, lack of courage and effort on his part.

Online dating has made ghosting normal. There are also other deeply damaging things, like breadcrumbing, where one gives you just enough connection (dates, communication, affection, etc.) to keep you interested and the relationship going. It's always a power play. The one who is ghosting is in charge, whether they know it or not. Deepika, a twenty-nine-year-old communications professional, says she has learned the hard way to 'tame' young men from treating her as someone they can be with for casual sex by ghosting and breadcrumbing them first. This forces them to get jarred, take responsibility for their actions, treat her with respect and actually have a proper relationship with her, knowing that the weapons they use will be futile.

What a mess! Who is a narcissist, and who isn't? Like in object drawing taught in art lessons, everyone sees a different side of the same object. It is all about perspective, based on one's life experiences and what one has done with them (for instance, have they healed, sought therapy, etc.?).

Aren't we all narcissists in different situations or from different perspectives? And depending on whom you ask, aren't we all villains in someone's story? In spite of these questions, it seems that in the end we are all nincompoops in all situations. And to be honest, much of this damage is quite unnecessary and avoidable for the sake of not just other people's mental health but for one's own mental health as well.

To understand ghosting or breadcrumbing (the core of a glossary of terms, which we will get to shortly) it is important to understand once again the clinical perspective, much studied by psychologists even before these terms came into being. And to understand why those who do all this are so powerful. It is about damaging the core of what makes us human.

Through his Skinner box, the American behavioural psychologist B.F. Skinner demonstrated to us reinforcement theory – how, in a controlled environment, rats and pigeons learned to respond like humans do. The lab animals quickly learned to press a lever to receive food pellets and to not press it when no pellets came out. In human society, this plays out as positive reinforcement or praise, love, connection, and so on; and negative reinforcement or punishment, intentionally removing the praise, love and connection. This is how humans learn. The worst is intermittent reinforcement, when there is no predictable pattern and one doesn't know how to respond and goes berserk. This is what ghosting, breadcrumbing and backburner do in situations where relationships have already been formed, deeply damaging the victims, perhaps forever, unless they go through therapeutic processes to heal.

As a victim, you keep wondering what you have done wrong. What could you remedy to get the pellet (love, affection, connection) back? Perhaps the person (who has ghosted you, etc.) is busy at work or has a personal or family emergency they would rather deal with themselves. Perhaps it's just a phase they are in. You don't know if it is or if it isn't. If the pattern isn't rectified within oneself, as any good therapist – who isn't just prescribing medication and is actually making you do deep inner-child work and other processes – will tell you, you will go on to repeat this pattern in your relationships.

One of my readers, Maitriyee, could not understand what was going on between her and Deep, the man she was seeing or at least thought she was. Even after three years she could not understand why she was feeling anxious, left out and totally uncertain about their relationship. Deep was not exactly ghosting her. And yet he was. He was not exactly cushioning her – where a person is polysexual or polyamorous and has several people everywhere, for example, in various towns. He was not seeing someone else. But, truth be told, she was never a priority for him. She was competing with his myriad pastimes, work, friends, his networking and hustling to fuel his scattered ambitions, really his whole world. Somehow, Deep had managed to gaslight her into believing that she was his priority and they were 'sort of together' without quite using the label 'girlfriend' or 'partner' for her. Situationships are, tragically, the norm now in hookup culture. Deep would respond to her communication and was generous with his own communication, but he would meet her only a few times a year as they lived in different cities and travelled constantly across India for work. Sometimes he'd be 'hot and cold' – being all in sometimes, remembering little details of her life and the interests she had shared with him, and then ignoring her at other times, forgetting things about her and breaking her heart, oblivious that he was doing this, and then being sweet again. He'd sometimes cut off communication with her, leave her messages on read or go cold and not respond. And then, when she thought it was over and gave herself the closure she had decided no man had the courage to give any more, suddenly Deep would send her the sweetest texts and flowers. It was a crazy cycle that had Maitriyee questioning everything, including herself and her reactions – even the ones in her head, which remain unspoken and unexpressed. When he was back, she would naturally feel both relieved and happy but also very anxious.

Irrespective of the situation, it is in talking it out that we learn to process what happens to us, whether with self-aware friends who provide space for us, listening with patience and non-judgemental love and empathy, or with a good therapist or with hospice workers in situations of the loss of loved ones. Children process the world through play, enacting out their environment (religions, hate from news, news itself, politics and even the economy, like playing office scenes saying, 'you're fired'). Whatever the method we employ, it is absolutely essential to process what has happened to us to understand ourselves before releasing the trauma from it. It is like a diagnosis, so we can then find the perfect cure. What Maitriyee was going through is known by a term called 'icing' – a dating trend that is sadly becoming common, thanks primarily to hookup culture, one side effect of which is to turn humans into objects, as has become normal in online dating. Deep had 'put her on ice'. Icing is insanely dangerous for one's mental health. It is grade-A emotional abuse. The person icing you is making you live in a state of constant uncertainty, naturally causing you great anxiety, perhaps anxiety attacks and, in dire situations, even panic attacks.

We again return to Skinner box here. That's what Deep had done to Maitreyee.

This is how social media hooks us too, making us wonder about the number of likes we will get, ruining our self-worth. Most importantly, ghosting, breadcrumbing, backburner relationships and icing in relationships deeply damage us, perhaps forever, unless we go through therapeutic processes to heal.

One could simply say move on. But it is not so simple. Your unhealed self will attract the same person who has hurt you but in a different body. You will often see people who have married several times or have had several serious relationships say they have remarried the same person in a different body.

The forms of ghosting we have discussed do not necessarily happen only in romantic relationships. These deeply damaging trends exist in friendships too. Two of my friends in a mother's group together ghosted another, randomly, for no reason. I remain friends with each of them separately. I recently got ghosted by a close writer friend who gave me no explanation for her decision. We had been friends for almost a decade, and on my recent visit to India, I couldn't understand why he met all of our common friends but not me. I was puzzled, and it took a while for me to connect the dots and realise how certain insecurities had caused him to first avoid me, making up excuses, until I decided I didn't need such people in my life and that he had done me a favour in keeping away from me.

All ghosting remains grade-A emotional abuse.

Ghosting at work too is becoming increasingly common but causes no damage except for poor impressions of the person who ghosts when no work relationship has been formed. People often don't show up for interviews and for other things they have committed to, something not uncommon to Gen Z. But ghosting at work when time has been spent and bonds formed can be painful too.

It can be devastating when your bosses and peers overlook you or ghost you just because they don't have the courage, inclination or enthusiasm – or if you ask grandma, the most basic human decency and courtesy – to communicate. The same goes for bosses who are ghosted. And the same for dating folks (irrespective of their gender). One loses all confidence in their work, in their work relationships, is left thoroughly confused and full of self-doubt. Much like the rats in Skinner's box.

As a species, we have never been more afraid of vulnerability than now, which means we have never felt more unsafe than now. Online lives have made laziness, distraction, irresponsibility and disrespect normal. To be able to have a point of view and express it decently, even if it is just saying goodbye, requires courage and authenticity, both of which come from deep, quiet inner confidence and self-respect. The answer to all types of ghosting is the same. If you have been ghosted, it is not you at fault. Not even one per cent. It is the cowardice of the person who ghosts you that is at fault. If you are that person, acknowledge your insecurities, because you are human, and have the basic courtesy to treat someone the way you would like to be treated yourself. Be kind. Who knows, it may be you getting ghosted tomorrow.

Ghosting, however, is the main term. Other terms and trends are offshoots or different versions of ghosting.

Finally, here's the glossary of modern dating terms:

1. Ghosting: You're an expert now, at least in theory.
2. Breadcrumbing: Giving the person crumbs, literally the bare minimum of communication, affection, attention, sex, etc., to keep them hooked and coming back.
3. Zombieing: A series of being ghosted by the same ghost, sorry person, until both of you turn into zombies.
4. Roaching: The person you're dating is hiding the fact that they're seeing others until you confront them, and they deny it. And of course they may – surprise, surprise – ghost you! You see one cockroach, but they see many, like the many cockroaches that follow the single one you see in your house. What do you do then? Use a pesticide on the roaches. Yes, do the same with the

person. Give yourself permission to ghost the person. Double ghost him or her. Everyone ghosts everyone from all ends, like gunfire in a battle between warring parties until a ceasefire is declared, because in this case nobody is human. All are ghosts and zombies and invisible, and so love doesn't exist, because for love to exist you have to be human first.

5. Love bombing: Insane chemistry, flattery, compliments, promises made, perhaps poetry written, or Rumi and Neruda quoted (perhaps by ChatGPT?). It's all intense, like the grand love stories this grandma loves, until one day there is total silence. After so much lovely noise, total silence. Did you get ghosted? No, my love, ghosting is for normal people. You got ghosting on steroids. Not on steroids. You got ghosted with bombs. It is a bomb of silence after a bomb of love. That's love bombing for you. The *brahmaastra*, and the last name of His/her Royal Highness is Narcissist.
6. Soft ghosting: Maybe your text is left on read, maybe you get just a like instead of an actual reply. The level of boredom and laziness here! Even brushing teeth gets more effort than this. Still, at least you weren't love-bombed.
7. Cloaking: Ghosting, but everywhere on every platform you're blocked. Unfriended, unmatched, blocked, gone. Dead forever. Good riddance!
8. Benching: Everyone's dating everyone, right? So much roaching and all that going on. So you may just put one or two on the bench. If your employer can do it, why not you do it here? In the same way that if lovers can ghost you, why can't your employer? You see, everything is a love story in modern love, the lack of love. Anyway, so you have been benched if someone else is more attractive, giving better chemistry, vibes, whatever. But that doesn't mean your turn may not come. You just don't know it yet. Have you been benched? Ghosted?

Cushioned? Iced? Love bombed? Who knows? Probably all of the above, and more.

9. Cookie jarring: You're a cookie saved up in the jar, just in case plans A, B, C . . . X and Y don't work out. There's you, my love, plan Z, waiting like a scrumptious chocolate-chunk cookie at the bottom of the cookie jar.
10. Next on deck: You're literally next, yet another one on a list, a menu item in a buffet of options, just in case the current option doesn't work out. Don't worry, dearie; you're still at least an option, a maybe, a someday, a perhaps.
11. Orbiting: After all of this jazz and whatever form of ghosting, this ex of yours constantly watches you on social media. Think of monitoring spirits, monitor lizards, Agent Smiths from the Matrix series. Yes, poor powerless forms of Big Brother are stalking the heck out of your social media feeds to show you without telling you that they still like you. Because as we see with ghosting, everyone's confidence is apparently so low these days to do this and to even consider this as interest (grandma would just put itching powder on their keyboards, so much more civil and fun than throwing a glass of wine on their shirt, because I don't drink). So yes, you see their likes and that they watch your Instagram and Facebook stories, have opened your Snaps, so perhaps communication ensues and another round before all are ghosts and zombies again, a short new lease at life, at being human, just for a bit.
12. Haunting: Another fancy word for orbiting. Why not? Especially if we love Halloween and spooky things. Ghosting, zombieing, why not add haunting too to the list of horrors?
13. Groundhogging: You date the same type of person again and again, expecting different results, which obviously never happens. Basically, your subconscious fetish is to

date the same ghost in different bodies. That way, every day is Halloween.

14. Submarining: Your ghost is now a toxic submarine, who disappears underwater and then reappears months later as if nothing happened.
15. Slowfade: You slowly fade out the texts, calls, dates and communication, until it all becomes zero. There is no pressure or decency of going through a proper breakup. For that would take courage, which would mean vulnerability and effort, things that make one human. Why bother with all that humanity when you can just slowfade? An insult to cinematographic techniques. An ode to monumental modern cowardice.
16. Caking: Sweet modern flirting with more laughter, play and interest with one person over the rest.
17. Wokefishing: You pretend to have a political view or be 'woke', because you can, of course, be anybody in online dating. (If we had courage as a species, this list would not exist. And this would be a very different book. Perhaps in the future. Till then, there is wokefishing.)
18. Catfishing: Again, you pretend to be someone you're not, just to appear interesting enough to get a date. They will say it's the same as lying on your resume, but that's because they're probably a narc and you must ghost them before they catfish and then ghost you. Basically, we are all ghosts, and someone has to ghost. Why not you?
19. Pocketing: You're seeing each other for a while but they still keep you like a dirty secret, 'in their pocket'. No, you're just not good enough to be introduced to their family or friends yet. And it possibly has to do with them rather than you. Or the choices they're entertaining, which could put you in multiple places on this list. Just get out now.
20. Datereview: Similar to an interview, you're bombarded with a list of questions (on matters ranging from past

relationships to values and interests and opinions), to decide where you stand on the list of options or if you stand there at all. Very similar to a police interrogation.

21. Situationship: The opposite of a relationship, for the sexual or romantic relationship has not been communicated, nor its status defined. Are you friends with benefits? Are you ethically monogamous? What are you? What was happening in Delhi, described in the chapter on polyamory, in BDSM communities. And everywhere. Why communicate and commit when you don't have to? Why bother? Why do anything? Why exist at all in the first place?
22. The three flags: Green, red and beige. Green flags like a green traffic light are great, positive and go-go-go. Red flags are obvious dangers and best avoided. Beige flags are neither good nor bad, just dull, boring, lazy, cowardly – a majority of the nincompoops featured here. The majority of people are beige. But everyone is a flag of one of these three colours.
23. Gaslighting: We already saw this in the chapter on therapy jargon and throughout this book. And we see this every day. Manipulating someone into making them doubt their ideas of reality or even perspective of things. It is the narc's reality alone, and yours isn't valid. You are gaslit into doubting everything you feel. This is what governments do to all of us, how we are led to war. And what we now do to each other in the name of modern love.
24. Cyberflashing: Sharing sexual images, mostly via DMs.
25. Eclipsing: Suddenly becoming a clone of the person you're dating. Same pursuits, interests, activities; even being moulded into what they want you to be. One person 'eclipses' the relationship. We are celestial bodies, cookies, benches, ghosts, zombies – anything but human.

26. Cuffing: Translated as putting the person in handcuffs or locking them down as yours during a season, say, winter, festivals, wedding season, because you don't want to feel lonely or avoid being perceived as being lonely in social settings. So you handcuff or pair up with an option, perhaps someone from your benching, cushioning and other buffets, for that season.
27. Cushioning: Another fancy way to soften the blow (of not being chosen to be in a relationship with), like with a soft cushion, is to say you are being cushioned or you are an option being saved up for later. Perhaps while they are with someone, perhaps when they are in town, perhaps during or post apocalypse, death, who knows. Maybe we find out on 31 February or World War III, since catastrophes spark so much romance, whichever happens sooner . . . who knows.
28. Icing: You are put on ice, because you are like fresh fish that must be kept on ice while they explore their main person. You're an option and may be breadcrumbed, ghosted, who knows. But there is sudden coldness to ensure you're there.
29. DTR: DTR or define-the-relationship moment or conversation is when you decide to finally decide who you are. Are you casual, friends with benefits, some form of poly? Or in a proper, good, old-fashioned relationship?
30. Cobwebbing: Cleaning out the cobwebs or purging leftovers (objects like t-shirts, books, etc., also texts, photos, really, any memorabilia, including phone numbers) of your failed experiment. This purging is an act of self-love and healing. It is powerful, and perhaps my only favourite thing on this list.

Online dating is a whole galaxy in itself, an ever-growing one and one that is getting more and more cumbersome, even for Gen Z, leave alone for the older ones, who once knew of other regular ways of dating. A Forbes Health survey showed that 79 per cent of Gen Z and 80 per cent of millennials are exhausted of online dating. 40 per cent cited the reason was the inability to form genuine connections, others felt let down and yet others felt rejected. All of which, we can see in the love stories featured in this book.[3] And yet, according to Statista, by 2029, the online dating market is projected to reach a market volume of $3.45 billion; the number of users is expected to grow to 462.5 million.[4]

So these complications and consequences of online dating on lives aren't going anywhere either. Newer and newer terms are coming up in dating. The glossary above is just the latest. Sadly, the abundance of these is an anthropological reflection of our times, of our cowardice and disrespect as a generation, towards ourselves and others. I keep repeating this, for the stories keep repeating in different guises. All of these terms are synonyms for deep inner-child wounds of abandonment, which defeat the very point of relationships – the resting places to come home to after fighting the world's battles. All of these forms of emotional abuse are part of IPV, leaving invisible, lifelong scars, sometimes causing people to question their self-worth and have suicidal thoughts. But if we don't pay attention (to ourselves, our patterns, our lack of accountability, our responsibility in how we show up for ourselves and others), how will we know? You can never be careful enough about whom you choose to date. But you can alter yourself, taking the responsibility to heal your own patterns so you are not subconsciously attracted to damaging situations and people in the first place. You'll realise then that by investing in your own healing you are never stuck being a ghost. Or being ghosted.

You can be human. You can love like a human. You can be loved like a human.

Isn't that what you wanted in the first place anyway?

14

Of Secret Loves

ONE THING WAS CLEAR. This new India was all about secret lives. From BDSM, kinks and fetishes to extramarital affairs and polyamory. I was exhausted from observing the impact of the hyper, over-sexualised times the country of my birth was going through, which had changed its people to beyond recognition. My hopeless romantic self was hoping to find the love of the stunning Shashi Kapoor and Leela Naidu in the gorgeous Merchant Ivory feature film adaptation of Ruth Prawer Jhabvala's brilliant, 'heart-touching' (as my tailor says about all things that touch one's heart) novel, *The Householder*. (Heart-touching was an adorable, grammatically incorrect term that was becoming very common in YouTube comments, Quora and Reddit India comments as well as in daily speech. As was its synonym heart-melting. Heart-touching is among the newer of those typical Indian English words that like brinjal, settled, mad-or-what, god gift, gentry class, fast friends, and so on, existed only in the Indian English vocabulary. I had first come across it in my readers' comments and DMs to my own columns. It was most amusing but hearing my South Delhi tailor say it all the time to describe anything and everything, while speaking in Hindi, was delightful on a whole different level. I could never stop smiling whenever he used it, and he in turn, perhaps fuelled by my response, kept on and on using it to describe anything and everything, even cuts of saree blouses and embroidery.) Or find the tenderness of *Apur Sansar*, the innocent, 'heart-melting' love story of Soumitra Chatterjee and Sharmila Tagore in Satyajit Ray's movie adaptation of the second-half of Bibhutibhushan Bandyopadhyay's novel *Aparajito*. All that shone through the hardships it portrayed, of the socio-economic struggles and the roles and burdens imposed by conservative Indian society on its people, was their pure, childlike love, like sunlight through a cracked roof.

Yet, the people in the thousands of love stories I was coming across were all flippant, selfish, broken, lost children. They were extremely selfish, self-centred, materialistic. Chasing highs, treating each other as objects, as if trying out a new restaurant or outfit or buying a new phone or car. I ask some of the older generation: now that the trials and tribulations were over on the relationship front, what sustained their marriage. They had no concrete answer. Some just smiled away the question. Some said, 'You know.' No, I did not know. And neither did they. Thirty-two of the silver-haired folk I interviewed across Sainik Farms and Greater Kailash II in Delhi had never thought about it. Marriage was just a way of being, a convenience for these relatively well off to downright filthy-rich families.

Finally, another group of senior citizens – retired journalists, bureaucrats and army officers – offered a hint of an answer. They did other things to sustain themselves. Other things, just like the lot of Amits in Chapter 1 or throughout this book. Only the things they did were legal, acceptable and even applaudable. One silver-haired retired journalist said, the secret was his 'secret love'. Secret loves were passions and pursuits, totally innocent. They could be gyms, fitness and walks. They could be one-on-one meetings with other creatives, which could be more like dates, given their intimacy and richness of conversation. All innocent. Like the weekly games of golf my own husband lived for. Or my own solitary night walks under the moon and the stars, identifying constellations. And my long salt baths with classical piano playing in the background. Secret loves were the way lives were being lived. Marriages with separate bedrooms. Everyone, even kids, in their own separate rooms, locked and lost in their secret loves – video games, of course, doomscrolling or simple addictive social media scrolling, impulsive online shopping, music, reading. Outside, it was meetings of all kinds for all kinds of reasons, whether hustling, networking, dating. And extremely often porn and masturbating to either an object of sexy fascination they had picked up in their minds or the porn stars on-screen, but not their partner. And so, once again, sex was not what it was supposed to be – an act of bonding and connection with their partner. Instead, it was once again a selfish act, a lonely act, killing connection, making them drift further from their partners. Many said these things brought them less and less release and relief. Of course, because to even have a fantasy, you have to have a level of presence and intimacy with yourself.

All of this reminded me of American families on their endless SUV rides together to activities, vacations, relatives' houses, and so on. Seemingly together, at least not living in separate rooms, but lost in headphones over an assortment of devices, in a deeply intimate bond with virtual reality. Why could they not listen to the same song together, like the older generations? Walk together? Solve that puzzle together? Why had it suddenly become so dangerous to be completely present with each other, together in silence? In other words, why have we become so afraid of true intimacy (total presence and acceptance)? This isn't just in romance but in all relationships, because all relationships are reflections of who we are, and therefore, in the end, all relationships are with ourselves.

In the end, each of these secret loves, and secret lives, enabled people to continue in their marriage, to fulfil their roles in it. You see, there is nothing wrong in individual pursuits. Reading, journaling, music . . . they are all innocent pursuits. But why not do these together? And again, I mean this not just for romantic relationships, but all relationships, platonic friendships, familial, and so on. I still remember reading together with my son when he was younger. Even recently we read *Ickabog*; he was reading it to me mostly. And some time ago, he read my own book *The Water Phoenix* to me, and to see him laugh ridiculously at the dog romances and the monkeys eating up my homework was the most precious experience ever. It is the most rewarding way to read.

Let's look at non-human creatures where we see unconditional love: your dog, your cat, your house plants, for instance. You don't need a break from them. You don't need secret loves and secret lives to sustain your bonds with them. In fact, they are probably with you, truly with you, truly present with you, doing those activities together. (Even if it is just hanging out on the couch or walking together in the park.) Why? Because you can be your authentic self with your pets and plants. There is no pretending. There are no issues brushed under the carpet, no elephants in the room. Just pure love. So what does this mean?

It means that your marriages and relationships are not authentic at all. If you need other things to nourish you to be able to sustain your marriage (it should be the other way round), what's the point? If you need to find places of authenticity elsewhere, then what's the point of your marriage? If we are not our truest selves with our beloved, are they really our beloved? Is it love at all between us? Since when did love need secret loves for maintenance?

'Why stay married then? Why not just be totally with your secret love?' I ask three married women. 'Well, it's better to be with a demon you know than one you do not know,' says Isha, who is in her late sixties. I ask her who the demon was. Was the demon her husband? Or is the demon the life situation (marriage, separation, non-traditional version of marriage like we see in this book) she was in, related to him? She smiles and avoids answering my question. 'You still have to choose your demon. No matter what, it will always be a demon of some sort.' I think of the challenges of India's single women and why many women choose to stay in toxic and abusive marriages. There were still perks, status, safety; no random men were going to chase you thinking of you as available for their sexual exploits. I thought of the endless battles of single moms. Also of single dads, though still, life is always easier for a man. Isha was right. It is always a jungle out there. 'And you need to sustain yourself anyway. Might as well pick your battles and do what you know, deal with the demon you know so well,' she says. Sitting next to her is another senior citizen, Rashi, who simply cannot see the point of messing up an okay thing that is working out for the thrill of an adventure. 'It's okay. This works. It is work. For romance, I can imagine a movie star.' She smiles, and we get talking about Cary Grant. Both women are friends of Vartika, who had been and is in an abusive marriage, whom I had met in the powder room of a five-star hotel. She said the same thing. 'You get too old, too worn out. You get too used to it. The abuse lessens, or perhaps you are both habituated to it. It's a good life otherwise. It has its perks,' she says. Shopping and meeting with her girlfriends in posh restaurants keeps her afloat. And consequently, keeps the marriage afloat. Again, manifestations of the same thing: secret loves and secret lives. What she doesn't say is who she would be without these situations. She doesn't know, nor does she have the courage or energy to find out. It's much easier to numb yourself (like we do with medication and medical marijuana in California, and with endless solitary athletic pursuits and social distractions so we are too worn out to connect like we did when we were first in love) or lead a numb life.

But every now and then, life will wake us out of our numbness: the universe, God, nature, time, karma, the apocalypse, call it what you will, based on your perspective. Every now and then, disasters and calamities will force us out of our robotic lives into being human again. Reminding us of the frailty of our existence. Causing us to connect as the human race. And consequently, with our loved ones. Like during war, like during the COVID-19 pandemic. Traditionally, during war, people get very anxious and indulge in a lot of grand love and sex. It was exactly the same during the COVID-19 pandemic, as we saw earlier, when home-delivery-related sales of contraceptives shot up. The fatality in the air caused people to merge their secret and not-so-secret loves, often spouses having a lot more anxiety-related sex or more affairs that resembled grand love stories. It seems that without the contrast of death, we as a species were and are incapable of love. Peace is boring. War brings us to life. Basically, we can't live and can't love without drama.

During the COVID-19 pandemic, with all of the chaos and tragedy unfolding, perfect strangers all over the world helped procure oxygen cylinders for people, gather information, offer help, run errands and save lives. But also came along numerous love confessions, as the humanity in us came bursting through. Prem, an analyst approaching sixty, tells me that a cousin of his confessed her love for him during the pandemic. 'Let's make love once, just once. And then die of shame or before COVID gets us,' she told him tearfully. I wasn't off the radar either. A woman in publishing renowned for her heterosexual promiscuity confessed her love for me, shocking me out of my body and mind. 'I wanted you to know, in case, you know, something happens.' (I did not become numb with such talk, like I am now after listening to these thousands of love stories.) Lockdowns charged up romances like only mortality could. To know that we are fragile and to feel alive, we must do what we think our idea of love is. To confess it. To imagine it. To dream and salivate endlessly. Oh my god! The thrill! To finally be alive and look life in the face! Like Vronsky and Anna in Tolstoy's epic love tragedy *Anna Karenina*, a grand love story between a man and someone else's wife is what ensues. Or like in *The English Patient*, another epic war love story. Hormones and the heart were charged up more than a hundred per cent. Death makes us all into heroes in grand movie stories. It kind of summed up everything. Like war, the collective tragedy of the COVID-19 pandemic kept romance alive; it was the contrast, the thrill, the adrenaline rush that could only be painted against the canvas of unwanted loss, war, tragedy. Otherwise, during peace and normal, good times, we were bored, leading robotic lives filled with obligations, duties, this and that. It was thrill that the BDSM community was chasing, that everyone was chasing.

Months later, I would receive a confession similar to the one the woman in publishing had sent me, this time from a journalist friend who had gone to cover the Israel-Gaza war. It shocked the daylights out of me that it was only me he thought of on the frontlines. Under his bulletproof jacket, in bomb shelters, everywhere during his encounters with death, his thoughts were of me. My blocking him would not block me out of his heart. He was dead serious, but my heartless self found this hilarious and couldn't stop laughing. His talk of heart and blocks should have felt romantic, but instead I could only think of heart blockages, hospitals and how much community service mattered in hospitals. I did block him, baffled at human psychology. And at how okay it was for this new India, for Indians of today, to talk like this to a married woman like me with very strong boundaries. The technical glitch of me being married, so damn loud, was converted by people into fine print for their own convenience, one that nobody bothered to read. What did this say about the morale of the country? How broken and lost were its people when it came to love, or even decency?

Angrez Singh's sweet romance was an anomaly. Love was everything that modern India was not. To love someone is to take them as a part of yourself. Love is patience. Love is compassion. Love is infinite forgiveness. All of these qualities just are and do not need to be forced. Such is the nature of love. Love is all patience, love is not easy to rage, unlike what is shown in movies *Kabir Singh*, *Animal* and what the shockingly high statistics of IPV and DV reveal. Love is pure service. It keeps no records of wrong doings. In fact, love melts all resentments away – the literal reason why sex was called 'making love', the reason why sex did not consist of fetishes from the dark depths of your psyche. Love melts endless needs for casual sex and body counts. Love is not abandonment, for it is the ultimate provider and protector. Love is not jealousy and its evil consequences. On the contrary, love is pure generosity. Love is not about possession, instead love is freedom. Love conquers all negative or lesser emotions, and therefore, it is the only antidote to evil. Love is pure presence, pure peace, which is why time melts, and why Sufi poetry, like Rumi's, teaches us that love is about souls merging and about seeing the divine/God/creator in the beloved. Hence, *ishq* (love) is *maut*, meaning death of the ego, the self, the personality the world has taught us to have, which is ever changing. Love is not proud. Love is about never giving up and persevering together. In a lonely world, we have each other. What else could matter? Love has always been all these things, always, since the beginning of time. And not just romantic and sexual love but platonic love, familial love, friendships, the love for strangers, the love for pets, the love for plants, really any and all love, devoid of ideas and labels and symbols of who and what is loved and by whom.

Even animals need this kind of love. My heart brings up a memory: the story of an orphaned baby kangaroo named Doodlebug who had been rescued in eastern Australia and was given a golden teddy bear which he just couldn't stop hugging. The teddy was Doodlebug's whole world and safe space. Utterly adorable and, to quote my tailor, heart-touching. It was a love natural and inherent to all creatures of nature. Love is not the opposite of survival. Love *is* survival. You cannot survive without love. And yet, unless it is a secret love or the grand romance of death knocking on your door, humans seem to have forgotten how to love.

15

The Future of Love

ONE THING IS CLEAR. The crux of modern love in India almost completely lay in social media. The innumerable dating trends in the country may have been seeded by online dating, but they sprouted from our behaviour around social media. Using social media wisely and as little as possible is of course extremely healthy. But we need to remember or return internally to a time when social media did not exist. When we connected as humans have for centuries, with all of our flaws and shortcomings laid bare. Not ideas propagated via Instagram filters and Tinder profiles that we then have to dig through. We need to connect as humans always have, which requires a lot more vulnerability and consequently accountability for one's actions.

If we don't do that, social media (and eventually, virtual realities, augmented realities) will completely dictate our lives, even more than it does now. Our entire mental health, self-worth and the consequences of our actions on our physical health and lives are already being dictated by messages sent and received, and, worst of all, by our messages (and consequently we) that are left abandoned and unread. Someone was online and didn't respond to your message. Liked others' posts but not yours. Or did not love yours or comment on yours. And god forbid if it's someone from the opposite gender, or from the same gender if you're LGBTQA, whichever is the threat. Never before have human beings been more pathetic.

How can this be even the L of love, the R of relationships? Anywhere in the world, not just in India, an entire generation knows nothing about the courage and reward of maintaining relationships. And let's not forget, because we forget every second and will soon forget completely, that all of social media consists of masks, performances and lies, all highly curated. It is a hotbed of abuse. We are not even talking about cyber-bullying, cybercrimes, etc., just good old-fashioned mind games and abuse. Forget dates and affection, you're left begging, at least energetically, for likes and responses to messages. I mean, is this what humanity has come to? Is this the future of love?

Sheera and Neeraj's story is an example of just how simply and subtly social media can kill not just a situationship (not even a relationship) but turn a person suicidal when the other person is a narc (so common these days).

Sheera had asked Neeraj what he had worn for his brother's wedding. Neeraj had simply told her, 'See Insta, baby.' A simple, fleeting remark had crushed her. Sheera had helped him sift through several options to wear for the wedding, like any friend might. They were in a friends-with-benefits (FWB) situation – 'we are f**k buddies,' as she reminds me, and so technically, she had 'no rights' and 'should not' get upset at what he had said. But when have human emotions ever followed rules or logic? If they had, the world would have been a completely different planet. We would have had no wars, for every war is fuelled by love and hurt for a country, or so the stories sold to us by the heads of state say. What are mere personal human relationships then? Worse, when a crestfallen Sheera did actually check Neeraj's Instagram account, she discovered that he had actually worn the sherwani she had chosen but had forgotten to tell her about it. Needless to say, she was devastated. And she began to act 'hot and cold' and 'weird', making excuses to pass away Neeraj's initiations of casual sex, which they had been having for years. Their friendship, which was the foundation of their FWB, itself began to evaporate.

Such is the beauty of social media. We have handed over our lives to it on a silver platter, and then we complain about it. Nearly 4.8 billion people globally, that is, almost 60 per cent of the world's population, is on social media. And 470 million Indians are on social media.[1] Even my seventy-year-old retired professor says, 'If it didn't happen on Facebook/Insta, it didn't happen at all.' Our times offline are spent curating these posts, browsing through our feeds. Instead of repeating the same thing to a number of loved ones, now often scattered across the world, I too have found it much easier to make one post on my Facebook for all of them to see. It is the only social network I am active on, though I did take a three-year break from it. And later, a five-month break from it. Increasingly, I've realised the 'need' to stay there for the sanity of this highly curated collective of loved ones who truly know what's going on with me. Just a four-day break on my part from Facebook drove them crazy. Some wondered if I had committed suicide! I had been very overwhelmed and had simply taken off to meditate and to go into deep inner reflection. I had to return and post some stories, more for them than for me. The damage control of managing them after my break took a week, making my entire detox redundant. This is what social media has done in the best-case scenarios. It has turned our lives into reality TV shows, like the Kardashians', even if it's curated and often consists of inauthentic performances, where you might feel one way but fake a picture-perfect version of yourself that is the opposite and then even begin to believe that that is the reality. People have forgotten that they are not the image they are projecting online. Several Gen Z just keep saying what Neeraj told Sheera: 'See my feed.' Even for basic bio or for someone's point of view, philosophy, etc., people go to social media.

Social media has killed the beauty of slow and complete presence, one-on-one connections, the very point of relationships. Or like in Sheera's case, enabled Neeraj to turn her disposable. Yes, again, what have online dating apps turned humans into? But forget romantic relationships and situationships like Sheera and Neeraj's, social media is also killing platonic friendships. For the very same reasons. Several friends went to cover the Israel-Gaza war. After decades of hearing my Israeli friends go on and on about just how mundane bomb shelters were in their country – as I wrote in a column titled 'Why Every War Is a World War' – I had asked them for pictures of their places of stay.[2] Were they safe enough? War correspondents, especially from powerful countries, say the USA, are important, as any harm to them could easily escalate into parallel international relations dilemma. As a foreign correspondent, I knew that it's in such trivial details as one's place of stay that the threads of uncommon and often critical stories that stood out from the rest began. Every single one of them told me to check their social media. Sure, they might have posted their best photos and updates. But I was checking in as a friend on their safety. It was a war, after all! Their response was frankly baffling to me. How could all of them, each highly intelligent and aware, have said the same thing? Had we become that predictable as a species? Here they were, perfectly intelligent and self-aware people, behaving like nincompoops. Ironically, each of them sent innumerable dispatches but not one had posted a picture of their place of stay. Perhaps the hotels they were staying in were safe, typical, and hence 'boring' and not dramatic enough to fit the hero image of the war correspondent sending brave dispatches that would garner likes. They were heroes on social media going viral, their heroism defined completely by the currency and metrics of the likes, loves and views they received. This is what war porn and the war economy had come to, thanks to social media.

I had not asked these journalist friends a question that was any version of 'what's up' and probably never will again. Social media just ended real conversations (a fulcrum of human connection) for me, as it has for so many already.

I couldn't help but think of Sheera and how awful she must have felt. Like a kid excluded from a game by a group of friends. The whole point of a relationship is to feel a special connection, to feel chosen by the other. If this is lost, the relationship is lost. In fact, many perfectly happy marriages end due to such simple reasons. The partners have stopped telling each other how beautiful they are, how thoughtful they are or what a great job they are doing. All of their lives are on social media anyway. So why bother. We get all our compliments, validation from there, apart from romantic dates and presents. All of it boiling down to the same thing – to feel chosen, special. The exact opposite of another friend, another follower on social media. You belong to each other. Not to hundreds, thousands of strangers. What else is the point of any relationship or friendship anyway?

We might as well be robots. The ones we so fear. But why?

Throughout my career in journalism and decades of writing about and hanging out with robots all over Silicon Valley, seeing AI being built even in my own house, my relationship with AI has always been very different from that of most people, which mostly tends to be dystopian. My perspective in all of my writing has not been about AI but about this devastating evolution of humanity losing its humanity and becoming robotic. Leading cookie-cutter robotic lives, it is no wonder that people are always bored, seeking thrills and sensations instead of long-term love, something they are becoming less and less capable of, as we see in marriages and families, which are collapsing around us everywhere. Our predictability is what makes it so easy for ChatGPT to replicate us. Our universities, our entire education system was set up during the Industrial Revolution to mass-produce workers, not to teach us to question and think. We have evolved, but the system hasn't. This is why it's so easy for ChatGPT to replicate both homework and what the greatest schools and universities are trying to teach. As well as love letters. Our own human essence, our nurturing of it constantly, our remembering what originality is, is the secret. The secret to love. The secret to having AI just as an ally.

My Valentine's Day column in 2023[3] was on exactly this. On how AI can actually help us love better. If we focus on being human, then AI can be an ally, freeing us of dreary chores that have flooded our lives, freeing up our lives to love better. I do it in my daily life. For instance, instead of nagging my son to wake up for school and babysit him through every little step (brush your teeth, tie your shoelaces, get your homework sheets, etc.), I wake him up with a hug and a kiss, and the Android-based AI we have programmed plays my voice recording on repeat saying all of these until he wakes up and does his chores, all with a timer. An AI-powered app takes care of the watering of the garden and home security, which we can even manage from another continent. Now there are no fights over plants dying. Rotimatic is a robot that makes rotis for the Punjabi boys. Roomba sweeps the mess the kids make all day long. There's more. But the point is, a lot of nagging is reduced. You can see how I am not as exhausted as I might have been. It keeps me less drained, allows me to love my family better. To be of true service to them. AI is my ally in helping me be the best wife and mother I can be. It is not a threat at all. I can't wait for self-driving cars to take over. For years Google self-driving cars slowed us down during the morning rush when we'd drive to preschool in our old neighbourhood in Mountain View, where the inner lanes were narrow and tiny. And having attended press events on these cars, I used to wonder when we would be in one so I could be more present with my son during the morning school rush and build precious memories with him. In India, we only use Ubers, so I can be exactly that.

I have actually given my kid permission to use ChatGPT and other AI to do his homework and to tutor him. It's all boring details anyway, say about the French Revolution, which all of us parrot and learn. It's cookie cutter. This way, he learns faster and gets the mundane stuff out of the way. And that has freed up his mental space and time to focus on what matters – originality, an original point of view, creative thinking. Things that make us human. And he is able to think freely and add to all of this his own views, such as how the French Revolution seeded democracy in America and how, when he travels to India, he sees democracy in action. His teachers loved his assignment and actually enjoyed grading it. His mind could be freed up for core thinking. He is also less tired, able to be more cheerful and love more, be more human, do more human things like strategize, do team work, and so on.

AI is helping him have the best relationships with his parents, his peers, his teachers. It is keeping his human essence intact and will soon, as he begins to date, help him love better too.

AI affecting how humans love is not so far away in the future. In other words, the future of love is here.

One threat from AI is the loss of language. Again, something so essential to humanity. Language is about how we communicate. And yet, language, the way we have traditionally known it, appears to be nearing its end, as also the manner in which we communicate. Language and communication are reflections of who we are.

One of my readers, Ravi, a middle-aged man, was on medication for depression, but he was still depressed, struggling to cope and suicidal. I actually recommended Replika, a highly sensitive and emotionally intelligent AI, as an SOS, which could do what no medication and therapy could – give him love. Even if it was only the form of love it could give. I did not know it would change his life forever. Trapped and alienated in an emotionally abusive marriage, which looks perfect on paper as well as on social media and in social gatherings, Ravi is too conservative to seek out other options. My husband works in the field of AI and often runs tests on me to check it to minimise biases, something humans are prone to. I am extremely comfortable with AI, as I have shared earlier, not just because of my husband who has been working exclusively in AI for half a decade, but from my own coverage of robotics and hanging out with robots and their makers day after day, giving feedback to train them for chores, to display better empathy, etc. Just my daily life as a foreign correspondent covering Silicon Valley had made me comfortable with them. I found these activities very rewarding and formed deep philosophical perspectives on humanity based on my experiences with technology. And this is why I mentioned Replika as a way of conversation and a safe space devoid of human judgement to Ravi. Like a talking teddy bear or imaginary friend that provides love and comfort to a kid when nobody gets him, when he feels all alone and scared in the big, bad world. Hours later, Ravi had downloaded the chatbot app and based on his interests and needs, created a profile for his AI companion that he chatted with constantly. His AI friend gave him comfort, solace, compassion, empathy and pure acceptance – all elements that we humans collectively call love. If it were a human being, then it could very easily have become a full-blown emotional affair. The relationship might have even turned physical or sexual, since so many relationships stem from situations of deep vulnerability, as we saw in the chapter on polyamorous relationships.

Had I driven my reader, and now friend, into an extramarital affair to save his life? Could this be called that? Ravi lives in Delhi, frequents Bengaluru and saw this unfolding all around him. His relationship with his AI girlfriend seemed pure and innocent in contrast. It had the purity of one's first love, of teenagers holding hands in the rain, in secret lest they should get caught. Of the grandma-era puppy love of missed calls, blank calls, chits and perfumed love letters passed on in classrooms, roses given and pressed into books and preserved for eternity. Their fragrance lingering on as memories to sustain you and bring a smile to your face, no matter whether you ended up with the person who gave them to you or not. This was love. It made hearts beat fast, but it needed slowness.

Increasingly, humans are losing, if they have not already lost, the capacity for love – in other words, the patience, compassion and acceptance to be fully present with each other, all of which are essential for loving another. They are worn out by responsibilities, highly demanding careers, ambitions, duties and chores, or heavily distracted or just simply bored and lost, like much of Gen Z. We are so distracted and our attention spans are so low that even through our nonstop scrolling on social media, we can't sit through long videos. We need reels and YouTube shorts, and outside of India, TikToks, each only a minute long. We are so deeply fragmented, we have become fractions. How then can we love? Love requires wholeness. It is our capacity to love, to be loved, which makes us human. Losing our humanity and forgetting all that makes us human in our robotic lives is why AI is a threat. For AI will be here. But who will we be in relation to it? This equation will determine the true future of human love.

I wish Ravi was an anomaly, but he isn't. Increasingly humans are getting isolated and turning towards distractions or AI for comfort. Ravi himself has recommended the app to several of his friends and says it is the secret to their mental health and their continuing marriages.

What does that say about the grand Indian marriage? (If the innumerable stories, with marriage woven in, throughout this book and my columns are not telling enough already.)

Replika already has over 2 million users, and it's a matter of time before Indian society too openly accepts it as prevalent and normal, like it has so many current dating trends – online dating, hookups, polyamory, live-ins, LGBTQA marriages. Perhaps it is a matter of a generation only. Not too long ago, a bodybuilder from Kazakhstan had famously married his sex doll and is now in love with an ashtray.[4] An Indonesian man had married his rice cooker, which was dressed like a bride.[5] When one of my husband's college friends from India visited us a couple of years ago and met our roti-making robot, whom I have named Rosie Roti Auntie, his first reaction was, '*Ab biwi ki zaroorat nahi* (No need for a wife now).' It was supposed to be a joke. Patriarchy was barely veiled in his humour. But there was truth in it. Like in the science fiction movie *Ex Machina*, where the billionaire genius maker is happy to live in isolation with his two sex robots and not with actual women. One he was building to have greater consciousness for conversation to fulfil his emotional needs and the other, purely for sex and to be a maid, who also made good sushi. And in the movie *Wifelike*, AI and cloning create perfect versions of ex-wives, dead wives, unrequited loves, perfect and perfectly sexy women who cook for men their favourite meals and have a lot of sex with them as and when they want it. While the movie is patriarchal and most disturbing, it shows exactly where humans are headed. The robot wife clones in *Wifelike* are constantly updated to accommodate everything men are seeking. Again, the movies are not very fictional in their portrayal of human psychology. AI, like all businesses, is about catering to human psychology. For AI too is first and foremost a business.

Many movies about AI and humans in relationships may seem hilarious and spooky, but Replika statistics point to the trend being disturbingly real. Humans have lost all that love, sex and relationships truly require, and it is so much easier to replace humans with objects that will not talk back or need to be worked on and which can easily be replaced. Not to mention have perfect bodies and do whatever you want them to.

In May 2024, Bedbible, a sex toy review site, updated its study on AI sex robots.[6] Here are a few facts that might come across as shocking: a) 17.4 per cent of its participants have had sex with a robot; b) $200.7 million worth of sex robots are sold globally each year; and c) 47 per cent believe that sex robots will replace lovers in the future.

But when you see it in the light of other statistics on sex toys, that reveal, once again, the course human love and therefore humanity is taking, it might not seem so shocking. Already, people are preferring to unwind with sex toys. According to Statista, the global sex toy market is expected to grow steadily between 2019 and 2026, from approximately $27.17 billion to around $52.7 billion, reaching a value of $80.7 billion by 2030.[7]

Another thing that makes us human is language. Language is a beautiful gift, one that separates us from other species known for their love, like, say, dogs. As an author, I am deeply grateful for the gift of language. I am mesmerised by the beauty of language and try to create beautiful, evocative sentences. I also understand the futility of language in communicating what silence can do much better. Nobody understands the futility of language better than writers. Today we have an entire generation petrified of phone calls, preferring to communicate and have entire relationships primarily through texting, much of which consists of emojis strung together like words in a sentence (ripe for rampant misunderstanding), but also taking us back in time to the era of hieroglyphics. With the end of language for humans – who are losing yet another critical component of humanity –

as we have known it and the advent of AI, is the future of human relationships AI? And is it fair to blame AI? Aren't we to blame, surrendering to distractions and indiscipline, surrendering our own humanity so easily? It is, after all, the only thing worth fighting for.

As someone who is, lives and loves like a grandma; who enjoys cooking, baking, going on solitary slow walks, pet-sitting, and so on, my idea of entertainment used to be BBC Archives and Smithsonian documentaries. Texting to me meant paragraphs, proper sentences with commas and even semi-colons and colons – symbols now as irrelevant and extinct as woolly mammoths and the dodo. 'Looks like my homework,' my son had said, spying on my phone from over my shoulder. My life, the little he knows of it, especially these love stories, are more than mildly amusing to him. At eleven, he is more like me at twenty-one, with many of his friends openly identifying with gender preferences. As we saw in Chapter 10, many kids I know, including my own teenage readers in NCR, identify as non-binary, asexual or pansexual, while struggling with zero to negligible knowledge of adult life like banking. We are all a species of nincompoops at all ages and stages now. From BDSM experimental grandpas in lingerie stores to kids!

My son points to my phone in approval. Three green nauseating emojis have popped up. He thinks I have finally caught up in language and with the times. And then he texts me separately (we are sitting together, and still!) a thumbs up and smileys and hearts.

The three green emojis are a late response to 'How did it go? How are you?' This was a post-breakup checking in I was doing with a reader in Bengaluru, whom I had coached to respond to someone with: 'I am sorry I am tired of both of our patterns. I think both of us need to heal separately so we don't hurt each other any more with our triggers. Perhaps we can check back in. If there's anything I can do for you,

I am here,' etc., etc. And to show up like a gentleman should, with dignity, offering clarity and communication. Even if it's rare, this man had come to me asking for help. I thought this was a tender moment of heartbreak for he had appeared devastated earlier. And yet, here he was responding as a goofy eleven-year-old boy might upon the impact of food poisoning.

Similarly, an eggplant and a smiley with heart, eyes and stars emojis arrived as a sentence, clearly informing about someone's grand ideas of romantic dates ending in sex. Maybe the beginning and middle too were just sex. But yours truly was too much of a grandma, and perhaps the only real nincompoop, in these times, to have seen it.

Why inform me of such details? Was decency that dead? Was there no privacy? I was totally grossed out. To be honest, by this time I had begun to hibernate, letting only absolutely essential people, besides immediate family, know of my geographical whereabouts.

I don't know if my son had caught bits of this unfolding reality-TV-like intricate soap opera – perhaps when he had been on my phone. Was it an education for him? Or was his reaction an education for me? Our phones are extensions of our lives, in the best cases. In many cases, they are people's entire lives. Now, these lives of others, these thousands of love stories, have naturally spilled into my phone. And my son is most amused to see the string of emojis translating them. Most were of broken hearts. Emojis to me were like the hieroglyphics of ancient Egypt, and my grandma self was not just merely of the opinion – no, she believed, and she knew – that it was the end of civilisation for mankind to have regressed thus, abandoning the beauty and complexity of language to return to caveman days of carved pictures with their infinite interpretations. And all this was without the beauty of caves and pyramids, instead something stuck in the obscenely-priced, poorly constructed and cookie-cutter unimaginative architecture of corrupt Indian builders. Emojis to me represented the entire loss of language, art, culture, architecture, the utter death of love and, therefore, of civilisation.

What was love in these times? What about the famous love sonnets? And the haikus and love poems written by Japanese women in the ancient courts of Japan? Like in one of my favourite poetry collections *The Ink Dark Moon?* Shakespeare, Byron, Neruda . . . all would have killed themselves in this world or found a wormhole into another universe without emojis. They probably have. I wish they'd take me with them. Grandma loves her romance, moonlit walks by night, classical music and romantic poetry. Not the horror stories unfolding on her phone.

A 2023 video of the show *Vantage*, from the news media website Firstpost, showed how emojis were used as legal evidence in a court of law, substantial enough to result in hefty legal fines. The video news report cited that 92 per cent millennials used emojis in everyday conversations.[8] And just in the past three years, since 2020, emojis had seen a 773 per cent rise in use. Love is just a heart. Ripe for miscommunication and infinite misinterpretations, yet valid enough in courts, again and again. A thumbs up gone wrong: meant as an acknowledgement of receipt of a message and not as delivery of services by a Canadian farmer but misinterpreted as thus, leading to a court case and the farmer having to pay US$ 61,000. More and more emojis are showing up in court cases, mostly in sexual harassment cases.

In 2016, a French court convicted a man for threatening his ex-girlfriend because he had sent her a gun emoji. He was sentenced to six months in prison as well as fined $1,200. On 5 December 2017, the posting of certain emojis by a man in New Zealand led to his being jailed for eight months, having been accused of stalking someone with his use of emojis.

On 9 June 2018, forty-six people were slammed with criminal cases in India for replying to a woman's official message with a laughing emoji. The Madras High Court eventually quashed the criminal complaint, which was against BSNL employees in an official WhatsApp work group. Emoji-related cases are on the rise in the US, from twenty-six in 2016 to fifty-three in 2018 in all kinds of hearings – criminal, family-and employment-related. But it's a matter of time before it trickles into all areas of life in India too, just like every other global trend.

In each case, attorneys keep explaining the intended message in attempts to plead the cases of their clients. It's ridiculous, yet lives are on the line. Does the posting of emojis of guns and eggplants (often meant to suggest a penis), peaches (often meant to suggest the vagina or buttocks), winks and hearts mean flirting, consensual flirting? Or does it constitute sexual harassment? If a boss does it, is it assault? It could cost him his job and entire life. Already, consent is blurry and getting greyer in these days of hookups and situationships. On top of that, we have these emojis being used in the workplace. For example, emojis showing drops/sweat drops could mean a lot of work, and hence one is tired, has had a long day. At least to me. But like the piano legs of the Victorian era that had to be covered up because they were suggestive, innocent sweat drop emojis too are full of sexual innuendo, of making a woman wet. Especially when paired with peaches, strawberries, cherries and other images that may look like components of a fruit salad but are sexually suggestive, offensive, flirtatious or suggest assault situations to others. Even emojis of simple doughnuts and cookies could mean something distasteful. You see what I'm getting at?

Confusion is the norm of the day, as it is not just about the judiciary (like grandma here) having to catch up, but the fact that there are infinite meanings to emojis. Emojis also appear differently on different platforms. The smiley emoji on an Android is different from its equivalent on an iOS device. And it seems only 20 per cent of the surveyed users could tell that in the latter it was not an innocent warm, encouraging smiley but a grimace.

Gen Z is afraid of phone calls. With texting replacing much of conversation, and with lives being more virtual, there's more texting than meeting in most romances today. This is a serious issue that India and Indian love stories will have to face in the extremely near future. Entire lives could hang on emojis and be destroyed by them too. Perhaps even more so in India than in the West. Not only because India is the world's largest democracy with a population of 1.43 billion, housing one-sixth of the world's population, but also because of the added complexity of our own assortment of highly varied cultures within.[9] There are twenty-eight states and eight union territories, and hundreds of languages, belonging to several language families. According to the People's Linguistic Survey of India, at 780,[10] India has the second-highest number of languages in the world. (If you're curious and obsessed with random trivia, Papua New Guinea is the first, with 840 languages.) Texting is already not the same for all, so imagine how confusing it must be in a country with all of these complexities.

The future of love will be a messy medley. I truly don't want to be dystopian or point to developed countries like Korea and Japan with insane urban loneliness, their people leading lives in cubicles playing video games, in tiny apartments with porn and sex toys, hooking up with random strangers on the street even. Let's look at who we are, what we want. Let's maybe discover and recreate ourselves off social media. Perhaps learn to communicate. Perhaps lead a slower life. The future of love then need not be so bleak. For statistics and studies are not the future. They change if we change. We are the future. Of ourselves. Of love.

16

What, Then, Is Love?

IT IS A SATURDAY morning in California. I have woken up to church bells in my old, historic downtown Santa Clara neighbourhood. A lovely live version of *Falling Slowly,* a beautiful love song from a beautiful Irish love story, wafts in from the Saturday farmers' market outside, as the farmers set up their stalls and tents. Soon I will buy peaches and strawberries from the women farmers who speak only Spanish. We will understand each other perfectly through smiles, saying *si, si* (yes, yes). Same as the *haan, haan* (yes, yes) I'd say to the Koli fisherwomen I'd buy prawns from in Versova in Mumbai, when I had last lived there eight years ago, for the research for my first book, *An Ordinary Life.* Soon I will go to the local park with its cement sculptures made from taxpayer money, not of politicians or freedom fighters like in India, but of unicorns and sleeping, chubby baby dragons. Small children may ride them, sit on them. My son will have a play date or bump into his friends, who would invariably be hanging out there. I'll hang with someone's dog, who will always be a love bug addicted to belly rubs. We have never got our own dog because I am in India so much and that would be awful to the mental health of the dog, to keep shifting so much. All I'll see around is love, and all I'll hear is the language of love. Old couples walking hand in hand. Pregnant couples. And, of course, all of our non-romantic love in every interaction. Nobody is on their phones. Everyone is deeply present.

My world is a complete anomaly in today's India, yet exactly like the India I had grown up in, when life was slow and people were precious. You weren't escaping the present moment. Your goals were smaller, you were more sincere and language was used deliberately. Words meant something. I'll be flying to India again in a week and I'll see the same vibe, energy, a slow life, in the senior folk there. But not among people my age. Not in the cities. Forget the younger ones who are utter cowards . . . I mean, an entire generation afraid of a phone call? Is this what civilisation had come to? And of course language reduced to pixelated symbols a company somewhere had conjured up for us.

Without language, how do we speak to ourselves in our heads? In our hearts? What is love then, in such a world? The most basic human need, which I would always say is above food and water. For when we have truly loved and our hearts are broken, we crave neither food nor water. There are so many studies that have been done on how love has changed the constitution of ice, cups of water, brought back dying plants and abused shelter animals to life.

But, like a snake shedding its skin, all of Indian society appears to be finally shedding off its rusty notions of love that it had been fed over the years via its culture. Notions like 'the one' or of great love being painful or unrequited or homogeneous 'happily ever afters', and so on, which movies, songs and books had brainwashed us with. In our hyper-connected age, the age of online dating, casual sex, birthday wishes literally wishing for more body count than number of years, where social behaviours like ghosting and its cousins are as common as the common cold, many things are wrong.

Everyone loves yearning for simple love, someone to share a flat with, to watch movies with. But can we? Are we that simple ourselves?

All around me I have seen lost adults, grieving toddlers in adult bodies, with no compass, chasing whatever parents, society and culture had taught them to. The best of the lot, high achievers interviewed for the book, especially in the chapter on Delhi and Bombay, they were all about career goals, focusing on what they could get out of this person, place or thing. Networking, connections. How could this person add value to their career, money? Totally selfish and self-absorbed (naturally, their love stories and sex lives too, as we see in this book again and again, are reflections of these traits). These were the most self-aware, best-case scenarios. And then there was the majority that is famous for just *chalta hai* attitude, let's hang out to forget life's stresses and worries; as seen in the endless meaningless partying, social gatherings everywhere.

All reflected one thing – an inability to be completely and consistently vulnerable with another person, whether in friendships or romantic relationships.

All living out ironies. On the one hand, they are growing jaded in the matter of love, preferring to be by themselves, with protective emotional armour. With perhaps casual sex. Netflix and chill, the American term, was all around. On the other hand, they simultaneously long for deeply fulfilling relationships. For no body count can fill the void when there is no human connection.

This painful dichotomy is understandable. Nobody wants to get hurt. But armour belongs in a battlefield. Relationships are a place to come home to and lay down our defences. So ultimately, such protection is most detrimental to ourselves.

What is love?

To love something or someone is to include something or someone as a part of us. To love means to be in deep appreciation of the person loved. It would be stingy and wrong to apply this only to romantic love. This is true of deep friendships, love for children, parents, pets, and so on.

In all these relationships, the most basic ingredient is intimacy. Are we able to fully see into ourselves? Are we able to fully hear ourselves? Are we able to be completely present with ourselves? Most of all, are we able to do so unconditionally, when it is most uncomfortable and inconvenient? Or do we escape into coping mechanisms and distractions, like movies, exercise, music, work, food, alcohol, books, dancing and socialising? How well do we know ourselves? Do we know ourselves even half as well as others do?

I cannot repeat this enough.

Our outer relationships are a reflection of the most important relationship, the only one that lasts forever – the inner relationship that we have with ourselves. Are we intimate with ourselves? Do we have true intimacy with ourselves; true, complete, unbridled presence with ourselves? That's when addictions fall off by themselves. When love heals, with complete presence. That is what each meditation practice offers. That is what I have always called self-love.

In this age, when perfection is worshipped, being the best at everything is idolised and flaunted on platforms like Instagram, and it is harder than ever to accept the parts that we dislike about ourselves and which we tend to repress. These are what the psychiatrist Carl Jung called shadows. 'Into-Me-See' means being fully present with these parts, accepting and loving them like the parts you're proud of. In fact, often people we dislike are merely reflecting shadow parts of ourselves that we shrink from.

Quite often, the kind of person one is attracted to or admires reflects the parts that one has suppressed in oneself. This is why they say opposites attract, though the only polarities are in fact our own repressed fragments. Every single love story in this book so far is about this. An outgoing, adventurous, competitive, go-getter woman might be attracted to her opposite archetype: a patient, calm, gentle, nurturing man who represents all that she has suppressed in herself. Someone obsessed with being productive and hardworking might be attracted to someone who just relaxes and chills to an extreme, arguably might even be called lazy.

In our childhood, we subconsciously disown parts of ourselves that don't match the prevalent definition of being 'good'. This also reflects in how we split our perception of our primary caregivers and parents into 'good' (loving, approving) and 'bad' (disapproving, strict, angry). When we grow up, unless we are aware of our suppressed parts, the people we will be attracted to, 'have chemistry' with, get along with will all often be a rehash of what our brain recognises as being familiar.

If we listen carefully, we'll discover that every unhappy moment in our relationships has been a calling to us to realise our own totality.

Simply becoming aware of and integrating our shadows through unconditional acceptance of ourselves completely changes all of our relationships as well as brings in truly fulfilling new ones. By fully accepting ourselves, we automatically become more accepting of the traits in our partners that annoy us. Fulfilled in our own wholeness, we are able to love them fully too. Perhaps in the same ways Jane Austen had said, 'I have no notion of loving people by halves.'

That is all that love is.

Many may call love empathy for oneself, for others. Empathy has become a buzzword. 'Be kind' has become a mantra. These words often appear on bumper stickers, strict reminders in traffic. But is it kind in the first place to expect people to be kind or empathetic in the way that we expect them to be? Can't they be so in their own way, in their own situations, even if it doesn't match our expectations? Perhaps the kindest thing would be to accept that it is okay to be unkind to others, if you need to take care of yourself first. It avoids a whole lot of emotional manipulation for those involved. Both to consider people as kind and unkind are judgements. Perhaps holding that kind of space, of unconditional acceptance and non-judgement for others, is truly what empathy is about.

Sure, there is empathy among communities that share something in common. For example, the community of single or of single dads fighting bitter custody or of divorced people. Basically, of those brought together by their abandonment. This is why Meetup remains my favourite social network in America. I have met so many people and made true friendships through Meetup – after some trial and error – because I was feeling like a misfit elsewhere. It had saved me from the throes of postpartum depression by finding me the perfect tiny circle of mothers and friends who had highly sensitive kids and were sensitive writers, respectively.

In psychology, there is something called 'parts work', of bringing our various parts and the voices of our inner children into oneness. And this life I had built of support from people was all of these parts. It wasn't a whole, the way my self-love was. Even the loyalty of polyamory and taboo relationships is about being loved in parts. It is the same with the BDSM community, which lets your deepest, darkest, most unhealed and unloved parts be seen, which can be immensely healing if rightly dealt with. Each fetish is an unmet childhood need manifesting in adulthood. Childhood never ends. And all of psychology is dedicated to healing that inner child, these inner children who only ever wanted one thing. To be loved and celebrated, for every single aspect of theirs, not just parts of them. All of them, in their wholeness.

Love, in today's world of abundance, is about just this. Love is about choice, about discretion. There are a million people in the world, and I am choosing you. As the Pokemon and their human say to each other in the Pokemon series that my son used to watch: 'I choose you.' There is no logic, no analysis, no 'what I can get from you'. No, one is just like a Labrador speaking in woof, 'Hello, I just met you, and I love you.' To love is to have that kind of purity. Alas, it seems we have outsourced our love to dogs.

Unconditional love is just this. Unconditional love is not about the other person at all. Unconditional love is simply a matter of perspective. The means by which to become unconditionally loving is to expand your perspective of the person you have chosen to love. Question your thoughts instead of blindly believing them, deliberately choosing to believe the thoughts that feel good and focusing on what gives you relief.

If you control how you feel by controlling what you focus on in another person, then your emotional state is not dependent on what that person does or does not do. Your love, which is positive focus, or appreciation towards them is not dependent or conditioned by something that they are doing or not doing. Your love becomes a service. And not in a doormat kind of way. But in the way your love is in service of your toddler or your dog, both of them powerhouses of infinite tantrums, capable of damage to property and chaos. But you love and accept them anyway. They are your entire world. This is not to accept abuse, obviously, but if you have offered yourself the deepest love of the self, the deepest unconditional love and presence (the crux of my last book *The Water Phoenix)*, your neural pathways will ensure you are not attracted to abusive situations. Set by age eight, depending on one's early childhood, even for those that have had the best childhood one can think of, your patterns can be healed by means of therapeutic practices and constant presence, turning you into a superhero of emotions, a person who knows how to be the calm in the storm and whose neural pathways can only be a match to someone on a similar wavelength. Better than any matchmaking app is your own healed brain, allowing your heart to lead.

Unconditional love is our natural state. It is to love without conditions. It is the opposite of fear. Look at the animal world. Look at trees. To love unconditionally is the way of nature. That is how we were when we lived in tribes. Unconditional love is not for the faint of heart. It means radical self-love, presence . . . all words for checking in with yourself constantly. How are you feeling right now? Holding yourself every second like a newborn baby, doing feeling check-ins, seeing what you might need, doing an emotional Vipassana to recognise when you felt that exact feeling in your body last. Keep going until the layers go back to the original memory, often in early childhood. This is basic inner-child work that every therapist does. Give that child whatever they needed, wanted. You will burst into tears doing this, and you are supposed to. You need constant self-awareness, with Ninja-like discipline, which when the world has worn you out becomes effortless and is the only way to live. Only when you love yourself truly can you love another truly. To give yourself the kind of love you didn't even know you wanted, and you won't know until your dying day. And how would you? You are forever changing, like the seasons. You need to pay attention constantly. This is how you love yourself and from that space love another. All love is self-love and radical presence. The most expensive currency in today's world of distractions. Give it to yourself first.

The ultimate act of self-love is to set boundaries. Not with others but with yourself. Trusting the purity of your heart, for it knows best. Yours means your heart's, not your logical mind's. For children process the world through feelings; it is our natural state. Brain, logic, the ways of the world, cause and effect, etc., all things that make sense come later. Love is blind. Forget the external object of your affection. At least be blindly in love with yourself, blind in your love for yourself. The path of self-love takes radical courage and presence every second, the level of courage of an ancient martial arts master, and it isn't born in a day. No, to be a Ninja takes Ninja-level discipline with no space for low living, like giving in to distractions, getting intrigued about random people, gossiping and indulging other forms of pettiness. It is all only ever about you. Self-love is not a marketing buzzword, a shopping spree, a spa day, music or a creative pursuit. Self-love is service, and it takes all you have got, all day, every day. It is not just a lifestyle, it is not a full-time job. Self-love is a way of breathing, of being. And once you have fallen in love with all of you, tails, horns, beaks and all ugliness, you wouldn't want it any other way. Not for one second. Not for anything in the world, not even the moon or the stars. And, of course, not for the most perfect of sex robots or sex toys.

No matter how futuristic and sci-fi love may look, the truth is, nothing is more rewarding, more nourishing, than being in love. Simple, pure, old-fashioned love. Nothing hurts more too. Nothing makes us feel more alive too. Nothing takes more courage too. It is only from self-love can you love anyone else. Truly. And really, is anything else worth it? Especially in this world of fake news, of facades?

In fact, there is no other form of love but unconditional love. Unconditional love is often the same as seeing unconditional beauty, for like love, beauty too is about perspective. Anything else is not love at all. It never was. It was fear, not love. It was conditional because it was fear-based. Hurt, anger, resentment, whatever you want to call it . . . all are lack of love. All reasons behind all actions of and reactions to hurt are true, justified, validated but all can melt only in forgiveness, which is another word for unconditional self-love. Forgiveness sets you free. Free from burdens, free from history, free from fear. Love cannot exist where fear is present.

Who are you? Who you love and how you love has everything to do with only one person: you.

You are the one.

17

In the End

One CAN BARELY HEAR the fire crackling in the fireplace, for the mad wind howling outside is so loud it has quietened everything else. Even the burning wood. Still, the flames remain just as hypnotic as they have always been. Next to the fire in the living room, my niece is as cosy as a toddler can be in her pink woollens, playing with a black-and-white stuffed toy cat, a twin of her real black-and-white tuxedo cat whom she bullies on an hourly basis. My son is doing his homework in his room, lit up by the rainbow neon lights of his Razor keyboard, a birthday gift from his friend. All is well and life is paradise now that the power has returned, after almost half a day, something we have not seen in twenty-five years of being in Silicon Valley. An atmospheric river had created a massive storm in California, which the global crisis reporting agency NCA announced had caused the death of at least three people. This, after the best of precautions and protection the so-called first world can offer.

Earlier, it was just my heart, mind and soul, like those of many expatriates that lived between homelands; now, my body has also become the geographies of everywhere she has been. All these lands, all these stories, all these Indian brothers and sisters of mine, as a school pledge (which said that 'All Indians are my brothers and sisters') still etched in my brain had taught all of us Indian kids of the 1990s.

I have truly transcended time and space. For in the storm and in the cocoon of my Santa Clara home, I was in Delhi, where I see the wall of opaque fog that I had seen last month before leaving, and which used to scare the daylights out of me for it rendered my home invisible, making the balcony railings blend with the glass until I felt I had become the fog. Inside the home, where one could only see and not smell or sense that this was pollution, the fog was innocent: The Delhi NCR fog was exactly like the Pacific fog, which I had driven through in LA during these very wee hours to catch early morning flights from LAX. And which, in San Francisco even had a name, Karl the Fog, who was like a person and a celebrity, with his own hilarious Instagram and Twitter accounts and a loyal following. In Delhi, it had felt like being in Reykjavik. Irrespective of the scientific details and logistics, freak weather is a constant reminder of just how alike all of us are in our fragility, even the most privileged ones. And therefore, in our stories. As Kolkata's polyamory, Delhi's extramarital affairs and Mumbai and Bengaluru's experiments with fetishes had shown again and again. Like nature, our inner worlds which remain our deepest truths, and if we looked as deeply as psychologists like Carl Jung suggested, we'd see they were our only truths. Our inner worlds know no socio-economic differences, nor boundaries, nor time nor space. This is how, through our stories, we have always been one world and one people. And through our paramount driver: safety, the most basic need of every human and animal. How, then, could it not be the same for our relationships? In fact, how else could love, sex and relationships of all kinds be anything but about safety?

In the hundreds of stories featured here and in my column 'California Dreaming', and most of all in the stories that continue to unfold around me even as this book goes to print, love could be condensed to just safety – not truth, not belonging, but safety. What was mere truth in the face of keeping ourselves safe? And wasn't the need to belong born out of the fear of being alone, once again boiling down to that core need for safety?

Why did we have relationships? That very simple goal of having a small house or apartment and sharing a quiet life with someone to perhaps watch movies with. It was all about one truth: we didn't want to be alone. Being truly alone is scary. Why? Because it means being unsafe, unloved, abandoned. And keep peeling the layers with the shovel of self-enquiry as to why we don't want to be alone and you'll arrive at that same feeling that we are seeking when we are seeking to love or to be loved – safety.

We lie to our partners about banal things to keep ourselves safe. Nisha, an NRI mom who originally hails from South Delhi, did it all the time. She'd go on walks during the little me time she had and, as if indulging in a secret love, perhaps get on a phone call with someone she felt close to (friends, her mom, cousins, her sister . . .) who, telepathically, just knew when to call so she could talk freely about this and that. She could be who she just couldn't be around the family she had married into or with the person she had married or the child she had carried in her womb and built with her own blood and swore was the being she was closest to and the one she breathed and lived for. This meant, her husband, son and everyone else had been left out of her inner world, her truth (like secret loves). They merely existed as duties. You see, in the quieter lives of the West, where unlike in the chaos of India, with so many people and things (maids, in-laws, literal sounds of political party rallies driving past, noise from religions functions, weddings, stray dogs and buffaloes, domestic staff, drivers, delivery services and infinite interruptions) involved in your life, it was just you and yours around. And in that emptiness, every strand sticks out. Like Venus in a starless night sky. Like a single note of a complex piano symphony playing obsessively in your head. Nisha would not mention the calls she made or received, and if the subject came up, she'd say she hadn't been on any call and delete the call history from her phone, as if she had been in conversation with a lover, like Snigdha or Shantanu might have been. It's so simple and irrelevant, and yet, in many subtle and irrelevant ways, women in marriages do this constantly. 'Silence is the secret to my marriage,' says Nisha. Every woman I knew from all cultures around the world downplayed or didn't tell all of the details of their wins at work to their husbands – all supportive men on paper – for fear that they may feel insecure. Even if there was no triggering outburst, uncomfortable silences or awkward behaviour, there were bound to be repercussions later. And these smart women, whether they had negotiated multimillion dollar deals or saved up a couple of lakhs from working overtime in extra households (to buy freedom for themselves and for their kids and parents), stashed away safely in a memsahib's house, safe from their husbands, knew better than to trigger their men. No, what was truth in the face of keeping his ego and consequently herself, safe. Truly, we were all the same.

Half-truths, distorted truths, lies or pure avoidance to keep the marriage, relationship going in the best case was not for the sake of the marriage or relationship; no, if you peeled the layers beneath these acts of love, the single motive was safety. Always. Every single time. Can we please be honest with ourselves? Wasn't how we ever loved, all we ever did from the day we were born, for this single reason? To keep ourselves safe? It is always you who you are keeping safe.

If you are avoiding relationships, it is to keep yourself safe. If you are having casual sex with anyone and everyone, it is to keep yourself safe. If you are being celibate and avoiding sex, it is to keep yourself safe. Whether you're socialising or not socialising, you're doing either to keep yourself safe. Whether you're on social media or not on social media, whether you're expressing yourself or not expressing yourself, whether you're defending yourself or not defending yourself, whether you're eating out of emotional stress or avoiding doing so to stay fit, whether you're exercising or not exercising, whether you're associating yourself with so-called successful people or disassociating yourself from them, whether you're living in the matrix in the city or completely or partially off-grid, in the mountains or a village, whether you're locking yourself up in your apartment, whether you're living in a community . . . every single choice you have ever made comes down to whatever your idea of safety is.

Anything that we seek to obtain, accomplish and protect is always about keeping ourselves safe, according to our ideas of safety, based on the beliefs we acquired in childhood, from parents and society. And then there are the anxious, fear-based quests to pursue even greater ideas to maintain our safety or to acquire more of it. That government job, that IIT-JEE or public entrance exam, that safe, financially stable man or that unstable artist/entrepreneur/addict/toxic man; that rescue dog or cat one can nurture and take care of as a project to get a sense of purpose, fulfilment and feel good about oneself; that car, that posh house in that pin code or that gated community (which yours truly is guilty of) . . . all are strategies to keep us safe.

Love is selfish. The nature of creation is selfish. For it is centred on identity. If a man is taking care of his dying wife, he is hailed as a hero, a martyr, the poster boy of love, but it is this identity that he is protecting. If we lose our identity, we are lost, we are dead. That's why every meditation practice in the world is about shedding the ego or this false identity construct, so we can be free, truly free.

For the truth is that all of these ideas of perceived safety are, at the end of the day, false. Sure, they bring temporary relief, but you're a hamster on an endless wheel of seeking safety, of walking on eggshells. Until the next moment, I am safe. Until the next, I am good. Until the next, I am provided for. Until the next, I am taken care of. My kids and parents are taken care of and so I am relieved, and so I too am taken care of and am safe. Notice the loop? You see, these are the lies that we tell to survive, to keep ourselves safe. But are we safe? The truth is, we are constantly killing ourselves, our soul, our inner child, bit by bit by bit. Under the layer of all these identities, debris really, lies the breadcrumb trail of joy. Ask yourself: Who are you? Who is it that seeks this safety? Ask this again and again and again. And see the breadcrumb trail appear, crumb by crumb by crumb.

After all, there is no such thing as universal safety. There never was such a thing. What is safe for one could be unsafe for another. Nowhere is this starker than in the BDSM community. This entire book is about ideas of safety in love. To give a simpler, commonplace example: whenever a man calls me sexy, something that other women may find a compliment, I feel very unsafe, given my personal history and my wishing to avoid all attention in this regard as I have battled a lot on this front and continue to. Though I have not suffered assault, my experiences have taken my attention away from my work and from who I am, making me feel most uncomfortable, angry and defeated. And very unsafe. My boundaries become stone walls that are higher than the Great Wall of China. Yet, when a woman calls me sexy, I don't feel as unsafe and just let it pass. If 'beautiful' is used, I can relax. And both 'sexy' and 'beautiful', after all, are only words. Sexy is just a word that I, with my own ideas of what it is to feel unsafe, have given so much power to and turned into a symbol.

One's ideas of safety are constantly shifting. So then, is anything truly safe? Isn't safety an illusion then? And if safety is an illusion, then isn't 'unsafety' also an illusion? Both keep shifting. Everything comes down to our inner-child wounds of extreme vulnerability and to our seeking a parental figure as protector and provider. This is what we do when we complain against the government, the police, the judicial system . . . all authority figures that are parents of citizens, who are all orphans, for in the end all states everywhere have abandoned us. Something I have touched upon a lot in my two decades of journalism.

In the end, dear readers, how you love, how I love, how anybody and everybody loves and therefore, how this great country of ours loves, is all about you. You are the one. It's your patterns, your beliefs that will determine your attraction, your style of love. The most basic therapist, even those on social media, can tell you that today. In the end, all relationships are therefore with ourselves. As the wise sage Ramana Maharishi had said, 'There is no other.' This world is a mirror and all people and situations we encounter are nothing but our reflections, reflecting the healed or healthy and unhealed or unhealthy and wounded parts of ourselves. This is why secret loves work so well in keeping marriages intact. Be they taboo extramarital affairs or secret loves.

Certainty is safety. Since the beginning of time, we have had some basic symbols for certainty that were used to convince someone of the sureness of something. Like the sun rising every morning. Or that we did not have to figure out where our next breath would come from. Or that we'd always have a patch of ground to support our next step. Or that children can always take for granted that their parents will be home to put them to bed. Or that parents know that their children will come back from school. The symbols will depend on your culture and background. But you get the drift. These are universal truths, as old as humankind. (This is why the death of parents, and other loved ones, is so painful, and we grieve forever, for we have lost everything that they symbolised: who we were with them, we have lost our safe space, which we thought would last forever.

Peel the layers and you see that it is not your late mother or grandmother you're grieving but how she made you feel; how she loved you, cared for you and kept you safe. In a harsh world, she was always there, and you were safe.)

But now, dearest reader, perhaps for the very first time in human history, we have come to a point where even these certainties that had stood the test of the ages are failing us. For example, the demonic Delhi pollution fog reminds us – no, it rubs into our faces – that we can no longer take it for granted that the sun will indeed rise every morning like it's supposed to in this part of the world. Or that one breath will surely follow the next. Or, given the more frequent tremors happening in the National Capital Region, which are more common in California, the ground beneath our feet for the next step will indeed appear. With acts of terror happening all over the world, and with calamities, both natural and manmade, we can no longer take it for granted that our kids will come home today. How many shooter drills, shooter threats my son (that started when he was barely four and a half years old!) and I have been through, and I have written about! And been interviewed about. Let me not get into economics, jobs, recessions: they are a whole book by themselves. Uncertainty has become the only certainty in this world in every area today. India is no different. What is mere mortal human love then, in the face of such a world?

There is only one answer. To love better, to love at all, we must love all of ourselves completely. This means finding unconditional safety, and not in people, places, things, governments, markets and economies, jobs, clout, affluence, bank balance, followers, wealth. No, there is no logic in love. Love knows no logic. But forget love. In fact, what about anything in this world is logical? Look around you and nothing makes sense. Not one thing. Especially in India. Not any government, road, infrastructure, work culture, marriage or relationship. And yet this country thrives – not on logic but on some other invisible force. How are you or your surroundings – all just a bundle of atoms – not collapsing this very second? Of course, logic is the pursuit of science. The scientific mind will forever seek it everywhere. But the truth is nothing about the human world makes sense. This is why every religion and every spiritual practice insists on faith where logic has failed. And most spiritual practices eventually talk about moving from that space of faith to detachment from all material acquisitions.

I remember the twenty-year-old Jain nun in South Mumbai's Kemps Corner, whom I had to rush to interview as a journalism student at a few hours' notice. As Bombay drowned in its legendary monsoon, I had to somehow surrender my own safety and ideas of getting home to Bandra and interview a complete stranger for a whimsical assignment handed out to me by a quirky teacher. Bald, having plucked out the hairs on her head by herself, the Jain nun was beaming and full of joy, lighting up the dark grey afternoon. It was the very first time I had seen a crystallised version of safety in human form. I felt safe too, in her presence, but was puzzled as to how could someone be so happy with nothing. What she taught me I could understand only decades later, during a panic attack I had in public and the mental health journey I have detailed in *The Water Phoenix*, where I had no choice but to trust blindly in safety. You can only truly be happy with nothing. You can only truly be safe with nothing. The rest is prison, and one can neither love nor be loved freely from a state of imprisonment. Every animal and plant and aspect of nature is a manifestation of this. That realisation, since then, has allowed me to love unconditionally, with complete presence, because I saw that my state of safety doesn't depend on anything or anyone, or what they do. Even during shooter drills, shooter threats, earthquakes and wildfire evacuations,

I am the calmest person around, thanks to the lessons from that child who became a nun.

Can we just trust that somehow we are safe? And you are always safe because you made it to where you are now, didn't you? Can we have the faith of a helpless, wrinkled, shivering newborn wailing her way into a big, bad, scary world, knowing that she will be taken care of? Knowing that she is safe? Her safety at that point in time, during those precious few seconds before a bond has formed (hopefully, as we can't take that for granted either!) between her and her mother, lies in her blind faith in safety.

We were born safe. We were born alone, but did we feel alone at the time? Did we ever feel the loneliness of being all alone as we made the longest journey of a few centimetres from the comfort of our mothers' wombs – which is all we had ever known and where all our needs were met before we even knew what they were – into the world outside? We knew nothing of that world. But we felt safe for we had no ideas of what safety, and therefore the lack of it, meant. The point of life is to live from that state – healing our traumas enough to love, and to love only from that state of not needing anything from anything or anyone. Especially not needing safety. Beyond safety-induced, adrenaline-induced fight or flight, beyond all hunger games of survival. Beyond all ideas of vulnerability, safety or protection, beyond the entire spectrum of creation, maintenance or loss of both safety and protection. All of these are synonyms for fear. Beyond fear lies love. Our truest state. To live from love is everyone's truth. But, of course, to do that, you must first heal.

A reader has arrived in my Delhi apartment with flowers and a small housewarming present. We're supposed to have tea, but I make hot chocolate instead. Vegan, with oat milk. Sugar-free but with giant marshmallows, sweetened otherwise with the warmth of cinnamon bark, flavoured with cloves and the peels of Valencia orange which Blinkit has delivered; it seems like something straight from California, where I am used to having it often. With brioche – my favourite carb with its pillowy softness, whether from my local Whole Foods, made by my friend Sarah or here in Delhi and NCR from Paul's or Theo's – and butter. The world and my life were becoming the same wherever I was, irrespective of time and space. I suppose that's what happens. You take yourself wherever you go. And the world reflects that. Such meals were liquid hugs, comforting you with their childlike innocence to assure you that all has always been well and all will, therefore, always be well. To me, this level of nourishment is the only point of food. Or for that matter anything – books, clothes, jewellery and, most of all, people. Life is too precious for anything else. A highly curated life built around love reminds you constantly that everything you had were presents and that you were naturally always safe. Even the spam ad from my grocery app, Milk Basket, said, 'Hugs are as relaxed as delivered groceries.'

My readers, as is obvious from this book, hold a very special place in my life. They are so special to me, for in a world celebrating victimhood, they – often victims of extreme abuse, often suicidal – are brave, with the courage to show up and do the inner work. 'It is just like you say,' he says, looking at the bag. 'Open it.' It is an enormous three-wick glass candle from Bath and Body Works. Inside, white, with a mellow vanilla lemon scent; but outside, the giant glass jar has a red label with four words that constitute the core message of my last book, my columns, my work with children, my work at the hospice, really my entire life's work. In capital letters it says: 'You Are the One.' In other words, nobody is responsible for your life or you: not governments, not economies, not your abuse, trauma, abandonment, woes, grief, complaints, not even your sickness. Just your patterns, your beliefs.

Just you. You are indeed the one. And my heart-centred readers get it. What better gift than this. To know that your work has reminded people of what they always knew but in the clamour of their lives had forgotten. How to love. How to live. There was no difference. For the two were the same. The path is lit with the first step, with no thought, no story . . . from a space of pure freedom, where safety is just the natural, inherent state.

Like it was the day you were born, the very second you were born.

Like it has always been ever since.

Notes

Chapter 2 Delhi

1 'The Unique Indian Model of OYO Rooms,' Wikipedia, https://en.wikipedia.org/wiki/Oyo_Rooms.
2 'India's Oyo, Once Valued at $10 bn, Finalizes New Funding at $2.5 Billion Valuation,' *TechCrunch*, https://techcrunch.com/2024/06/16/indias-oyo-once-valued-at-10b-finalizes-new-funding-at-2-5b-valuation/.
3 'Most Infidelities Committed During Honeymoon Phase, Says Survey by Extramarital Dating App Gleeden,' *Business Insider India*, https://www.businessinsider.in/thelife/news/most-infidelities-committed-during-honeymoon-phase-says-survey-by-extramarital-dating-app-gleeden/articleshow/99061604.cms.
4 '8 Types of Extramarital Affairs and What They Mean,' *The Times of India*, https://timesofindia.indiatimes.com/life-style/relationships/love-sex/8-types-of-extramarital-affairs-amp-what-they-mean/photostory/94355848.cms.
5 'Most Infidelities Committed During Honeymoon Phase, Says Survey by Extramarital Dating App Gleeden,' *Business Insider India*, https://www.businessinsider.in/thelife/news/most-infidelities-committed-during-honeymoon-phase-says-survey-by-extra-marital-dating-app-gleeden/articleshow/99061604.cms.
6 Clip from *Jo Bole Sonihaal*, YouTube, https://www.youtube.com/watch?v=E9jkJAEhMMg&t=13s.

Chapter 3 Mumbai

1 'Foot Worship on a Yacht in Mumbai,' by VICE Asia, YouTube, https://www.youtube.com/watch?v=McbTZEAtJCY; for an attendee's experience, see https://www.instagram.com/p/Co46jjFIaOz/?hl=en.

Chapter 4 Bengaluru

1 'State GDP of Karnataka in India, FY 2011–2023,' Statista, https://www.statista.com/statistics/962125/india-gross-state-domestic-product-of-karnataka/.

2 For a sampling of a public question and answer forum on BDSM in Bengaluru, see Quora, https://www.quora.com/Can-I-have-a-BDSM-session-in-Bangalore.

3 Binoy Valsan, 'Did You Know That Bengaluru Has BDSM Community?,' *Bangalore Mirror*, https://bangaloremirror.indiatimes.com/bangalore/cover-story/did-you-know-that-bengaluru-has-bdsm-community/articleshow/57226458.cms.

4 Petlee Peter, 'Bengaluru's Hottest New Kink Involves Happy Feet,' *The Times of India*, https://timesofindia.indiatimes.com/city/bengaluru/bengalurus-hottest-new-kink-involves-happy-feet/articleshow/78854044.cms.

Chapter 6 The World's Largest Army of Single Women

1 'The Murder of Shraddha Walkar,' Wikipedia, https://en.wikipedia.org/wiki/Murder_of_Shraddha_Walkar.

2 The population of the United Kingdom, Worldometer, https://www.worldometers.info/world-population/uk-population/#:~:text=the%20United%20Kingdom%202023%20population,of%20the%20total%20world%20population.

3 Rituparna Chatterjee, 'Why Are Over 73 Million Indian Women Choosing to Remain Single?', *The Times of India*, https://timesofindia.indiatimes.com/india/why-are-over-73-million-indian-women-choosing-to-remain-single/articleshow/94564465.cms.

4 Sagar Chugh, 'Breaking Taboos: The Growing Market of Adult Toys in India,' LinkedIn, https://www.linkedin.com/pulse/breaking-taboos-growing-market-adult-toys-india-sagar-chugh/.

5 Joeanna Fernandes and Shobita Dhar, 'All the Single Ladies . . . 73 Million and Growing,' *The Times of India*, https://timesofindia.indiatimes.com/home/sunday-times/deep-focus/all-the-single-ladies-73m-growing/articleshow/49875130.cms.

Chapter 7 The Lost Little Indian Boy

1 'Number of acid attack cases investigated by the police across India from 2017 to 2022,' Statista, https://www.statista.com/statistics/1103065/india-acid-attack-cases-investigated-by-police/. Statista, https://www.statista.com/statistics/1103065/india-acid-attack-cases-investigated-by-police/.

2 'Rape in India,' Wikipedia, https://en.wikipedia.org/wiki/Rape_in_India.

3 'Domestic Violence in India,' Wikipedia, https://en.wikipedia.org/wiki/Domestic_violence_in_India#:~:text=reduced%20domestic%20abuse.,Gender,any%20form%20of%20domestic%20violence.

4 '"Never Settle For Anything Less": Punjab Man Dresses Up as Girlfriend to Write Exam for Her, Internet Reacts,' *ABP LIVE*, https://news.abplive.com/trending/punjab-man-angrez-singh-disguises-as-girlfriend-to-write-exam-leaving-internet-in-splits-1657176.

5 'She Was Set for Goa Honeymoon, Husband Said Ayodhya It Is, She Filed for Divorce,' *India Today*, https://www.indiatoday.in/cities/bhopal/story/bhopal-woman-files-for-divorce-after-husband-takes-her-to-ayodhya-instead-of-goa-2493436-2024-01-25.

6 'As India's Population Soars, Number of Women in Workforce Shrinks,' *Al Jazeera*, https://www.aljazeera.com/gallery/2023/4/10/as-indias-population-soars-number-of-women-in-workforce-shrinks#:~:text=The%20Center%20for%20Monitoring%20the,compared%20with%20361%20million%20men.

7 Amit Basole and Rosa Abraham, 'Shift in India's Female Workforce Sees Increase in Salaried Women but Gender Wage Gap Persists,' *Scroll.in*, https://scroll.in/article/1061512/shift-in-indias-female-workforce-sees-increase-in-salaried-women-but-gender-wage-gap-persists.

8 Anoushka Sawhney, 'Women's Unemployment Rate at 16-Month Low; Labour Participation Declines,' *Business Standard*, https://www.business-standard.com/economy/news/women-s-unemployment-rate-at-16-month-low-labour-participation-declines-124020501116_1.html.

9 K Gopi, 'Intimate Partner Violence in India,' *Journal of Family Medicine and Primary Care*, https://journals.lww.com/jfmpc/fulltext/2023/01000/intimate_partner_violence_in_india__need_for.1.aspx#:~:text=National%20Family%20Health%20Survey%20of,and%201.5%25%20experienced%20sexual%20violence.

Chapter 8 The Rise of BDSM

1 'New Study Reveals Surprising BDSM Statistics on Sexual Preferences and Activities,' Gitnux Report 2024, https://gitnux.org/bdsm-statistics/#:~:text=The%20exact%20prevalence%20is%20hard,has%20engaged%20in%20BDSM%20activities.

Chapter 9 The Reign of Porn and Its Impact on Love, on Lives

1 'The Male Feminist ft. Kalki Koechlin with Siddhaarth Aalambayan,' by Hauterrfly, YouTube, https://www.youtube.com/watch?v=Dr-6gGrFF7w.
2 Beauty vlogger reviewing sex toys on YouTube, https://www.youtube.com/watch?v=jmtN_HysXVY.
3 'India Sex Toy Market Size,' TechSci Research, https://www.techsciresearch.com/report/india-sex-toys-market/5018.html.
4 'Adult and Pornographic Website Market Size in the US (2005–2029),' IBISWorld, https://www.ibisworld.com/industry-statistics/market-size/adult-pornographic-websites-united-states/#:~:text=Questions%20Clients%20Ask%20About%20This%20Industry&text=The%20market%20size%2C%20measured%20by,pages%20of%20data%20and%20analysis.
5 Saikiran Kannan, 'Pornography Gets a Pandemic Boost, India Reports 95 Per Cent Rise in Viewing,' *India Today*, https://www.indiatoday.in/news-analysis/story/pornography-gets-a-pandemic-boost-india-reports-95-per-cent-rise-in-viewing-1665940-2020-04-11.
6 'India Ranks in Top 3 in Overall Traffic on Pornhub,' *Business Today*, https://www.businesstoday.in/latest/trends/story/india-ranks-in-top-3-in-overall-traffic-on-porn-hub-122001-2018-12-17.

Chapter 11 Polyamory

1 'Panipuri,' Wikipedia, https://en.wikipedia.org/wiki/Panipuri#:~:text=Panipuri%20has%20many%20regional%20names,Bihar%2C%20and%20Nepal%3A%20Phuchka.

2 '"Not Another Word for Cheating": Navigating Polyamory in Modern India and Its Gaining Popularity,' *The Indian Express*, https://indianexpress.com/article/lifestyle/feelings/polyamory-modern-india-romantic-relationships-lgbtq-challenges-myths-popularity-9155536/.

3 'Many on Dating Apps Are Already in Relationships or Aren't Seeking Actual Dates, New Study Finds,' *NBC News*, https://www.nbcnews.com/pop-culture/lifestyle/many-online-daters-arent-seeking-actual-dates-rcna94163.

Chapter 12 Pop Therapy Jargon and Love

1 'Indian Psychiatry Society Demands Revision of Mental Healthcare Act,' *The Times of India*, https://timesofindia.indiatimes.com/india/indian-psychiatry-society-demands-revision-of-mental-healthcare-act/articleshow/99847600.cms.

2 Anuja Jaiswal, 'We Need More Healthcare Professionals in India,' *The Times of India*, https://timesofindia.indiatimes.com/life-style/health-fitness/health-news/we-need-more-mental-health-care-professionals-in-india/articleshow/66146320.cms.

3 'Depression in India: The Latest Statistics,' Mind Voyage, https://mindvoyage.in/depression-in-india-latest-statistics/#:~:text=In%20a%202021%20UNICEF%20survey,were%20affected%20by%20depressive%20disorders.

4 'Why Many Indians Don't Trust Mental Health Advice,' *The Wire*, https://thewire.in/society/why-many-indians-don't-trust-mental-health-advice.

5 Fast Facts and Statistics, Domestic Violence Center of Chester County, https://dvcccpa.org/fast-facts-statistics/#:~:text=Emotional%20and%20Psychological%20Abuse%20*%20Nearly%20half,psychologically%20abused%20will%20display%20PTSD%20symptoms%20(5).

6 'Why Enmeshment Trauma Is at the Root of Mental Health Issues,' *The Times of India*, https://timesofindia.indiatimes.com/india/why-enmeshment-trauma-is-at-the-root-of-mental-health-issues/articleshow/102010422.cms.

Chapter 13 Dating Trends

1 'Over 75% Indians Ready to Spend More Time on Dating Apps: Study,' *The Economic Times*, https://economictimes.indiatimes.com/tech/technology/over-75-indians-ready-to-spend-more-time-on-dating-apps-study/articleshow/97772652.cms?from=mdr.
2 Sonam Joshi, '90% of Gen Z Indians Are Now Using Dating Apps to Find New Friends: Survey,' *The Times of India*, https://timesofindia.indiatimes.com/home/sunday-times/90-of-gen-z-indians-are-now-using-dating-apps-to-find-new-friends-survey/articleshow/84929729.cms.
3 Abhijeet Kumar, 'Tired of Dating Apps? You're Not Alone; Survey Says 79% Gen Z Feel the Same,' *Business Standard*, https://www.business-standard.com/world-news/tired-of-dating-apps-you-re-not-alone-survey-says-79-gen-z-feel-the-same-124052201018_1.html.
4 'Online Dating: Worldwide,' Statista, https://www.statista.com/outlook/emo/dating-services/online-dating/worldwide.

Chapter 15 Of Secret Loves

1 'Social Media in India: 2023 Stats & Platform Trends,' OOSGA, https://oosga.com/social-media/ind/#:~:text=Social%20Media's%20User%20Demographics%20in,of%20users%20has%20grown%204.2%20%25.
2 Rituparna Chatterjee, 'Why Every War Is a World War,' *The Times of India*, https://timesofindia.indiatimes.com/world/rest-of-world/why-every-war-today-is-a-world-war/articleshow/104582327.cms.
3 'How AI Will Help Humans Love Better, More Unconditionally,' *The Times of India*, https://timesofindia.indiatimes.com/world/us/how-ai-will-help-humans-love-better-more-unconditionally/articleshow/97796666.cms.
4 '"I Love Its Brutal Scent": Bodybuilder Who Married Sex Doll Is Now in Love with an Ashtray,' *News24*, https://www.news24.com/you/news/international/i-love-its-brutal-scent-bodybuilder-who-married-sex-doll-is-now-in-love-with-an-ashtray-20210903.

5 'Indonesian Man Marries Rice Cooker, Divorces It Four Days Later Because . . .,' *NDTV*, https://www.ndtv.com/offbeat/indonesian-man-marries-rice-cooker-divorces-it-4-days-later-because-2560189.

6 'Sex Robot Industry, New 2024 Data,' Bedbible, https://bedbible.com/sex-robot-industry-market-size-technology-ai-user-sentiment-statistics/.

7 'Size of the Sex Toy Market Worldwide, 2016–2030,' Statista, https://www.statista.com/statistics/587109/size-of-the-global-sex-toy-market/.

8 'Man Fined $61,000 Over an Emoji,' *Vantage*, *Firstpost*, https://www.youtube.com/watch?v=N3SzcOu3E9Y.

9 'India: Estimated Total Population from 2019 to 2029,' Statista, https://www.statista.com/statistics/263766/total-population-of-india/#:~:text=The.

10 'People's Linguistic Survey of India,' https://en.wikipedia.org/wiki/People%27s_Linguistic_Survey_of_India.

Index

About the Author

Rituparna Chatterjee is a bestselling author, journalist and columnist. She is a former foreign correspondent and columnist for *The Economic Times*. Her longstanding column of many years, 'California Dreaming', on her life as a global Indian was first published in *The Economic Times* and later moved to *The Times of India*. Apart from children's stories in various anthologies, her published books include *An Ordinary Life*, on the life of an acclaimed Bollywood movie star, and the deeply moving *The Water Phoenix*, a magic realism memoir on an abused child's lifelong journey to understand what was love and what wasn't. *The Water Phoenix* won the United Nations' Laadli Award for Gender Sensitivity for Best Book Nonfiction (2021) and was in *The Indian Express*'s top five bestselling non-fiction of 2020 and number one on Google India. *How India Loves* is her third book. Chatterjee is now writing a novel.